Sharing America's Neighborhoods

Sharing America's Neighborhoods

∾ THE PROSPECTS FOR STABLE RACIAL INTEGRATION

INGRID GOULD ELLEN

HARVARD UNIVERSITY PRESS
Cambridge, Massachusetts, and London, England 2000

Library of Congress Cataloging-in-Publication Data

Ellen, Ingrid Gould, 1965–
    Sharing America's neighborhoods : the prospects for stable racial integration / Ingrid Gould Ellen.
        p. cm.
    Includes bibliographical references and index.
    ISBN 0-674-00301-2
    1. Afro-Americans—Housing.   2. Race discrimination—United States.   3. United States—Race relations.   4. Neighborhood—United States.   I. Title.

HD7288.72.U5 E45 2000
305.8'00973—dc21   00-038929

Contents

Acknowledgments

This book began its life as a dissertation and has followed me as I have moved through a number of institutions. It started to take shape as I finished up my graduate work in public policy at Harvard. There, the Joint Center for Housing Studies generously provided me with office space and other support, and I owe them a great debt. In particular, I want to thank then executive director Bill Apgar for his steady guidance during my search for a topic, and Chris Herbert and Nancy McArdle for early discussions and help.

During the next two years, I moved to Washington, D.C., to undertake the empirical work. The first year, I had the good fortune of being a visiting scholar at the Urban Institute. The institute generously provided me with an office, knowledgeable and friendly colleagues, and a powerful data set without which I could never have undertaken an analysis of the scope that I did. I am enormously grateful to Susan Weiner and Al Gillespie for assisting me with the institute's Underclass Data Base. During the second year, I had the privilege of being a visitor in the Economic Studies division of the Brookings Institution, where I again received office space, support, and valuable advice from senior fellows and other visitors.

The cooperation of the Census Bureau was also instrumental in my empirical research. Dan Weinberg and his staff at the Division of Housing and Household Economic Statistics gave me access to a unique data set that provided the core of my analysis, allowed me to clog their system with my various programs, and were always there to solve the inevitable technical problems that arise in empirical analysis.

I must also thank the U.S. Department of Housing and Urban Development, which provided me with a research grant to support this work. Thanks also to my colleagues at Yale and New York University, and to my editors at Harvard University Press, who have aided me in turning my dissertation into a book.

Most importantly, I owe tremendous debt to the members of my dissertation committee, who reviewed countless proposals, outlines, and preliminary drafts, and consistently offered me guidance and direction. Alan Altshuler provided healthy skepticism and superb political analysis, both of which pushed me to think a good deal harder about my project. Denise DiPasquale spent untold hours advising and encouraging me and gave me invaluable help with the empirical analysis. John Kain generously shared with me his vast knowledge and experience in the field and guided me in my empirical design. And Richard Zeckhauser, my advisor and the chair of my committee, brought to the project his extraordinary gift of always seeing the issue from a slightly different angle and never failing to ask the essential question.

Finally, I must acknowledge my incredibly supportive family. My parents have provided both editorial help and countless hours of babysitting. My children, Audrey and Jacob, have helped motivate me to think about the neighborhoods they will grow up in. And the greatest thanks of all goes to my husband, David, who has been with me throughout this project and has always managed to find the time and patience to lend his sensitivity and unparalleled analytical skills.

Sharing America's Neighborhoods

CHAPTER ONE

Introduction

The conventional wisdom on racially integrated neighborhoods in the United States is that they are exceedingly rare and where they exist, exceedingly transitory. Racially integrated neighborhoods cannot stay that way for long, according to popular belief, because as soon as the black population in a neighborhood has reached some "tipping" point, whites move away in droves—a phenomenon commonly referred to as "white flight." Integration is viewed, as Saul Alinsky once said, as no more than the time between when the first black moves in and the last white moves out (Sanders 1970).

Yet while this conventional view of racially mixed neighborhoods is largely accurate as a description of the country's past, and while there is no denying that the United States remains a remarkably segregated country, this account has become inaccurate and misleading in a few important respects. First, racially mixed neighborhoods are no longer as rare or as unstable as people tend to think. Nearly one-fifth of all neighborhoods in the United States were racially mixed in 1990, and 15 percent of non-Hispanic whites and roughly one-third of blacks lived in such communities. And these neighborhoods do not seem to be merely transitional. Over three-quarters of neighborhoods that were integrated in 1980 remained integrated in 1990. Most importantly, perhaps, both the number of racially mixed communities and their degree of stability has increased markedly with time. Chapter 2 offers a more detailed empirical examination of the extent and stability of racial integration in the United States today, as well as some analysis of trends over time. As discussed earlier, integrated neighborhoods are defined in this book by demographic make-up and not necessarily by social interaction.

Second, to the extent that neighborhood racial transition does still occur, the conventional view that such transition is fundamentally caused by "white flight" misunderstands the true dynamics of racial transition. White flight—that is, the decisions of whites living in integrated neighborhoods to move out of those neighborhoods—is not nearly as significant a contributor to neighborhood racial change as what might be termed "white avoidance": the decisions of whites living in all-white neighborhoods *not to move into* an integrated neighborhood.

It is not hard to see why white avoidance is likely to be a more dominant cause. Nearly one in five Americans moves every year, for all sorts of reasons entirely unrelated to race (such as a new job or a wish for a larger home). With this many people moving naturally, white flight need not take place to produce racial transition—even dramatic, sudden transition. For even if whites move out of integrated neighborhoods at the same rate that they move out of all-white neighborhoods, integrated neighborhoods will become quickly all-black if there are no new whites moving in to replace them. Subsequent chapters in this book demonstrate, both on theoretical and empirical grounds, that racial composition does matter more in "entry" decisions than in "exit" decisions; thus white avoidance plays a considerably more important role in neighborhood racial change than does white flight.

One important reason that the conventional emphasis on white flight persists, despite the lack of empirical support, may be that the whites who exit mixed neighborhoods because of racial considerations are easily identifiable and therefore obvious targets for media stories about transitioning neighborhoods. We hear, for instance, about John Dunham, a white plumber in Illinois who moved from his hometown in suburban Chicago because of "the blacks" (Terry 1996), and Terry Wells who fled Oceanside, California, on account of the area's changing ethnic mix (Holmes 1997). The many more whites who choose not to move into mixed neighborhoods because of racial considerations are a statistical abstraction who are rarely identified and never interviewed.

Finally, the conventional view is conspicuous in its neglect of black household decision making. Integrated neighborhoods are assumed to become all-black because whites run away from them (or more accurately, avoid moving into them). Yet change occurs not simply because whites resist racially mixed areas; blacks must also move into them instead. Because of some combination of discriminatory barriers, fear of racial hostility, and perhaps a desire for cultural affinity, blacks rarely move into all-white neighborhoods. And this fact naturally makes their demand for housing in integrated neighborhoods somewhat higher.

With that said, however, the conventional view is not all wrong on this point. Racial change, when it occurs, is indeed driven more by white avoidance than by blacks' special attraction to integrated neighborhoods. Consider that survey evidence consistently shows that blacks simply care less about neighborhood racial composition than whites (Farley et al. 1978; Farley et al. 1993; Bobo and Zubrinsky 1996). Thus, while the empirical evidence given later provides some additional insights into the residential attitudes and behavior of black households, the focus throughout is on white decisions, because it is these decisions that are more central to the story of racial change.

If white household decisions—particularly the decisions of whites not to move into integrated neighborhoods—are central, the critical question arises: what is the dominant motivation underlying such avoidance? There are at least two conventional answers to this question. The first is that white avoidance is primarily motivated by racial prejudice against blacks, pure and simple—whites avoid mixed neighborhoods because they simply do not want to live among black neighbors (Berry and Kasarda 1977; St. John and Bates 1990; Weiher 1991). The second common explanation is that white avoidance is primarily motivated by class-based preferences for affluent neighborhoods, which tend to be more white. As one group of researchers has written: "All people—white and black, rich and not so rich, are willing to pay, and substantially, to avoid class integration" (Leven et al. 1976, p. 203). Thus, the typically lower incomes of black households pose a "serious barrier to achieving racial integration in neighborhoods" (p. 202).

While there is an important kernel of truth to each of these explanations of white avoidance (and therefore of racial transition), I believe that both—especially the conventional class-based preferences explanation—fall short as the primary explanation. It is no doubt true that whites are generally better off economically than blacks. But the notion that white avoidance can be explained primarily by white preferences to live among more affluent people cannot be sustained in light of the empirical scrutiny undertaken in this study and elsewhere. Such a notion is also contrary to our shared intuitions, rooted in the long history of race relations in this country, that racial attitudes—specifically, negative race-based attitudes of whites toward partly or all-black neighborhoods—obviously still matter in residential decision making.

The racial prejudice explanation cannot be dismissed so easily. Many accounts suggest that it was the dominant motivation underlying white avoidance in the past, and it may still be today. But Chapter 3 sets forth an alternative hypothesis, one that affords a central role to white households' negative racial attitudes but offers a more complicated account of how such attitudes drive neighborhood transition. Specifically, the hypothesis, which builds in part on the work of Richard Taub and his co-authors as well as other researchers, is that whites avoid integrated neighborhoods because (1) they tend to assume, based on past evidence, that mixed neighborhoods will not stay that way for long and will become predominantly black, and (2) they automatically associate predominantly black neighborhoods, rightly or wrongly, with poor neighborhood quality (poor schools, high crime, and so on) and on that basis stay away. To put the second proposition another way, whites use the racial identity of the majority of a neighborhood's inhabitants as a signal of poor neighborhood quality. I refer to these two propositions collectively as the "race-based neighborhood stereotyping" hypothesis.

Personal accounts may help to illustrate. Consider Andrew Formus, a white resident of Matteson, Illinois, a suburb outside of Chicago that has rapidly transitioned from 12 percent black in 1980 to 48 percent black in 1996. He says he is comfortable with the racial mix but worried about crime. As he explained in 1997, "It doesn't bother me at all seeing blacks in the area. It's just the crime that comes with it" ("Why Can't We Live Together?" 1997). Patricia Backus, a village trustee in the town, instead stresses property values: "We are proud of our diversity. But historically, communities that have re-segregated are not as successful. Housing values drop, people move away. We want to avoid that" (Terry 1996). Finally, Paul Pfingston stresses the schools: "One of the big concerns that I had about the community was the education and decline in the quality of the education that our students were receiving" ("Why Can't We Live Together?" 1997).

Despite the commonsense notion that neighborhood considerations matter, little work has been done to develop a thorough understanding of how they matter and when, and what their significance implies about the stability of racial integration in different communities. And as will be discussed later, most accounts that stress worries about community quality in neighborhood change tend to view race as being ultimately irrelevant to white residents. According to the race-based neighborhood stereotyping hypothesis, however, the way that people evaluate neighborhoods is strongly shaped by racial considerations.

Naturally, there are grounds for skepticism about the true motives of whites. As one black, upper-middle-class resident of Matteson has explained it, "What [white] people are really saying [when they express concerns about property values and crime] is, 'I really have a fear of that 6-foot-five inch, 250-pound man with big lips moving next door to me" ("Why Can't We Live Together?" 1997). While such skepticism cannot (and should not) be entirely dismissed, this book aims to go beyond such anecdotes and speculations about motives and inspect the actual behavior of white residents.

Whether this race-based neighborhood stereotyping explanation for white avoidance is morally distinguishable from racial prejudice is a complex question. Is white aversion to black *neighborhoods,* that is, morally distinguishable from a white aversion to blacks *as individuals?* Fortunately, this question does not need to be answered to get at the central aim of this book—understanding why and when integrated neighborhoods racially transition. But if one wants to consider the case for government intervention to promote stable racial integration on social justice grounds (as well as an economic grounds), a topic this book explores in its final chapter, this question cannot be entirely ignored. In this spirit, a few brief observations are worth making here.

First, whether aversion to black neighborhoods is morally distinguishable from aversion to blacks as individuals ultimately depends, to a large degree, on the extent to which the neighborhood stereotypes that whites appear to adopt are true. If it were really true, for example, that black neighborhoods, controlling for income and wealth, were of inferior quality to white neighborhoods, there might be a case—as Orlando Patterson argues—for concluding that nothing racially motivated, and thus morally objectionable, is going on (Patterson 1997). The emphasis on "might" is important here, for even if it were true that black neighborhoods were generally worse, any such discrepancy may well be explained, to a significant degree, only by factors that themselves are rooted in objectionable attitudes. For example, one obvious reason black neighborhoods might be worse is that they have been unfairly denied the same political power as white neighborhoods to attract the necessary resources to sustain and improve neighborhood services and conditions.

At the other extreme, if it were *never* true that black neighborhoods are worse than white neighborhoods (again, controlling for income), then, under the race-based neighborhood stereotyping hypothesis, race is clearly being used by whites as a wholly illegitimate proxy for neighborhood quality—one based on the same kind of insidious assumptions about black inferiority that underlie racial prejudice against individuals. With that said, it is at least worth considering whether a world in which racially motivated neighborhood stereotyping predominates may still be preferable to a world in which individually targeted racial animus predominates. For the race-based neighborhood stereotyping hypothesis predicts that where whites are persuaded—contrary to their neighborhood prejudices—that a particular mixed neighborhood will in fact remain racially stable or that the neighborhood's quality will not decline, they will be quite willing to live in and among black neighbors. Given the twentieth-century history of segregation in this country, this is no minor observation.

In any event, as explained earlier, the moral evaluation of race-based neighborhood stereotyping is not an essential element of this book's focus, and neither therefore is the empirical question of whether and to what extent racial composition is in fact a reliable indicator of neighborhood quality. Yet it is at least worth observing that the answer to this empirical question is far from clear. It is true, for example, that black neighborhoods on average have higher crime rates, older housing, and inferior schools than white neighborhoods. But the evidence presented later suggests that these differences largely disappear once we control for socioeconomic status. Finally, whatever the moral implications of race-based neighborhood stereotyping, it is plainly *analytically* distinct from individually targeted racial prejudice (hereinafter referred to as simple or pure racial prejudice) and may ultimately justify different policy responses.

As mentioned, Chapter 3 sets forth in more detail the various theoretical claims regarding the causal mechanism by which mixed neighborhoods transition and concludes with a full presentation of the race-based neighborhood stereotyping hypothesis. The chapters that follow embark on a lengthy empirical examination of the dynamics of racial transition. The aim of these chapters is primarily to test the race-based neighborhood stereotyping hypothesis as the dominant explanation for white avoidance and to a lesser extent, to demonstrate the priority of entry over exit decisions.

The first of these, Chapter 4, explores how stable, racially integrated areas differ from those that are quickly gaining black population and on their way to becoming largely minority. Relying mainly on 1980 and 1990 census tract data from thirty-four different metropolitan areas, it finds little empirical support for any of the traditional hypotheses about racial change. Most notably, neither the initial size of the black population in a neighborhood nor its level of social and economic deprivation appears correlated with the pace of racial change in that neighborhood.

To truly understand the dynamics of racial change, however, one ultimately needs to move from studying neighborhoods in the aggregate to studying the individual decisions that underlie such change. Using a special data set that links households to their individual neighborhoods, Chapters 5 through 7 attempt to do just that. In particular, Chapter 5 examines how racial composition and change affect household satisfaction with a neighborhood. Chapter 6 then explores how racial composition affects the actual decision whether to remain in or exit a neighborhood. The findings of these two chapters are quite consistent, and both provide considerable support for the notion of race-based neighborhood stereotyping. In general, they conclude that people—both whites and blacks—are considerably less concerned about the racial mix of their neighborhood than is commonly assumed and than surveys of racial preferences suggest. In particular, neither households' evaluations of their neighborhoods nor households' probability of leaving them appears to be influenced by current racial mix. *Changes* in that racial mix however,—and thus, implicitly, expectations about the *future* racial mix and neighborhood character—are connected to household satisfaction and mobility for certain white households, in particular, homeowners and households with children. (Significantly, black households with children appear resistant to growing black populations, too.) It would thus appear that an increasing black population raises white households' concerns about future property values, school quality, and general neighborhood conditions and leads to some "white flight." Still, the magnitude of the rate of white departure is small, and the evidence does not suggest that such departure itself destroys integrated communities.

Chapter 7 examines the entry of households into neighborhoods and finds that race is far more central to these decisions. Consistent with race-based neighborhood stereotyping, it also finds that the typical white resident who decides to move into a racially diverse area is young, single, childless, and a renter—in other words, less invested in a community's long-term conditions and quality of life. Significantly, this finding is contrary to the conventional belief—rooted in a focus on "white flight"—that homeowners are more likely to live in integrated neighborhoods because of their lack of easy mobility.

Along the way, the empirical analysis in these chapters yields other interesting results not directly related to the testing of my core hypothesis. One powerful and somewhat surprising result, for instance, is that blacks are more likely to move into units vacated by other blacks, even after the price and quality of the unit and the racial mix of the neighborhood in which the unit is located are taken into account.

The final chapter summarizes the key findings of the book and explores their implications for the likely efficacy of traditional policies used to promote the stability of racially integrated neighborhoods. More fundamentally, the chapter also explores the moral and economic justifications for government intervention to promote racial integration. I accept the assumption that if it were true that the vast majority of integrated neighborhoods remained stable over time, or that the neighborhood transition that does occur is fundamentally the product of truly benign private preferences for ethnic clustering and imposes no social costs, it would be hard to justify government intervention or even concern.

But the key findings of this book, together with certain other general observations, suggest that there may be a good case to be made for modest government intervention to promote the stability of racially integrated neighborhoods. As a matter of political morality, white avoidance resulting from race-based neighborhood stereotyping cannot reasonably be characterized as the playing out of benign private preferences for ethnic clustering on the part of whites. Rather, race-based neighborhood stereotyping, although arguably preferable to individually targeted racial animus, is still a byproduct of the country's long history of private and public racial discrimination—a history from which certain obligations may still flow. There may also be an economic case for modest intervention, given the social costs imposed by segregation.

Lastly, to the extent that there is justification for modest public action, the chapter outlines the kinds of policies most likely to be effective in light of this book's empirical findings. Specifically, it suggests that government policies to promote integration are most promising when they are (1) aimed at encouraging outsiders to move into mixed areas, rather than deterring current residents from leaving; (2) race-neutral to the extent possible; and (3) respectful of personal liberty.

As explored in greater detail in Chapter 8, two sets of policies that generally meet those criteria are community betterment projects and public information campaigns. The findings here also suggest that integration is much more likely to endure if it happens at a more moderate pace and if it occurs in outlying, suburban communities rather than in central city neighborhoods. Finally, while efforts to combat racial discrimination in housing markets do not directly address white avoidance, they may nonetheless play an important indirect role.

A single study could hardly attempt to explain everything about racial and ethnic patterns of settlement in this country. Thus, the scope of this book is naturally limited. Three particular ways in which it is limited are worth emphasizing at the start. Each represents an important question that merits future study.

The first important limitation is that in this book I do not intend to offer any bold *historical* claims about neighborhood racial transition. In particular, while I demonstrate that racially integrated neighborhoods are more common and more stable than they have been in the past, I do not make definitive claims about why this is the case. The data used here simply do not extend far enough back in time. With that said, it is tempting to speculate that whites' greater tolerance of racial mixing over the last ten to twenty years can be explained by the fact that race-based neighborhood stereotyping has replaced simple racial prejudice in recent decades as the dominant force behind neighborhood racial change. Anecdotal accounts suggest that in earlier decades racial animus loomed large in white decision making. By contrast, in more recent years, survey data indicate that white households—or at least their stated preferences—have become strikingly more tolerant of racial diversity. Consider that the proportion of whites who said they would move if a black household moved in next door has fallen from 44 percent in 1958 to just 1 percent in 1997. But again this is hardly definitive. (Another possibility, for instance, is that overt market discrimination has become less prevalent in recent decades and that as a result there are now fewer all-white neighborhoods to which white households can flee.) Future studies should more systematically explore the question of how, if at all, the motives underlying racial change have shifted over time.

A second self-imposed limitation of this book is that for the most part it addresses only blacks and whites. Yet in 1990, Latinos made up 9 percent of the U.S. population and Asians constituted 2.9 percent. Clearly, a picture of our cities and suburbs that ignores these groups is an oversimplification. Yet there is at least some justification for this restriction, other than space constraints. For while Hispanics and Asians live separately from other racial and ethnic groups, their segregation levels do not approach those of blacks. And the underlying dynamics of neighborhoods shared by non-black minorities and whites seem clearly distinct from those shared by blacks and whites. Most significantly, perhaps, much of the segregation of non-black minorities appears to relate to their immigrant status. With passing generations, and rising incomes, these groups appear to become substantially more integrated (Massey and Mullan 1984; Massey and Denton 1985; Alba and Logan 1993; Logan, Alba, and Leung 1996; Ellen 2000a). Moreover, Latinos and Asians have not experienced the same centuries-long history of enslavement and oppression in this country that African Americans have, and thus their residential separation does not deliver the same affront to our nation's sense of racial justice.

Finally and most important, the study of racial transition in racially mixed neighborhoods addresses only *part* of the overall story of why we remain a remarkably segregated society—despite the very real progress documented in this book. The other critical question, of course, is why so few racially integrated neighborhoods arise *in the first place*—again, despite some very real progress. If the story of racial transition in already integrated neighborhoods is mainly a story about white decision making (and specifically white avoidance on account of race-based neighborhood stereotyping), the story of the paucity of new integrated neighborhoods is mainly the story of black decision making, in particular, the story of why more blacks do not move into white neighborhoods. While answering this question is not the focus of the book, Chapter 3 offers a brief analysis in order to provide some context.

As explained earlier, however, I do not regard these self-imposed limitations as undermining the core propositions that I defend in this book—propositions that I hope advance our understanding of race and neighborhood decision making.

In summary, this study presents the following portrait of America's neighborhoods: a majority are racially segregated, but at the same time, a substantial and growing minority are well integrated, and not just fleetingly, but typically over many years. Moreover, this book also concludes that to the significant extent that racial transition does still occur, it seems to have more to do with race-based neighborhood stereotyping than with other, more disturbing and perhaps less addressable causes such as racial hatred.

This portrait hardly tells the story of an ideal society that has become entirely color-blind. Again, overall levels of segregation remain extraordinarily high. But it does tell a more optimistic story than that emphasized by many researchers and widely shared by the public—a portrait according to which there are only three kinds of neighborhoods: the permanently all-black, the permanently all-white, and the exceedingly rare (and not-long-for-this-world) integrated neighborhood.

The true story of racial transition is also more dynamic than is commonly believed. The argument here is that when transition occurs, it seems to be chiefly the result of the reflexive everyday decision by tens of thousands of white households, when moving in the normal course of events, to remain in predominantly white neighborhoods. The critical implication of this fact is that contemporary segregation in the United States is not a relic of the past, but rather the result of ongoing contemporary decisions. The pessimistic corollary is that segregation has been reproducing itself in every generation. A more hopeful perspective, however, is that this high level of mobility also suggests enormous potential for change.

The Extent and Stability of Racial Integration in the United States

This chapter presents an empirical overview of racial integration in the contemporary United States. It reports on the number and proportion of integrated neighborhoods that exist in the country as a whole; it looks at trends in the extent of integration over time and explores the existence of regional differences; and it examines the stability of racial mixing during the 1980s as compared with earlier decades. Before launching into any of these inquiries, however, certain key terms must be defined.

What Is a Stable, Racially Integrated Neighborhood?

Over the past few decades, sociologists and demographers have paid considerable attention to the question of how best to measure racial segregation (Duncan and Duncan 1955; Winship 1977; James and Taeuber 1985; Massey and Denton 1988). In sharp contrast, surprisingly scant attention has been paid to the question of how to conceptualize neighborhood racial integration (Ellen 1998; Galster 1998; Smith 1998). For racial integration is not simply the opposite of segregation. Racial segregation is a concept applied to an entire city or metropolitan area, and it measures the degree to which different groups are spatially separated. The most common measure of segregation, for instance, the dissimilarity index, estimates the proportion of blacks (or whites) who would have to move into different neighborhoods to produce a perfectly integrated city. Unfortunately, such a measure does not tell us how to determine whether a particular neighborhood is racially integrated, a determination that is critical to any assessment of the state of neighborhood racial mixing. Thus, before presenting any empirical results, this section aims to clarify what in fact we mean when we use such terms as "neighborhood," "racial integration," and "stability." Similar definitions are offered in Ellen (1998).

While people talk about "neighborhoods" all the time—good ones, rough ones, transitional ones—there is little agreement on exactly what the term neighborhood means, even from a theoretical perspective. In the sociological literature, neighborhoods tend to be defined according to four basic elements: natural geographical boundaries; ethnic or cultural characteristics of residents; shared use of local facilities, such as shops or schools; and psychological unity of residents (Keller 1968).

Political scientists, in contrast, view neighborhoods as an arena for political organization and activity (Altshuler 1970; Berry, Portney, and Thomson 1993). Economists have focused on the concept of externalities—the costs or benefits imposed on external parties (Segal 1979; Galster 1986b). The neighborhood is the area over which "environmental changes initiated by others are perceived as altering the well-being that a given individual derives from the given location," with an individual's neighborhood extending as far as the individuals or facilities that affect her satisfaction with the community (Galster 1986b, p. 246).

Others have abandoned general rules altogether, taking the position that a neighborhood is simply defined by people's perceptions. As the report prepared by the National Commission on Neighborhoods put it in 1979: "Each neighborhood is what the inhabitants think it is." But even if we could operationalize this concept, studies have found that residents do not necessarily agree on the boundaries of their neighborhoods (Hunter 1974). Some find, for instance, that poorer residents tend to move in "smaller radii," suggesting that neighborhoods might be smaller for poorer residents (Altshuler 1970, p. 127). Another study of neighborhoods finds that people often see their communities as extending precisely to the point where they personally perceive that the socioeconomic status of residents shifts (Coleman 1978). They define their neighborhood, that is, in a way that makes it *feel* socially homogenous to them.

As interesting as these theoretical discussions are, when undertaking a large-scale quantitative analysis, one must rely on statistical neighborhoods for which data have been collected. For the purposes of this study, as with most other studies of neighborhood composition and change, census tracts are used to approximate neighborhoods. Census tracts, which typically include between 2,500 and 8,000 people, are probably closest in size to what most envision as a neighborhood, and they have the practical advantage of supplying more data than other alternatives. And a majority of past researchers have used tracts as a base for their analysis, so it is easier to do historical comparisons when using the same unit of analysis.

Nonetheless, many argue that tracts can be misleading and can easily conceal considerable separation that would be evident on the block level (Taeuber and Taeuber 1965; Farley and Frey 1994). These smaller units, containing just a few hundred people on average, are more homogenous and thus yield more sensitive (and certainly higher) measures of segregation. To give an example, one study of Seattle in 1950 reports a segregation index of 63 when computed from block data and just 17 when computed from tract data (Jahn 1950). (The segregation index used here is the dissimilarity index, which ranges from 0–100, with 0 representing perfect integration and 100 maximum segregation.) A much more recent analysis of Dallas, meanwhile, finds that just 30 percent of the blocks contained within racially mixed census tracts are integrated (Jargowsky 1994).

These figures are quite compelling, and consequently, this study supplements its tract-level analysis with a small study of block groups in Washington D.C. (collections of individual blocks that usually contain between 250 and 550 households) to see if the results hold at this more intimate level as well. (See Chapter 4.) Still, it is not evident that neighborhood integration requires racial mixing on every street. Some random clustering will naturally occur even in an entirely color-blind world. Moreover, even if individual streets are racially segregated, when part of a racially mixed area, their residents are likely to interact with people of different races at stores, schools, playgrounds, and bus stops.

"Racial integration," like "neighborhood," is a term that is widely used in both popular and academic literature but is rarely defined precisely. In part, this lack of specificity is due to the fact that most researchers exploring racial patterns of settlement have focused not on evaluating integration, but on measuring segregation.

As with many policy issues, it is essential to decide whether to focus on process or results. When considering the fairness of a given income distribution, for example, one can be concerned with either the underlying equality of opportunity (process) or the ultimate distribution of wealth (results). In the case of integration, one primarily concerned with process would likely describe as integrated a city in which all households choose their neighborhoods freely and without regard to their own race or the race of their neighbors. If, in contrast, the focus is on outcomes, one will take racial integration to be more about resulting racial distributions, without regard to how they came about. Most researchers and commentators have typically viewed integration as concerning results, and the same approach is used here. This is not to suggest that process is unimportant. As explained in Chapter 8, how certain residential patterns come about is critical to the assessment of the costs of racial segregation and the case for government intervention. But regardless of how a neighborhood has achieved its racial mix, I still consider it to be integrated if minorities are present in sufficient numbers.

But what constitutes sufficient? Is a neighborhood that is 1 percent black and 99 percent white integrated? If not, then what threshold level of minority presence is required? When considering a racially integrated neighborhood, many tend to envision a community that is half black and half white. And indeed, several researchers use the 50–50 mark—plus or minus a few percentage points—to define integration (Lee and Wood 1991; Jargowsky 1994). Yet in a country where only 12 percent of the total population is black, such an approach hardly seems fitting.[1] According to this strict definition, only about one-fourth of the nation's population could theoretically live in "integrated" neighborhoods. The remaining three-fourths would live in communities with no black residents at all. Certainly, this is not the result we would expect in a perfectly color-blind world.

At the other extreme, we might define an integrated community as one with the same share of blacks and whites that exist in the general population, plus or minus say five percentage points. (This is effectively how the dissimilarity index, the most popular measure of segregation, views integration, since it considers the extent of segregation to be the divergence from a perfectly even distribution of minority residents.) This strategy is certainly appealing, but it too has drawbacks. For example, such "integrated" neighborhoods would include those that are 8 percent black but exclude those that are more than 18 percent black. Yet a neighborhood in which one group vastly outnumbers another is not what most people envision when thinking about integration. Several researchers argue further that the definition of integration should vary across counties and metropolitan areas depending on each area's racial mix (Saltman 1990; Maly and Nyden 1996; Smith 1998). But again, while appealing in concept, this comparative approach will lead us to classify an even greater number of overwhelmingly white neighborhoods as integrated. Should a neighborhood that is 1 percent black and 99 percent white ever be considered racially integrated, even in Salt Lake City?

This study settles on something of a compromise. "Racially integrated" neighborhoods are taken to be those in which the black population constitutes between 10 percent and 50 percent of the total population. This definition reflects the general feeling that integration should be about sharing spaces on relatively equal grounds but also takes into account the fact that blacks make up just 13 percent of the total population of metropolitan areas around the country. Any definition of integration will be somewhat arbitrary. Nonetheless, the basic results elaborated below are largely the same when using alternative definitions of integration (Ellen 1996).

It is important to stress that the definition of integration used here reflects merely the demographic makeup of a community and says nothing about the nature of social relations. One can imagine a neighborhood composed half of black families and half of white families where there is virtually no contact between the two groups—"elbows together and hearts apart" in the words of Reverend Martin Luther King Jr. (Washington 1986, p. 118). The white households shop at one store and the black households another; the white commuters ride one bus, the black commuters another; the white children use one playground, the black children another. Should this neighborhood be considered racially integrated, or is there some minimum level of social interaction required to qualify it as integrated?

Several authors argue that socially stratified communities should not be considered truly integrated; an integrated neighborhood, that is, should involve more than a mere geographic mixing of races (Molotch 1972; Helper 1986; Saltman 1990). According to Molotch (1972), true integration should involve "biracial interaction," defined as non-antagonistic social interaction, and "transracial solidarity," meaning that blacks and whites interact freely and without constraint. Of course we need to be realistic in our assessment of the degree of social interaction that occurs in residential neighborhoods. There are many all-white communities in which people have little meaningful contact with their neighbors. But certainly, we should expect that there be no social barriers preventing blacks and whites from interacting on the same basis with one another as they do with those within their racial group. As important as this question of social interaction is, it is virtually impossible to examine in a study like this, which extends to such a large number of neighborhoods.

One final point to re-emphasize is that the chief aim of this book is to explore neighborhoods shared by whites and blacks. Given the growing numbers of Hispanics and Asians in many major metropolitan areas, such a focus may seem misplaced. Yet Hispanics and Asians are still far less segregated than blacks, and to the extent that they are residentially isolated from non-Hispanic whites, it appears to be largely a function of their lower incomes and immigrant status. Middle-class Asians and Hispanics appear to be quite integrated, for instance, while middle-class blacks are almost as segregated as poor blacks (Massey and Mullan 1984; Massey and Denton 1985; Alba and Logan 1993). In any case, this chapter does provide a brief examination of integration in the context of a multiethnic world. And the analysis throughout the book tries to be sensitive to the existence of these other minority groups and the ways in which their presence might shape the behavior of non-Hispanic whites.

The third concept that needs clarification is "stability," or more fundamentally, how to measure racial change. A key consideration here is the relevant time period over which neighborhoods will be examined. Because this study, like most others, relies on decennial census data, change is generally examined over a ten-year period. For added certainty, however, 1970 data are utilized as well to learn how many integrated tracts are stable over a twenty-year horizon.

A second issue is which population—blacks or whites—to focus on when assessing racial change. In a world populated only by blacks and whites, such a distinction would be meaningless. But with significant non-black minorities, a growth in the black population and a decline in the non-Hispanic white population may represent two very different sorts of shifts. Most prior studies consider changes in the level of black representation (Steinnes 1977; Guest 1978; Logan and

Stearns 1981; Logan and Schneider 1984; White 1984; Lee 1985; Stahura 1988; Lee and Wood 1991). The drawback with this method is that it cannot distinguish between a tract in which blacks are replacing Hispanics and one in which blacks are replacing whites. Given that fleeing whites are typically considered the greatest threat to integration, our measure of integration should surely distinguish between a neighborhood in which the white population is stable and one in which it is declining. Thus, following Denton and Massey (1991) and Galster (1990b), this study examines changes in the non-Hispanic white population rather than the black population.[2]

As for the actual measurement of change, this study uses the difference between the proportion of non-Hispanic whites present at the beginning of the decade and the share present at the end of the decade. This same convention—typically applied to blacks—has been adopted in many prior studies of racial change (Logan and Schneider 1984; Lee 1985; Galster 1990b; Lee and Wood 1991; Galster and Keeney 1993). An alternative is to consider the percentage growth in the given population (Taeuber and Taeuber 1965; Denton and Massey 1991). Unfortunately, however, this method does not reveal how a group is changing relative to the overall population. A 10 percent growth in the black population should surely be viewed differently when the white population has grown by 10 percent as well.

A third possibility is to consider the percentage change in the proportion of blacks or whites, with a neighborhood that shifts from 40 to 50 percent black viewed as undergoing a 25 percent change. The problem with this strategy is that it overstates change in neighborhoods with small black populations. Consider that a shift from 5 percent to 10 percent black is viewed as a 100 percent change, while a move from 50 percent to 55 percent black is understood as a mere 10 percent change. While a change of five percentage points perhaps should be considered differently depending on the initial level of representation of the group, it seems extreme to view these two changes as so dissimilar. A preferable approach, and one that is more consistent with theories of racial change, is to consider them equivalent.

In summary, racially integrated neighborhoods are represented here by census tracts that are between 10 and 50 percent black, and racial change in those neighborhoods is measured by the increase or decrease over a ten-year period in the proportion of neighborhood residents that are non-Hispanic white. As to how to classify census tracts as either changing or stable, Lee and Wood define stable tracts as those that experience no more than a five-percentage-point change in their proportion of blacks (Lee 1985; Lee and Wood 1990; Lee and Wood 1991; Wood and Lee 1991). Given the ten-year time span, however, this seems too strict, so a threshold of ten percentage points is used here instead.

Data Description

As noted earlier, this chapter relies heavily on the analysis of data drawn from census tracts. Unfortunately, this book was completed prior to the 2000 census, so the analysis relies on data collected in the 1970, 1980, and 1990 decennial censuses. The focus is on 1980 and 1990, mostly because they are more recent and have yet to be explored in depth, but also because of limitations of the 1970 data.[3]

The census data used are taken from a special data set prepared by the Urban Institute (the Underclass Data Base, or UDB) that links 1970 and 1990 data forward and backward to the 1980 census tract boundaries (Tobin 1993). By using this data set, it is possible to examine changes in neighborhoods over time, from 1970 through 1980 to 1990. Without such a data set, boundary changes between decennial census years make comparisons in many neighborhoods impossible.

Most of this chapter reports results from the full set of metropolitan areas nationwide. (Metropolitan areas consist of central cities and their surrounding suburban areas.) When examining the stability of mixed neighborhoods, however, the analysis is limited to the thirty-four metropolitan areas that in 1990 had total populations of over a million, black population shares of greater than 5 percent, and Hispanic population shares of less than 30 percent. Metropolitan areas in which Hispanics represent more than 30 percent of the population are omitted because the presence of large numbers of Hispanic residents could potentially cloud the primary aim of studying the interaction between black and non-Hispanic white residents. By limiting the analysis to metropolitan areas with significant black populations, we also ensure that the definition of an integrated neighborhood is reasonably consistent. Finally, by choosing generally large areas, we can generate a large sample size—the sample includes 40.5 percent of all census tracts defined in 1980. Table 2.1 presents a list of the thirty-four metropolitan areas.

Table 2.1 Selected characteristics of metropolitan areas included in sample

Metropolitan area	Region	Population, 1990	% Black, 1990
Atlanta, Ga.	South	2,833,511	26.0
Baltimore, Md.	South	2,382,172	25.9
Bergen-Passaic, N.J.	Northeast	1,278,840	8.3
Boston, Mass.	Northeast	2,870,669	7.3
Charlotte, N.C.	South	1,162,093	19.9
Chicago, Il.	Midwest	6,069,974	22.0
Cincinnati, Ohio	Midwest	1,452,645	13.1
Cleveland, Ohio	Midwest	1,831,122	19.4
Columbus, Ohio	Midwest	1,377,419	12.0
Dallas, Tex.	South	2,553,362	16.1
Denver, Colo.	West	1,622,980	5.9
Detroit, Mich.	Midwest	4,382,299	21.5
Fort Lauderdale, Fla.	South	1,255,488	15.4
Fort Worth, Tex.	South	1,332,053	10.8
Houston, Tex.	South	3,301,937	18.5
Indianapolis, Ind.	Midwest	1,249,822	13.8
Kansas City, Mo.	Midwest	1,566,280	12.8
Middlesex, N.J.	Northeast	1,019,835	6.9
Milwaukee, Wis.	Midwest	1,432,149	13.8
Nassau/Suffolk, N.Y.	Northeast	2,609,212	7.4
New Orleans, La.	South	1,238,816	34.7
New York City, N.Y.	Northeast	8,546,846	26.3
Newark, N.J.	Northeast	1,824,321	23.2
Norfolk, Va.	South	1,396,107	28.5
Oakland, Calif.	West	2,082,914	14.6
Orlando, Fla.	South	1,072,748	12.4
Philadelphia, Pa.	Northeast	4,856,881	19.1
Pittsburgh, Pa.	Northeast	2,056,705	8.2
Rochester, N.Y.	Northeast	1,002,410	9.4
Sacramento, Calif.	West	1,481,102	6.9
San Diego, Calif.	West	2,498,016	6.4
St. Louis, Mo.	Midwest	2,444,099	17.3
Tampa, Fla.	South	2,067,959	9.0
Washington, D.C.	South	3,923,574	26.6
Average		1,694,633	15.3

Source: U.S. Bureau of the Census (1990).

The Extent of Racial Integration

Table 2.2 presents an overview of the extent of racial integration in the country in 1990. Neighborhoods are classified into four categories: less than 1 percent black, 1–10 percent black, 10–50 percent black, and at least 50 percent black. As implied by the first column, of U.S. neighborhoods nationwide, over 8,000 were "integrated," or 10–50 percent black. In fact, close to one-fifth of all tracts were racially integrated. A more relevant reflection of integration is arguably the share of the population (both black and non-Hispanic white) that live in these areas. In the second and third columns of Table 2.2, we see that 15.4 percent of the non-Hispanic white population in metropolitan areas lived in integrated communities, while more than 80 percent resided in areas that were predominantly white. The proportion of black residents living in racially mixed communities was considerably larger, amounting to nearly one-third of the total black population.

This table makes evident that integration is rare, yet it also illustrates that a considerable number of integrated neighborhoods do exist and are perhaps more common than most studies of racial segregation suggest. Certainly these numbers seem surprisingly large in a country described by some as being characterized by residential apartheid.

The evidence also indicates considerable growth in integration over

Table 2.2 Distribution of Neighborhoods and Population by 1990 Percentage Black (all metropolitan areas)

Neighborhood type	% of neighborhoods	% of total NHW population	% of total black population
Less than 1% black	30.8	36.3	0.8
1–10% black	38.0	46.7	12.9
10–50% black	19.0	15.4	32.4
At least 50% black	12.2	1.7	53.9
N	42,412	148,069,316	25,768,131

Source: Ellen (1998).

Notes: NHW = non-Hispanic white. Neighborhoods classified as 1–10 percent black in this book are in fact at least 1 percent black and less than 10 percent black. Neighborhoods classified as 10–50 percent black are at least 10 percent black and less than 50 percent black.

time. Table 2.3 shows the proportion of whites and blacks living in neighborhoods with different racial compositions in 1970, 1980, and 1990.[4] Between 1970 and 1980, the share of whites living in integrated areas increased by 14 percent, while between 1980 and 1990, it rose by a full 30 percent.[5] Meanwhile, the proportion of blacks living in majority black tracts has fallen from over two-thirds to just 53.9 percent, while the proportion living in integrated tracts has risen from 25.7 to 32.4 percent.

Perhaps the most striking shift has occurred in the exclusively white neighborhoods. As shown, the proportion of whites living in census tracts in which less than 1 percent of the population is black declined from 62.6 percent in 1970 to 35.6 percent in 1990, suggesting that increasingly few communities totally shut out minorities.

Pessimistic observers might question the significance of this latter change, arguing that whites in these neighborhoods typically remain an overwhelming majority. And surveys of racial preferences suggest that whites tend to remain comfortable in areas as long as they form such a majority. It is only when the black population grows to 10 or 20 percent that white households begin to exhibit serious discomfort. Still, as John Kain has argued (1985, p. 267), the "difference between none and several is enormous." And such modest levels of racial mixing may pave the way for more substantial integration. For one thing, black households tend to be reluctant to be the very first of their race in a white neighborhood. According to one recent survey, whereas only 38 percent of black households are willing to move into an all-white neighborhood, the percentage willing to move in jumps to 95 percent when just a few other blacks are present (Farley et al. 1994).

Table 2.3 Distribution of white and black population by percentage black in 1970, 1980, and 1990 (all metropolitan areas)

	% of white population			% of black population		
Neighborhood type	1970	1980	1990	1970	1980	1990
Less than 1% black	62.6	48.5	35.6	0.6	0.9	0.8
1–10% black	25.0	37.9	47.1	6.6	10.2	12.9
10–50% black	10.5	12.0	15.6	25.7	26.7	32.4
At least 50% black	1.9	1.7	1.7	67.1	62.2	53.9
All neighborhoods	100.0	100.0	100.0	100.0	100.0	100.0

Source: Ellen (1998).

For another, as noted above, there is evidence that racial hostility declines with interaction, especially when people are of similar social status. Thus, white households living among even a small share of black neighbors may grow less resistant toward racial integration.

There is no comparable nationwide data for the years prior to 1970. But one study considers a sample of 64 metropolitan areas and finds that there was comparatively little change during the 1960s. The fraction of whites living in tracts that were less than 1 percent black declined between 1960 and 1970, but the fraction of whites living in mixed tracts rose only slightly while the fraction of blacks living in majority black tracts actually *increased*. Over the 1960s, that is, whites experienced a modest increase in integration, while blacks became more concentrated. This seeming paradox is probably explained by the fact that the black population in metropolitan areas grew at a much faster rate than did the white population during this decade, and the growth occurred largely within existing black neighborhoods (McKinney and Schnare 1989). The evidence on integration for years prior to 1960 is even thinner, but most research has suggested that cities became more segregated during the first half of the century (Pascal 1967; Lieberson 1980; Cutler, Glaeser, and Vigdor 1999).

In short, the evidence seems to suggest that on average, blacks became progressively more concentrated in our cities and metropolitan areas between 1940 and 1970, experienced a small increase in integration in those locations over the 1970s, and had a somewhat larger increase during the 1980s. White residents, meanwhile, have generally experienced an increase in exposure to blacks in each of the three decades since 1960, with the rate of increase accelerating in each subsequent decade.

Measuring Racial Stability

This analysis has so far said nothing about the long-term stability of this growing group of integrated neighborhoods. All of the neighborhoods that were integrated in 1980 might have become largely black by 1990. Indeed, such a pattern was taken to be the norm in the past, because racial tipping or transition seemed to occur so consistently in racially mixed neighborhoods. As a result, few early studies even recognize the possibility of racial stability, much less explore its prevalence. The authors of one classic study of racial change in Chicago, for instance, actually omit as outliers the few tracts in which the proportion of blacks decreased between 1940 and 1950, stating that there are only "isolated instances of tracts with mixed white and Negro populations in which the Negro proportion failed to increase" (Duncan and Duncan 1955, p. 11). In more recent years, a number of studies have begun to question the inevitability of succession and to explore the pace of racial change, but the studies have so far focused on the 1970s (Taub, Taylor, and Dunham 1984; Lee 1985; Lee and Wood 1990; Denton and Massey 1991; Lee and Wood 1991).

One way to measure racial stability is to consider the share of tracts in each racial category in 1980 that remained within the category by 1990. Of the 2,773 tracts in the sample that were racially integrated in 1980, over three-fourths (76.4 percent) remained integrated in 1990, while 16.6 percent became majority black and 7 percent changed to predominantly white. These figures hardly suggest relentless and inevitable succession. Still, there is considerably more movement within the integrated category than there is within the segregated group. A total of 89 percent of the tracts that were predominantly white in 1980 remained predominantly white in 1990, and 97 percent of the majority black tracts remained largely black in 1990.

Of course, a neighborhood might change a great deal and still remain within a given racial category. Thus, a more accurate picture of stability is given in Table 2.4. This table shows the proportion of tracts in each category of racial composition that experienced sub-

Table 2.4 Percent of neighborhoods undergoing change between 1980 and 1990 by 1980 percentage black (34 MSA sample)

% Black in 1980	NHW loss	Stable	NHW gain	Number of neighborhoods
Less than 10% black	21.2	78.4	0.4	11,590
10–50% black	46.1	49.5	4.4	2,773
At least 50% black	12.3	83.3	4.4	2,816
All tracts	23.7	74.6	1.7	17,179

Source: Ellen (1998).

Notes: NHW = non-Hispanic white. Tracts undergoing non-Hispanic white loss are those in which the percentage non-Hispanic white *declines* by at least 10 percentage points. Tracts undergoing non-Hispanic white gain are those in which the percentage non-Hispanic white *increases* by at least ten percentage points.

stantial white loss, significant white gain, or remained stable between 1980 and 1990. As discussed, tracts are considered to be "transitional," or to be experiencing significant white loss, if their proportion of non-Hispanic whites falls by more than ten percentage points over the decade. Similarly, tracts in which the proportion of non-Hispanic whites increases by more than ten percentage points are classified as white gain tracts.

The table reveals a pronounced difference between integrated and non-integrated communities. Roughly 80 percent of both predominantly white and predominantly black tracts were stable over the decade, compared to less than half of the racially integrated tracts. And a full 46 percent of these racially mixed tracts experienced a loss in white population share. Still, this picture does not suggest the relentless and inevitable loss of white households. Indeed, even when using a more narrow definition of stability (a change of less than five percentage points), a substantial fraction of integrated tracts (40 percent) fail to lose whites.

Ten years is not that long a time period. Thus, I also look at integrated tracts over the course of two decades. As expected, a greater share of mixed tracts lost white population over this longer period. But a considerable number still appear stable. Of the 2,058 census tracts that were racially integrated in 1970, 61.3 percent remained integrated in 1980 and 56.9 percent remained integrated in 1990. And 36 percent had not lost a significant share of their white population by 1990 ("significant" again being gauged as more than ten percentage points).

Is Integration Becoming More Stable?

Accounts of earlier decades suggest far less stability for racially integrated neighborhoods. Consider one author's claim in 1957 that "the only interracial communities in the U.S. . . . are those where limits exist upon the influx of non-whites" (Grodzins 1957, p. 36), or another statement in 1975 that "the process of succession is rarely, if ever, reversed" (Aldrich 1975, p. 334). But has integration in fact become more viable over the years? A comparison of the 1970s and the 1980s suggests that it has. As shown in Table 2.5, the average 1970–1980 decline in the proportion of white residents in racially mixed tracts was 18 percentage points, compared with a mean loss of 10.5 per-

Table 2.5 Comparison of 1970–1980 and 1980–1990 change in racially integrated census tracts

	1970–1980	1980–1990
Mean loss in percentage white	18.0	10.5
Percent of integrated neighborhoods that remain integrated at end of decade	61.0	76.4
Percent of integrated neighborhoods that do not lose substantial white population over decade[a]	44.5	53.3
Number of racially integrated tracts examined in each decade	2,058	2,773

a. Tracts in which the proportion of whites present either declined by less than ten percentage points or increased.

centage points for similar tracts a decade later.[6] Moreover, while 61 percent of the tracts that were racially integrated in 1970 remained integrated by 1980, that proportion rose to 76.4 percent between 1980 and 1990. Finally, the proportion of integrated tracts that did not lose a substantial share of whites between 1970 and 1980 was 44.5 percent, compared with 53.3 percent between 1980 and 1990. In short, it seems clear that racially integrated neighborhoods were more stable during the 1980s than they were during the 1970s.

Figure 2.1 shows the difference between the two decades in a little more detail. It compares the mean loss in white population share over the 1980s with that occurring during the 1970s, for each decile of black population (0–10 percent, 10–20 percent, and so on). As shown, the loss of white population during the 1970s was consistently larger, especially for tracts between 10 and 60 percent black. The pace of white loss also appears to have been more directly related to the size of the black population during the 1970s. The mean white loss during the 1970s for tracts that started out as between 30 and 40 percent black was significantly greater than for tracts that started out as between 10 and 20 percent black. During the 1980s, by contrast, there was no appreciable difference in the rate of white loss between such moderately and substantially integrated tracts.

Part of what is driving the larger mean losses during the 1970s is the existence of a greater number of integrated tracts that experienced

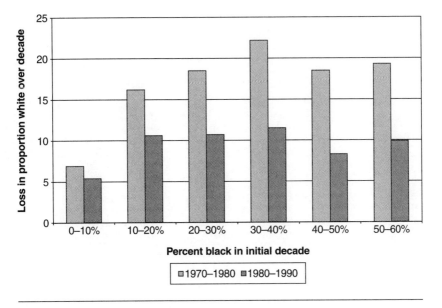

Figure 2.1 Mean loss in proportion white, 1970–1980 and 1980–1990

dramatic white loss. Figure 2.2 shows the 90th percentile of white population loss during the two decades and provides some additional insight into the difference between the 1970s and 1980s. The percentile curves are constructed by ranking tracts in each decile according to loss in white population share. Specifically, if the 90th percentile of white population loss for tracts between 20 and 30 percent black is 50 percentage points, this means that 90 percent of the tracts that were initially between 20 and 30 percent black experienced a white loss smaller than 50 percentage points.

As shown, the difference between the 90th percentile curves is quite striking, with substantially fewer integrated tracts experiencing a dramatic loss of white residents during the 1980s. Consider that during the later decade, 90 percent of the tracts that started between 20 and 30 percent black in 1980 experienced a white loss of less than 30 percentage points; during the 1970s, the 90 percent cut-off fell at nearly twice this level, or 55 percentage points. But the more limited scope of racial change during the 1980s is not the only difference between the two decades. There is also a substantial difference in the median white

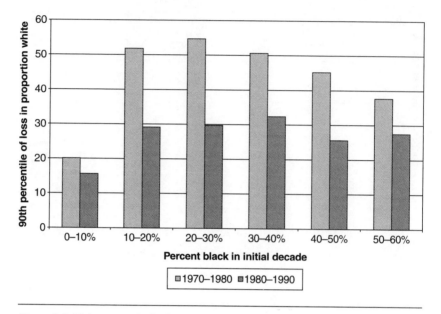

Figure 2.2 90th percentile for loss in proportion white, 1970–1980 and 1980–1990

loss. During the 1980s, for instance, the median white loss for census tracts that are initially between 40 and 50 percent black was 7.4 percentage points. During the 1970s, the median white loss for this set of census tracts was 23.1 percentage points, or in other words, more than three times as great.

Once again, this study did not have access to data for decades prior to 1970. But two other studies suggest that racially integrated neighborhoods were even less stable during the 1950s and 1960s than in the 1970s (White 1984; Wood and Lee 1991). Wood and Lee (1991), for instance, report that 38.9 percent of mixed tracts were either stable or lost more blacks than whites between 1970 and 1980, up from 27.7 percent between 1960 and 1970 and 28.4 percent between 1950 and 1960.

Contrary to this general trend of increasing stability of racial mixing, the evidence seems to suggest that integration was actually *more* stable during the 1940s than in the 1950s. In their study of thirty-eight cities, for instance, Wood and Lee (1991) find that integration was more stable during the 1940s than in later decades, with the share of tracts that were stable or lost more blacks than whites during this decade amounting to 38.5 percent as compared to approximately 28 percent during the 1950s and 1960s, respectively. In their now classic study of ten cities, Taeuber and Taeuber (1965) uncover a similar trend—integrated tracts were significantly more likely to gain non-white population between 1950 and 1960 than they had been between 1940 and 1950.[7] The authors attribute the difference largely to the housing market, and particularly the reduced residential construction during World War II, which meant that whites had fewer opportunities to move out of urban neighborhoods during the 1940s. When residential construction surged during the 1950s, whites fled to the suburbs in large numbers, and urban neighborhoods became increasingly black. (It is possible too, that some of the greater instability of integration during the 1950s was due to the Supreme Court's decision in *Brown v. Board of Education.* Sharing neighborhoods with blacks was suddenly much more threatening to many white households when it also meant sharing public schools.)

Accounting for a Multiethnic World

Although the chief aim of this book is to explore the nature and dynamics of neighborhoods shared by blacks and whites, this section briefly considers the question of racial change within a multiethnic world. To consider other, non-black minorities like Hispanics and Asians in analyzing patterns of integration is to complicate the process a great deal. But to fully understand today's world, such populations cannot be ignored. Non-black minorities made up 14.1 percent of the total population in metropolitan areas in 1990, up from 9.9 percent in 1980.

For simplicity, non-black minorities—primarily Hispanics and Asians—are treated here as a single group. (Black Hispanics are treated as blacks and not as Hispanics in this framework, because their settlement patterns are closer to those of non-Hispanic blacks than to those of Hispanic whites; see Denton and Massey 1989.) The world is thus made up of three different racial/ethnic groups, and seven different kinds of neighborhoods:

- All white (non-Hispanic)
- Predominantly black

- Predominantly other minority
- Mixed, white and black
- Mixed, white and other
- Mixed, black and other
- Mixed, multiethnic (all three groups present)

To define these neighborhood categories, minorities (that is, blacks and non-black minorities) are considered "present" if they make up at least 10 percent of the population in the tract. Since they compose a so much larger share of the nation's population, non-Hispanic whites are typically considered "present" if they make up at least 40 percent of the tract's population. A predominantly black or other minority tract is one in which the minority group in question composes a majority of the population (and the remaining minority group makes up less than 10 percent).[8]

Table 2.6 looks at the share of non-Hispanic whites living in neighborhoods of different types. Recall that Table 2.2 reported that 83 percent of non-Hispanic whites in 1990 lived in communities with insignificant black populations (of less than 10 percent). These figures make evident that a large number of these households were in areas with Asians or Hispanics. Indeed, only 61.7 percent of the white population in 1990 lived in predominantly white areas. Consistent with

Table 2.6 Distribution of non-Hispanic white population by type of neighborhood, 1980 and 1990 (all metropolitan areas)

Neighborhood type	1980	1990
Homogenous		
All white	72.3	61.7
Predominantly black	1.4	1.3
Predominantly other	1.2	1.8
Mixed		
Mixed, white and black	9.0	10.4
Mixed, white and other	13.1	19.4
Mixed, black and other	0.6	1.1
Mixed, multiethnic	2.3	4.2
All neighborhoods	100.0	100.0
N	141,209,308	148,069,316

Source: Ellen (1998).

the findings above, Table 2.6 also shows clearly that integration is becoming more prevalent. The share of non-Hispanic whites living in all four types of mixed neighborhoods increased over the decade. The growth in the proportion living in the mixed white and black tracts, however, was the smallest.

A key question is whether the neighborhoods shared by blacks and Latinos or those shared by blacks, Latinos, and whites are any more stable than those with blacks and whites alone. Table 2.7 attempts to answer this question by presenting a full racial transition matrix using this seven-way neighborhood typology. The picture here of racial dynamics is consistent with those found elsewhere, with the largely black and minority neighborhoods being far more stable than those that are shared by whites and blacks. Just under 60 percent of the neighborhoods that are shared by non-Hispanic whites and blacks in 1980 remain mixed white and black neighborhoods in 1990, while over 90 percent of the predominantly black communities remain predominantly black in 1990. Significantly, however, almost as many black-white neighborhoods by 1990 had developed into multiethnic communities with a substantial non-Hispanic white population as had become largely black.

Notably, the pace of white loss appears to be greatest not in the mixed black-white communities but in the multiethnic communities. Over a third of the census tracts that are initially classified as "multiethnic" lose non-Hispanic white population and end up as black-other communities. Further analysis confirms this general pattern, revealing that 62 percent of multiethnic census tracts lost a significant share of their non-Hispanic white population compared with 44 percent of the black-white communities.[9]

Growing Integration versus Persisting Segregation?

At first blush, the results reported in this chapter appear counter to those of authors who study racial segregation. In their important book on the subject, for instance, Massey and Denton (1993) describe segregation in contemporary America as being a system of "Apartheid" that has shown "little sign of change with the passage of time" (p. 2). Looking specifically at the 1980s, they write that "there is little in recent data to suggest that processes of racial segregation have moderated much since 1980" (p. 223).

Table 2.7 Neighborhood racial transition matrix, percent of neighborhoods in each category in 1990 by 1980 type (34 metropolitan areas)

1980 type	NHW	Black	Other	NHW/black	NHW/other	Black/other	Multiethnic	Total
NHW	75.6	0.2	0.0	6.4	15.2	0.1	2.5	100.0
Black	0.0	91.3	0.0	1.8	0.0	6.5	0.4	100.0
Other	0.0	0.0	70.1	0.0	3.8	24.3	1.7	100.0
NHW/black	5.8	17.2	0.0	58.5	1.6	2.6	14.3	100.0
NHW/other	2.2	0.2	9.9	0.5	69.6	4.4	13.2	100.0
Black/other	0.0	4.5	1.4	0.5	0.1	91.5	2.0	100.0
Multiethnic	1.7	3.0	2.5	3.4	5.1	35.7	48.7	100.0

Source: Ellen (1998).
Note: NHW = non-Hispanic white.

Part of their claim is undeniably true—racial segregation remains extreme and continues to be "a fundamental cleavage" in American society (Massey and Denton 1993, p. 223). Consider that the average index of dissimilarity (segregation index) in our sample of thirty-four metropolitan areas was 70 in 1990, indicating that in the average metropolitan area, 70 percent of blacks would have to move in order to achieve total desegregation.[10] But there have been notable signs of change in recent decades.

To start with, average indices of segregation did fall during the 1970s and 1980s. Massey and Denton focus only on very large metropolitan areas, but more recent analyses of larger numbers of metropolitan areas uncover real declines. In the broadest study to date, Cutler, Glaeser, and Vigdor (1999) examine all metropolitan areas with at least one thousand black residents and report that the average index of dissimilarity fell from 72.6 in 1970 to 62.9 in 1980 to 55.9 in 1990.[11] Farley and Frey (1994) examine a somewhat smaller set of metropolitan areas (232) during just the 1980s and find that the average dissimilarity index fell from 69 to 65. (This latter study relies on block groups, which are smaller than census tracts and therefore tend to yield higher segregation scores.) These declines may not be as rapid as one would like, but they do represent a significant departure from the consistent increases seen in the years following World War II.

Even so, these changes may seem relatively small in comparison to those reported earlier in this chapter. There I had shown that between 1970 and 1990, the proportion of non-Hispanic whites and blacks living in integrated communities had increased by nearly 50 and 30 percent, respectively. Moreover, the evidence here shows the stability of integrated neighborhoods to be increasing—even in a more limited set of large metropolitan areas. Consider that the mean loss in the proportion of whites living in integrated communities fell by over 40 percent between the 1970s and the 1980s.

In short, we see small but significant changes when considering measures of segregation and more substantial changes when examining integration. The key here is that the tools used to measure segregation are analytically and conceptually distinct from those used to assess integration. The various indices of segregation measure the extent to which blacks and whites reside in distinct neighborhoods in a given city or metropolitan area. While they give a good feel for how far a city is from the ideal of perfect integration, and provide a useful barometer with which to compare over time and across *cities,* they do not tell us the share of people living in integrated *neighborhoods* in that city or what happens to these diverse neighborhoods over time.[12]

The literature on segregation effectively conveys the extreme degree and persistence of racial segregation in our cities and metropolitan areas. What is sometimes lost, however, is the fact that integrated neighborhoods do indeed exist. This chapter hopefully makes clear that there are a substantial (and more importantly, an increasing) number of stable integrated neighborhoods in this country. Quite simply, Saul Alinsky's classic description of racial integration—as merely the time between "the entrance of the first black family and the exit of the last white family" (Sanders 1970, p. 86)—rings much less true in the 1980s than it did in earlier decades.

CHAPTER THREE

Toward a Theory of Racial Change

The previous chapter demonstrated that there are a growing number of stable racially integrated neighborhoods in the United States. At the same time, most mixed neighborhoods still do lose white population, and many fairly rapidly. Thus, several questions arise. First, what causes many integrated neighborhoods to lose white residents? Second, why is it that some mixed neighborhoods rapidly transition to predominantly black while others remain relatively stable? And more fundamentally, what role does race play in residential decisions? Clearly, these questions do not have a simple answer. Ultimately, any complete account of the causes of racial transition will necessarily embrace myriad different factors, including housing market discrimination, white household prejudice, voluntary ethnic clustering, class-based preferences, concern for neighborhood quality, and so on. Here, however, the focus is on identifying the *predominant* cause of racial transition.

As set forth in Chapter 1, this study suggests that the predominant cause of racial transition is white households' decision—when moving in the ordinary course of events—to avoid racially integrated communities. Furthermore, the study hypothesizes that such white avoidance of racially mixed neighborhoods is rooted primarily in certain negative race-based stereotypes that whites hold about the future quality of such neighborhoods–and not on any categorical unwillingness to live among black households. This hypothesis, referred to here as the race-based neighborhood stereotyping hypothesis, builds in part on (and therefore owes a debt to) the work that Richard Taub, D. Garth Taylor, and Jan Dunham have done on crime and neighborhood change in Chicago.

Neighborhood Racial Change in the Past

The popular view of neighborhood racial transition has been greatly shaped by the experience of American cities (in particular, certain Northeastern and Midwestern cities) during the first few decades after World War II. Racial transition in these cities was rapid and widespread. A typical example was the Mattapan neighborhood in Boston, which will be discussed later. It changed from 99.9 percent white in 1960 to 48 percent black by 1970 and 85 percent black in 1976 (Soutner 1980). Or consider one census tract in Chicago where the proportion of black residents rose from 16.5 percent in 1940 to 96.9 percent in 1950 (Duncan and Duncan 1957). More broadly, in all but one of Chicago's census tracts with non-white proportions of between 25 and 75 percent in 1940, the non-white proportion increased by more than 20 percentage points over the decade. Similarly, in the four Northern cities examined by Taeuber and Taeuber (1965), during the 1950s the average racially mixed neighborhood experienced an increase of 38 percentage points in the proportion of non-white inhabitants.[1]

How did such dramatic and sudden change take place? During the postwar era, the black population in many Northeastern and Midwestern cities expanded rapidly. Between 1940 and 1970, the growth of the black population in these cities grew by an average of 4.7 percent each year, largely fueled by migration from the rural South (Cutler, Glaeser, and Vigdor 1999). Over a decade, this increase added up to substantial change; during the 1950s, for instance, the non-white population grew by 84.2 percent in the cities of Minneapolis and Newark and by 189 percent in Milwaukee (Leven et al. 1976). Yet widespread discrimination confined blacks to only a handful of neighborhoods. Pressure naturally built for expansion, and when a certain neighborhood (for one reason or another) became open to blacks, the demand was extraordinary. The role of discrimination in greatly increasing black demand and therefore in contributing to the paths and patterns of racial transition was recognized by Charles Abrams some fifty years ago. If integration in neighborhoods was to persist, it was necessary, he suggested, "to ease the pressure for housing by all minorities." In a world with "no race covenants and no exclusions practiced, there might be a more even distribution of minorities in all neighborhoods and no fear of a shift in racial composition" (Abrams 1947, p. 26).

During the postwar era the notion of whites closely living among blacks—even a few—was quite foreign in the North, and fears and prejudices were great. As a result, whites living outside of the neighborhoods that became open to blacks stayed away, and those living inside them moved away, causing rapid racial transition. (As suggested earlier, the relative importance of white avoidance versus white flight in this earlier era is outside the scope of this study. In any event, the evidence seems inconclusive. Two studies of Cleveland and Chicago identified neighborhoods that were racially changing during the 1950s and 1960s but did not exhibit elevated rates of household turnover (Molotch 1969; Guest and Zuiches 1974). The implication, of course, is that the racial change that occurred resulted from white avoidance and not white flight. Other studies in these years, however, do suggest accelerated white departures.)

The "white flight" dynamic in these cities was exacerbated by the discriminatory scare tactics employed by speculating realtors. These realtors, dubbed "block-busters," pressured whites to sell their homes quickly and at much reduced prices. The case of Mattapan has been well documented. During the late 1960s, real estate agents called white households in Mattapan—on a daily basis, by some accounts—and tried to scare them into selling. One anonymous agent described his practices at the time:

We were told you get the listings any way you can. It's pretty easy to do: just scare the hell out of them. And that's what we did. . . . It got to the point that to have fun while we were working, we would try to outdo each other with the most outlandish threats that people would believe. . . . I'd go down the street with the [black] buyer and ask, which house do you want? He'd pick one and I'd ring the doorbell and say, these people want to buy your house. If the lady said no, I'd say the reason they're so interested is that their cousins, aunts, mother, whatever, it's a family of twelve, are moving in diagonally across the street. And they want to be near them. Most of the time, that worked. If that didn't work, you'd say their kid just got out of jail for housebreaking, or rape, or something that would work. (Anonymous, cited in Levine and Harmon 1992, pp. 195–196)

Panic selling ensued, whites fled, and these agents made substantial profits. Agents often purchased a property from a departing white family and resold it within one or two weeks to a black family at twice the price, earning substantial commissions on both sales as well.

The case of Mattapan illustrates how discriminatory bank practices may also have helped to accelerate racial transition. In the wake of the assassination of Martin Luther King Jr., Mayor Kevin White convinced twenty-two local banks to resuscitate a loan fund that they had set up a few years earlier to aid urban renewal. Called the Boston Banks Urban Renewal Group (BBURG), the newly rejuvenated consortium made available $50 million in mortgages insured by the Federal Housing Administration to help blacks buy houses in better neighborhoods. For political and economic reasons, however, the banks limited their loans to a well-defined inner-city district composed of Roxbury, Dorchester, and Mattapan (Levine and Harmon 1992).[2] All of the increased black demand was thus focused on a few neighborhoods, and pressures for transition became even greater.

As Gamm (1999) points out, however, BBURG could not have been the sole culprit. For the BBURG line did not in fact include the entire Mattapan neighborhood, and panic selling was just as rapid outside as it was inside of the line. Still, perceptions are critical, and the popular belief seems to have been that Mattapan was singled out. Thus, the funds made available through BBURG probably contributed to the general sense of panic and accelerated racial change both in Mattapan and throughout South Boston.

As suggested earlier, the conventional view in the postwar era (and beyond) held that the predominant reason why whites avoided and/or fled these neighborhoods (and why the scare tactics of block-busting realtors worked) was that white households held deep-seated prejudices against blacks and simply did not want to live among them. As an editorial in the *Baltimore Sun* argued in 1955, "The real villain is prejudice, which makes a whole neighborhood flee because of one Negro family" (Dorsey, cited in Orser 1994, p. 90). Accounts of departing whites suggest that whites simply could not imagine living near to blacks under any circumstances. "Their way of life is so different from ours," said one middle-aged white woman in Detroit in 1956 (Sugrue 1996, p. 217).

The common complaints were that blacks were lazy, more prone to violence and sexuality, and less apt to keep up their homes (see, for example, Orser 1994). Fears of racial intimacy and intermarriage were often paramount. White neighborhood groups continually warned of "rapacious black sexuality" and the risk of racial intermarriage (Sugrue 1996, p. 217). As one white resident of Chicago complained in 1954, integration meant that blacks would intermarry with whites and thus send the "whole white race . . . downhill" (Hirsch 1983, p. 196).

As the Mattapan example makes clear, block-busters made every attempt to play upon these racial biases. They would claim that the black families moving in had violent histories, and they would play into the sexual fears of white households by emphasizing that the new black families included younger men. They even went so far as to fabricate past rape charges (Levine and Harmon 1992; Sugrue 1996). Similarly, some accounts describe block-busters as deliberately choosing irresponsible black tenants to move into homes in white neighborhoods to confirm white stereotypes about blacks not keeping up their homes (Orser 1994).

Despite its clear importance, white prejudice against blacks was not the only motivation for white avoidance and/or flight in these years. Consistent with the race-based stereotyping hypothesis, some accounts describe white residents who were generally supportive of the inter-racial living but were worried about declining property values (Orser 1994; Sugrue 1996, p. 215). And evidence from case studies of racially changing neighborhoods in the 1950s suggests that departing whites were no more racially prejudiced than those who stayed behind (Mayer 1960; Fishman 1961).

On the heels of this pervasive neighborhood racial change in the 1950s and 1960s, Thomas Schelling (1972) developed his elegantly simple model of the white flight phenomenon—a model that remains, some thirty years after its initial publication, the chief theoretical tool with which neighborhood racial transition is analyzed and understood by economists and most other social scientists (see e.g., Clark 1991; Farley et al. 1978; Schnare and McRae 1978).[3] The model assumes that whites dislike sharing their neighborhoods with blacks and remain in a community only as long as its black population stays under individual tolerance thresholds.[4] The model also assumes that blacks are much less sensitive to racial composition, but that they are probably wary of being too small of a minority. Finally, the model allows for a range of white tolerance thresholds. Given these assumptions, the model generally finds only a narrow band of stable racial integration. In brief, as the most prejudiced whites leave, the proportion of black residents inevitably rises above the tolerance threshold of the next most prejudiced group of whites in the community and therefore prompts them to leave. This "tipping" process continues until the neighborhood becomes all black.

The powerful simplicity of Schelling's model, together with its consonance with apparent reality, struck a chord. And the message was clear: in a world where a substantial share of whites have a categorical dislike of living among blacks, racial integration will inevitably unravel.

In truth, as noted above, white attitudes were probably far more complicated than Schelling's abstract model suggested, even in those years of widespread transition. But if Schelling's model—predicated as it is on the notion of white flight and a categorical refusal of whites to live among more than a specified number of blacks—represented a simplification then, it seems likely that the model is further from reality today. Many recent commentators have noted (at times in an exaggerated fashion) the marked racial progress we have made over the last few decades (Patterson 1997; Thernstrom and Thernstrom 1997). In terms of racial attitudes, consider for example that in 1997, 61 percent of whites voiced approval of marriages between blacks and whites. In 1958, only 4 percent of white Americans voiced similar approval. White Americans today also report virtually no objection to voting for a qualified black candidate for president. In the 1997 Gallup Poll Social Audit, 93 percent of both blacks and whites reported that they would be willing to vote for a black candidate. As recently as 1958, meanwhile, only 35 percent of whites said that they would be willing to vote for a black person for president (Gallup Poll Social Audit 1997). What is more, as Orlando Patterson (1997) has pointed out, African Americans are a growing, and arguably dominant, force in the nation's popular culture: its music, its dance, its sports, and so on. There is also good reason to believe that white prejudice has lessened with respect to housing in particular. Whites consistently report a greater willingness to live in racially integrated communities, and, as shown in Chapter 2, a growing number of integrated neighborhoods are indeed remaining stable over time.

This progress in racial attitudes since Schelling, related changes in the nature of housing discrimination and enforcement, and the simple passage of time make this a ripe time to revisit the phenomenon of neighborhood racial change in the contemporary United States and to analyze its predominant causes afresh (Yinger 1995; Turner and Wienk 1993).

Explaining Contemporary Neighborhood Racial Transition

There are of course various contenders for the predominant cause of racial transition today. Putting aside for the moment the issue of the relative importance of white flight versus white avoidance (that is, "exit" decisions versus "entry" decisions), this section outlines three alternative hypotheses for the dominant motivation underlying white resistance to integrated neighborhoods: benign ethnic clustering; pure prejudice; and class differences. The section also addresses certain other factors that have been offered as accelerating the process of racial change.

Benign White Clustering

One possible major cause of white resistance to racial mixing is a "benign" desire on the part of whites to live among other whites–the same kind of benign desire that underlies ethnic clustering by non-white minorities such as Cubans or Koreans. The salient feature here is that such desires are not a function of any affirmative dislike of other groups. The argument is that Koreans, for example, cluster because they wish to live among others who share their customs and language and not because they have deep-seated prejudice against whites.

Both evidence and common sense, however, suggest that whites' motivation to resist sharing neighborhoods with blacks does not stem from some conventional ethnic desire to live exclusively among other whites. For one thing, whites are fairly willing to live among other minority groups—in particular, Asians (Bobo and Zubrinsky 1996). Further, it is difficult to understand what the interest in such clustering would be when whites themselves are the dominant group in our society. What customs and ways of life can whites not enjoy by virtue of living in a mixed neighborhood?

Given these arguments, such benign white clustering is not presented here (or generally elsewhere in the literature) as a real contender for the dominant cause of racial transition. The two remaining possibilities—pure prejudice and class differences—need to be taken more seriously, however.

Pure Prejudice

A more plausible primary explanation for white avoidance is that it is motivated by racial prejudice against blacks, pure and simple. The idea is that whites believe that blacks are racially inferior (or just "different") and simply do not want to live among them. This belief may rest on specific invidious assumptions about the characteristics of blacks such as that blacks are lazy. Or it may rest on more inchoate grounds. According to some studies, even after controlling for income and class, blacks are viewed as inherently inferior, and having black neighbors is viewed as inherently undesirable (Berry and Kasarda 1977; St. John and Bates, 1990; Weiher 1991).

As discussed, pure racial prejudice tends to be offered most frequently as the primary explanation for racial transition in the past. And this is not unwarranted. As also discussed, such individual-based prejudice has played a large role in shaping past neighborhood dynamics (and residential patterns more generally), and such prejudice may still explain the motivations of many white households today. But this study suggests that race-based neighborhood stereotyping is a more useful framework to understand the motivations of white households today. I return to such stereotyping later in the chapter.

Class-Based Explanations

An alternative claim is that what really drives racial transition are class differences, that is, whites' desire to live among more affluent people or in more affluent neighborhoods (Pascal 1967; Leven et al. 1976; Clark 1986; Muth 1986). The argument comes in two basic varieties (which overlap considerably). One variation, which focuses on the affluence of the neighborhood, views racial transition as fundamentally a process of income transition, whereby housing units and neighborhoods are filtered down from one income group to a lower one. Because whites do in fact have higher incomes than minorities, they are typically found in the group able to afford the move to those neighborhoods with larger and newer homes, better schools, and safer streets (White 1977; Anas 1980). In these models, white and black households are concerned with housing size and quality and with their neighborhood environment, but they are indifferent to the race of their neighbors.

The second version of the class-based story holds that households are most concerned about the "quality" of their neighbors, but significantly, they gauge such "quality" in terms of class. Charles Leven and his co-authors take the position that most whites do not mind living among blacks as long as they are of similar income and similar class. Racial separation, in their view, is driven by the simple fact that black households have lower incomes on average than their white counterparts and that were black earnings to rise substantially, racial segregation would largely disappear. In their words, "achieving racial integration may be substantially easier than achieving integration by economic class" (Leven et al. 1976, p. 202).

While income differences surely account for some of today's segregation, studies have consistently found that they explain a fairly small share (Marshall and Jiobu 1975; Kain 1976; Farley 1986; Darden 1987; Massey and Denton 1987; Galster 1988; Denton and Massey 1988; McKinney and Schnare 1989; Farley 1995). After all, middle-class blacks are often found to live in largely black areas, despite the obvious fact that ample white households exist of similar means. Clark (1986) points out rightfully that inter-racial differences in wealth (as opposed to just income) need to be explored before any definitive conclusions can be reached. But surely, such differences in wealth—significant though they are (Oliver and Shapiro 1997; Conley 1999)—could not explain the full extent of segregation.

Thus, while it certainly seems reasonable to assume that class plays some role in the process of neighborhood racial change, the role is not likely to be a large one. Again, this study suggests that race-based neighborhood stereotyping is far more important to explaining racial change.

In addition to these core hypotheses about the dominant motivation underlying white resistance to integrated living, there are a few other factors that have been offered in the literature as at least contributing to the rate of neighborhood racial change. These hypotheses do not make claims about the underlying motives of white avoidance, and thus they are not necessarily alternatives to the notion of race-based neighborhood stereotyping. But they do suggest some interesting ideas about the causes of the variation in the pace of racial change across different integrated communities and so bear mentioning. The first and most important is housing market discrimination.

Housing Market Discrimination

While the blatant block-busting techniques that were commonplace in the 1950s and 1960s have largely disappeared, housing market discrimination persists and plays a critical role in the overall story of segregation patterns in the United States. By discrimination, I mean the specific acts of sellers, landlords, realtors, lenders, and other marketplace actors to keep blacks out of white neighborhoods by refusing to sell, rent, show, or lend money for housing to blacks (Yinger 1995).[5] Such housing market discrimination is generally unlawful under federal and state anti-discrimination laws, but it persists nonetheless in part because of inadequate enforcement.

Popular writing on racial segregation often confounds such marketplace discrimination with white household prejudice—perhaps because both keep blacks out of white neighborhoods. But marketplace discrimination against blacks must be sharply distinguished from racial prejudice of white households. Racial prejudice, while morally repugnant, is not against the law. It is not against the law, for example, for a white resident in a particular neighborhood to dislike blacks and even to express that fact to the world and thereby make blacks feel extremely unwelcome in that neighborhood. Indeed, far from being unlawful, such morally suspect, hostile thoughts and words are generally constitutionally protected. But they still have the effect of keeping blacks out of white neighborhoods. For who, after all, enjoys living in a neighborhood where he or she is disliked and unwanted? (Similarly, it is not against the law, nor could it be, for white households not to like blacks and, for that reason alone, to choose not to move into a mixed neighborhood, or to choose to leave such a neighborhood.)

It is important to note too that while prejudice is considered here as a leading candidate for the dominant reason why whites resist integrated neighborhoods, racial discrimination is not. For realtors do not, for example, systematically deny whites the opportunity to move into integrated communities if they want to live there. It is possible that they may encourage or "steer" whites to live in largely white areas, but the evidence on steering is that the differences between neighborhoods shown to black and white customers is small (Yinger 1995, p. 55).[6]

With that said, discrimination plainly does still constrain white decision making in at least two important ways and thus plays a vital, albeit more indirect role in the dynamics of racial transition. First, housing market discrimination alters the range of choices faced by white households by helping to sustain the existence of all-white communities. It thereby affords white households a place to which they can flee from racially mixed communities (Yinger 1978; 1995). Second, as described below, the first proposition of the race-based neighborhood stereotyping hypothesis is that white households tend to assume mixed neighborhoods eventually become all-black. But this assumption is largely rooted in the fact that, historically, all mixed neighborhoods did eventually become all-black—a fact that, as typified by the postwar experience described earlier, was driven in large part by discrimination. In short, it is possible that the rate of racial transition in a community is shaped significantly by past and present lender and realtor practices in the metropolitan area (Vandell and Harrison 1976; Yinger 1978).

Finally, as discussed later, housing market discrimination does still play an important *direct* role in the other half of the overall story of segregation patterns in the United States—the story of why so few neighborhoods become integrated in the first place.

Social Solidarity

Another potentially relevant factor in understanding racial transition, which has been raised by a few authors, is the degree of solidarity of the existing (largely white) population within a community. The hypothesis is that communities with high levels of attachment—in particular, a strong core of long-term residents—are less likely to experience rapid racial change because the white population will be more comfortable remaining there and more effective in resisting further racial change (Logan and Stearns 1981; Logan and Schneider 1984).[7] One measure of such cohesiveness is the degree of ethnic homogeneity of the white population.[8]

Demographic Forces

Another commonly voiced idea is that the pace of racial change is shaped by larger demographic forces. Taeuber and Taeuber (1965) and others following them, for instance, stress the relevance of the relative growth rates of the black and white populations in the particular metropolitan area (Lee 1985; Lee and Wood 1991). Others point to the importance of the underlying mobility of the white population and maintain that neighborhoods with residents who move less often—for instance those with large stocks of owner-occupied housing—are likely to be more stable (Steinnes 1977; Schwab and Marsh 1980; Sugrue 1996, pp. 234–246). Again, these demographic claims may be perfectly consistent with the various possible dominant causes of transition; the point is that these demographic forces may powerfully shape the rate of change.

Race-Based Neighborhood Stereotyping Hypothesis

One of the problems with the popular emphasis on white flight (rooted in the postwar experience) is that it views neighborhoods as static entities in which their inhabitants would, but for the presence of blacks moving in, remain the same over time. From such a perspective, the only relevant decision is whether white inhabitants decide to leave for racial reasons: if they leave, there is white flight and the neighborhood transitions rapidly; if they stay, there is no white flight and the neighborhood does not transition.

But of course neighborhoods are not static; they are dynamic, with people moving in and out of them all the time in the normal course of events and for various reasons. People move out of their existing neighborhoods, and into certain new ones, because they want a bigger house, or because of a new job, or of course, because of racial considerations.

To properly understand neighborhoods as dynamic entities is to realize that the racial composition of a neighborhood is necessarily a function of four sorts of decisions: (1) white household exit decisions, (2) white household entry decisions, (3) black household exit decisions, and (4) black household entry decisions. As discussed, the focus in developing the race-based neighborhood stereotyping hypothesis is on white household decision making. Again, this is not to suggest that black household decisions are irrelevant, but rather that they are less likely to be the driving force behind racial transition. Consider, for example, that survey data consistently show that black households are far more open to a variety of racial mixes.

Again putting aside for now the relative importance of white "entry" versus "exit" decisions (i.e., "avoidance" versus "flight"), the next critical issue that arises is what best explains white resistance to mixed neighborhoods. The hypothesis emphasized here–which also finds support in the data–is that white resistance is based primarily on certain negative race-based stereotypes that white households maintain about the future quality of such neighborhoods and not on any categorical unwillingness to live among black households, even significant numbers of them.

The first salient point is that what white households seem to fear most is the prospect of living, in some isolation, in a predominantly black neighborhood. And such fear can prompt white households to avoid a community that is 10 percent black even though they are perfectly content with this particular level of integration. In short, the suggestion is that many whites do not mind living together with minorities, as long as the numbers of these groups promise to remain relatively fixed. Unfortunately, whites tend to assume that modestly mixed neighborhoods do, in fact, become rapidly predominantly black—an empirical (and potentially self-fulfilling) assumption that is based on having witnessed (or heard of) rapid transition in the past.

The second point is that households seem ultimately to care less about the racial composition of their neighborhood—fixed or changing—than about various quality of life indicators, such as public safety, school quality, community stability, and in the case of homeowners, property value appreciation. This is not to suggest that race is irrelevant, however. Far from it. For people (primarily whites, but potentially blacks as well) tend to hold powerful stereotypes about the social, economic, and physical characteristics of largely minority neighborhoods. Specifically, black neighbors are too often thought to bring with them, or at least to portend, a deterioration in school quality, public safety, and general neighborhood quality. In other words, it is not necessarily that white households dislike living next to blacks per se; it is that many white households, rightly or wrongly (and even perhaps, with some regret), associate predominantly black neighborhoods with diminished neighborhood quality and resilience. In sum, then, racial change has come to serve as a powerful, but not completely certain, signal for a change in the strength of the community, and as such, is one of the determinants of how people assess the area's future.[9]

Significantly, it is not clear that racial transition does in fact bring these changes. For example, the evidence is mixed with respect to housing prices. Many studies have found that if anything, property values rise as a result of neighborhood racial change (though they may fall in the short run) (*Research Report on Integrated Housing in Kalamazoo* 1959; Laurenti 1960; McEntire 1960; Ladd 1962; Karlen 1968; Muth 1969; Berry 1976; Kiel and Zabel 1995).[10] (To the extent that predominantly minority neighborhoods do offer inferior neighborhood amenities, it is almost certainly because these neighborhoods are typically less affluent, often lack the political power to ensure proper governmental attention to such matters as law enforcement and schools, and are overlooked by private firms.)

Generally, then, the contention that white decision making is driven by race-based expectations about the future quality of mixed neighborhoods (on the assumption that they will become all black) has something in common both with accounts that emphasize white household prejudice and with those that emphasize class-based preferences for superior neighborhood amenities. It shares with the pure prejudice approach the fundamental notion that white decision making is fundamentally based on morally suspect, negative race-based stereotypes, albeit stereotypes about black neighborhoods rather than about blacks as individuals. White avoidance, in short, is not the result of benign color-blind forces. But the race-based neighborhood stereotyping hypothesis also shares with more class-based explanations the notion that what people ultimately care about most is the quality of their neighborhoods, not racial composition. In short, race still matters, but as a signal of neighborhood quality.

In this latter respect, the race-based neighborhood stereotyping hypothesis builds on the important work of Richard Taub, D. Garth Taylor, and Jan Dunham. These researchers persuasively argue that Schelling's racial equilibrium points—that is, points at which racial composition will not change as a result of people moving—are merely theoretical. Points of actual, or what they call "practical," equilibrium will be determined not only by the distribution of racial tolerance levels in the neighborhood, but also by the level of competition for housing in the community and the relative magnitudes of black and white demand. If people feel that the local housing market is weak or crime is rampant, Taub and his colleagues maintain that they are more likely to expect a neighborhood to tip and to act on those expectations, rather than on current reality. Ultimately, however, racial considerations are not really the controlling concern of either white or black households. It is instead "the concrete realities of crime and deterioration" (Taub, Taylor, and Dunham 1984, p. 181).

But the race-based neighborhood stereotyping hypothesis also departs from this work in a few key respects. Most notably, it affords a greater role to racial considerations. According to Taub and his co-authors, the "apparent effects of racial issues . . . are negligible once we take account of other factors." But according to the theory here, race does not disappear so easily. To some extent, this difference of emphasis follows logically from another important difference in emphasis: Taub, Taylor, and Dunham focus primarily on the exit decision. As discussed later, it follows that they afford a smaller role to race.

It is also useful to note here that the race-based neighborhood stereotyping hypothesis is consistent with what appears to be a trend toward redefining the role that race plays in various sectors of society—a trend that emphasizes that "race matters," but not because all whites are necessarily acting out of traditional racist attitudes. Rather, whites tend to use race as a proxy, a morally if not always empirically illegitimate one, to signal legitimate, non-racial concerns. In the area of criminal justice, for example, Randall Kennedy (1997) has powerfully argued that race continues to play an important role in the administration of criminal justice—whom the police decide to stop and search, whom juries are more likely to convict, and so on. But this is not necessarily because police officers or juries have an animus-based desire to single out African Americans for punishment. Police officers—or at least most of them—are ultimately concerned with controlling crime (Kennedy 1997). Still, rightly or wrongly, they do often use race as a signal of criminality, just as white homeowners use race as a signal for neighborhood quality.[11]

Finally, it is important to re-emphasize that on its face, the race-based neighborhood stereotyping hypothesis is a theory about current racial transition and makes no grand historical claims about the growing stability of integrated neighborhoods in recent decades. But the discussion here has clearly insinuated a possible explanation for the growing stability: that (1) race-based neighborhood stereotyping allows for more racial stability than does prejudice-driven white flight and that (2) neighborhood stereotyping has over time come to dominate over pure prejudice as an explanation of white household attitudes. Naturally, there are other possible historical explanations that merit further study. For example, it could be that simple racial prejudice really does drive neighborhood change but that whites have grown less prejudiced and to that extent, transition has diminished.

Unfortunately, the data presented in this book are generally not able to address this issue directly, and so it remains for a future study to examine. The one exception is some suggestive data in Chapter 4 that may indicate a shift from prejudice to neighborhood stereotyping, or at the very least a shift away from a world where racial composition directly predicts the rate of white loss.

In any case, this race-based neighborhood stereotyping hypothesis generates many predictions about the pace and nature of racial change—predictions that can be tested empirically and are tested in future chapters. The rest of this chapter is devoted to discussing such predictions.

Exit versus Entry

Surprisingly few discussions of racial change explicitly distinguish between the decision to leave a neighborhood and the decision to move into one; instead they seem to assume that the factors affecting one decision are identical to those influencing the other. Yet the motivations behind these two actions can be quite distinct. Arguably, a white household is more likely to remain in a neighborhood that is 20 percent black than it is to move into one. For to be provoked to move out of a neighborhood, a household's distaste for racial integration must at least exceed the cost of moving. In-movers, in contrast, need not have quite as great an antipathy toward racial mixing, since these households have already settled on moving somewhere; it is just a matter of deciding where.

Moreover, the race-based neighborhood stereotyping hypothesis suggests that the desire to leave a neighborhood should be less influenced by racial composition than the wish to move into one. For potential white in-movers do not have direct experience with the neighborhood's crime levels or school quality in order to build rational expectations about the neighborhood's future quality. Nor does it accord with common sense to suppose that these whites are out in the world doing exhaustive empirical research on mixed neighborhoods in order to obtain the necessary neighborhood-specific information about school quality, crime, and other relevant neighborhood characteristics. Race-based neighborhood stereotypes may be all they have.

By contrast, residents already living in a community have considerable information about that neighborhood's quality and future prospects. They are likely to have a sense of the teachers at local schools, the community activities available for adults and children, the level of property crime in the community, and the manners and attitudes of the people, if any, who hang out on local street corners and/or at local establishments. Thus their decision to move or stay is likely to be much less influenced by present racial composition than is the decision by less informed outsiders about whether or not to move in.

The implication in turn is that entry decisions are much more likely to be the driving force underlying neighborhood racial change.[12] Yet to the extent that past models have distinguished between exit and entry, they have tended to emphasize the decision of whites to exit a neighborhood. Schelling, for instance, focuses on the decision of whites to leave a neighborhood and the decision of blacks to move in. The departure of whites is what ultimately drives his model. As long as some minimum threshold is met, he assumes that their places will be taken by blacks or "by whites and blacks in proportions that reflect what is happening to the neighborhood" (Schelling 1972, p. 161). Similarly, as mentioned above, Taub and his co-authors also focus on exit decisions and consider entry, or the ratio of black to white demand, to be exogenous in their simulations, and in their empirical analysis, to be simply the current racial composition in the community (Taub, Taylor, and Dunham 1984).

As mentioned earlier, this focus on exit may have led Taub and his co-authors to understate the role of race in residential decision making. Yet, even with respect to exit decisions, race may still play a part. It is certainly true that whites living in a mixed neighborhood have direct experience with the present quality of that neighborhood–and thus a more rational basis for building expectations about the future quality of that neighborhood. Still, under the race-based neighborhood stereotyping hypothesis, even households living in integrated neighborhoods react to racial composition—or at least changes in that composition. Specifically, white households living in an increasingly black neighborhood are likely to fear that their neighborhood will become largely black and will thereby undergo a fundamental deterioration in quality not yet visible. But such an assumption about the quality of predominantly black neighborhoods is, again, necessarily based on stereotypes and not direct experience.

Implications for the Pace of Change across Communities

Although economists, sociologists, and demographers have been studying neighborhood racial change since the 1950s, few have explored the roots of the differences in rates of racial change across integrated neighborhoods. The reason is simple: as an empirical matter, racial tipping (that is, rapid racial transition to an all-black community) has been considered virtually inevitable and universal—a view that was solidified by the experience of many cities during the 1950s and 1960s and that has found support in many surveys of racial preferences.

But as shown in Chapter 2, there are significant differences across communities, and they warrant explanation. The race-based neighborhood stereotyping hypothesis offers some insights. In particular, the hypothesis suggests that white attitudes toward an integrated area are shaped greatly by their expectations about its future, and such expectations are influenced by a wide variety of factors. First, people base their predictions about future racial composition not only on present racial composition, but on other considerations as well. For example, if a community borders on the central area of black concentration, observers are far more likely to predict that it will become majority black than they would another that is far out in the suburbs and surrounded by largely white communities. Similarly, it seems likely that households living in metropolitan areas in which structural decline has typically accompanied minority growth in the past would be more likely to make this connection in the present. The number of years that a community has been racially mixed is also bound to be a powerful predictor of the future course of change. People are undoubtedly more likely to believe that a community that has been 10 percent black for two decades will remain roughly 10 percent black than one that is also 10 percent black today, but was all white just a few years ago.

Past models of racial change have failed to take into account the influence of such expectations. In Schelling's simple world, for instance, mobility decisions are made entirely on the basis of preferences for present racial composition. There are no expectations and no compensating factors. People decide whether or not to move solely as a result of the number of blacks on their block or in their community. Schelling notes that an individual's tolerance level in his model could be interpreted as "the percentage black at which, projecting the trend . . . , he makes his decision to leave." But he acknowledges that the interpretation is only valid if the decision, and implicitly, the projected future growth, are "purely a function of the percentage black in the neighborhood and not any other indices that might influence his decision" (Schelling 1972, p. 161).

Expectations about the connection between racial composition and the quality of the neighborhood are likely to vary too. Thus, for example, even if people believe that two communities will have the identical racial composition five years from now—say, 15 percent black— their expectations about the condition of the neighborhoods might vary sharply. In one case, they might have faith that in the face of racial change, school quality and property values will remain high, while crime will stay low. The presence of a large and established institution such as a hospital, military base, or university might engender such faith, since these institutions are likely to keep the streets busy and less vulnerable to crime. Most importantly, such institutions generate a continual flow of well-off people who want to live in the surrounding communities. Observers have noted for years that the neighborhoods surrounding college campuses are often fairly stable, diverse communities. (Consider Hyde Park, Berkeley, and Cambridge.) But most onlookers have attributed this phenomenon to the liberal attitudes of the student and faculty populations. A more accurate explanation might be that local housing markets are bolstered by the knowledge that these large and durable institutions are nearby.[13]

In short, when white residents have more secure expectations about the future quality of life in a community, they are more likely to tolerate racial mixing. It is less clear however, how the *present* quality of life in a neighborhood will influence how households react to racial change. On the one hand, present neighborhood quality is probably a very good predictor of future strength, and thus one would expect residents of better neighborhoods to be more secure about their area's future. On the other hand, those living in higher-quality neighborhoods have more to lose from the changes that they believe are linked to racial change.

Notably, the class-difference model also offers some predictions about the types of neighborhoods likely to change more and less quickly. Most critically, it predicts that integrated communities in which blacks and whites are of more equal status should be more racially stable. It also suggests that wealthier communities—areas with more expensive homes and higher homeownership rates—should be more stable too since they are less likely to be threatened by lower-income minorities in the first place. Significantly, according to the race-based stereotyping hypothesis, neither the size of the black population in an integrated community nor its average socioeconomic status should necessarily influence the likely course of change. Moreover, as will be discussed later, the extent of owner-occupied housing is predicted to be *negatively* correlated with stability—the opposite prediction from that offered by the class-difference model.

What about pure racial prejudice? If, as is the case in Schelling's world, racial preferences drive racial change, then the proportion of blacks currently living in a neighborhood should be critical to the pace of racial change. In truth, because prejudice levels vary across households, and because households may sort themselves according to racial preferences, we may not expect to see such a perfect relationship. The most racially tolerant white households, that is, will be those living in racially integrated communities, while the most prejudiced will be those in the predominantly white areas. To the extent that this is true, present racial composition may not in fact be so closely related to subsequent course of change in a community. In reality, however, residential choices are constrained; households consider a wealth of factors in choosing a neighborhood, and many residents have lived in their communities for many years. Thus, the idea that households would be perfectly sorted across neighborhoods according to their racial preferences is simply not realistic. And if pure prejudice is the dominant factor underlying neighborhood racial transition, then the initial racial mix should be linked to subsequent racial change. The only other factor that should be relevant is the level of prejudice of the existing population. It is, of course, difficult to measure racial attitudes. Some have found that more educated people tend to be more tolerant, so this theory would probably predict that tracts with more educated residents should be more stable. It might also predict that tracts in Northern cities would be more stable, since at least in the past, people who identify themselves as from the South have generally been more prejudiced (Greenfield 1961).

Variation in Whites' Willingness to Live in Integrated Areas

If the race-based neighborhood stereotyping hypothesis is accurate, we would expect considerable variation across households in their willingness to live in integrated communities. For one thing, some households are likely to care more about future structural strength than others and are thus likely to be more fearful of a growing black population. One would think, for example, that homeowners are apt to be less willing to live in integrated communities than renters, not because they are more prejudiced, but because they obviously have a greater economic interest in the community and are likely to live there longer. (Homeowners move only about one-third as often as renters.) Significantly, this assumption runs directly counter to the conventional prediction that homeownership acts as a "healthy vaccine" against neighborhood change, since owners move so much less often than renters (Schwab and Marsh 1980, p. 388; Steinnes 1977; Hirsch 1983; Sugrue 1996). If racial prejudice is the dominant motivating force underlying racial transition, that is, we would expect neighborhoods with more homeowners to be more stable.

Another relevant factor should be the presence of children. Households with children are bound to be more sensitive than others to neighborhood racial change because of their heightened concern about the environment in which they are raising their children—the safety and cleanliness of the streets; the existence of parks, playgrounds, and other local amenities; and most significantly, the quality of local education. Because of the paramount concern about school quality, the theory would predict that households with children attending public schools should be the most sensitive to racial change. Yet households with children also face higher moving costs than others because they have to take their children away from their schools, friends, and community activities. Thus, they might have to reach a greater level of discomfort before they are willing to move.

There are other (and arguably more inherent) differences across households that are likely to be significant too. Households believing more strongly than others that minority neighbors bring with them a deterioration in neighborhood strength, for instance, should be more averse to racial mixing—and it seems safe to assume that white households (due to prejudice) are more likely than blacks to hold such beliefs about the weaknesses of minority neighborhoods. Of course, black households may share such beliefs and therefore try to avoid largely black areas. Consider Rosemary Lomax, an African-American nurse, who reported to the *New York Times* that she supported the efforts that her racially integrated town (Matteson, Illinois) was making to recruit whites. "It's not about making Matteson lily white," Ms. Lomax argued. "It's about keeping property values up" (Terry 1996).

Other theories of racial change pay relatively little attention to the kinds of white households likely to be more or less open to racial mixing. But the implications of the theories seem clear. In a world where pure prejudice predominates, white residents who are less racially prejudiced should be more willing to live in integrated communities. And if the class difference model is accurate, then less affluent white households should be more open to racial integration, either because they can afford fewer alternatives or because their incomes are closer to those of neighboring blacks.

Why so Few Neighborhoods Become Integrated

As mentioned earlier, the story of racial transition is the story of neighborhoods that have become open to blacks, and for one reason or another, eventually become predominantly black. But with respect to the overall patterns of segregation and integration in this country, this is only half of the story. The other half is the story of why the majority of neighborhoods, despite some very real progress, remain predominantly if not exclusively white.

For the most part, this study does not address this dilemma, though others certainly have (Galster 1988; Massey and Denton 1993; Yinger 1995). Still, a few casual observations are worth making. First, if racial transition is the mainly a function of white moving decisions, the persistence of exclusively white neighborhoods is mainly a function of black household moves. This follows simply from the fact that an exclusively white community cannot become integrated unless black households move in. So why don't black households move into predominantly or exclusively white neighborhoods more often? Here housing market discrimination does play a direct and critical role.

Certainly there is no denying that marketplace discrimination played a forceful and dispositive role in constraining black mobility in the past. In the public sector, public housing was explicitly segregated by race. Even more critically, perhaps, the Federal Housing Administration (FHA), which insures long-term mortgages made by private lenders, recommended the use of private, restrictive covenants that prohibited black occupancy and taught its underwriters to avoid "inharmonious racial groups." Evidence suggests that until the passage of the Fair Housing Act, private lenders commonly refused to serve blacks (Helper 1969; Jackson 1985; Massey and Denton 1993).

There is also no denying that such marketplace discrimination continues to be widespread. The 1989 Housing Discrimination Study (a national fair-housing audit study sponsored by the U.S. Department of Housing and Urban Development) found that blacks and Hispanics encountered some form of discrimination in roughly half of all their housing transactions.

Yet perhaps because of changes in enforcement or in underlying attitudes, the nature of discrimination has changed in recent years. Realtors rarely simply reject black clients who walk through the door; instead, to the extent that discrimination still exists, it has become more subtle. While the 1989 Housing Discrimination Study found widespread discrimination, it also found that minority home seekers do not face "insurmountable" marketplace barriers to predominantly white neighborhoods when they attempt entrance. Black auditors responding to newspaper advertisements of homes for sale, for instance, were almost always able to obtain some information about housing units in white areas (Turner and Wienk 1993). In the end, as the Housing Discrimination Study showed, a black family that is determined to move into a predominantly white area will succeed. Thus it seems that many black families are not making the attempt.

Such evidence, as well as other factors, have led many to conclude that the predominant reason that blacks seldom enter white neighborhoods must be benign ethnic clustering for which we should have little moral concern (Schnare 1978; Kantrowitz 1979; Clark 1986; Patterson 1997). It is certainly plausible that black clustering plays a role (see Patterson 1997). Yet while black clustering undeniably accounts for some amount of racial segregation, the segregation levels of blacks are so much higher than that of other ethnic groups that we would have to assume, implausibly it seems, that their desire for clustering is exceptional—far beyond that of even recent immigrants, such as Mexicans and Koreans, whose foreign language and customs make such clustering natural and perhaps even advantageous (Kain 1976; Massey and Denton 1993; Bobo and Zubrinsky 1996). Furthermore, as will be discussed in Chapter 7, surveys of racial preferences have shown that blacks, if anything, prefer *not* to live in majority black communities.

A variant of this argument is that blacks have different preferences than whites for non-racial attributes of neighborhoods, such as housing and school quality. The empirical evidence provides little support. Once income, family size, and age are taken into account, there appear to be only very small differences in neighborhood preferences across racial groups (Galster 1979).

There are far more plausible explanations for blacks' ongoing absence from white communities. One certainly is that even if discrimination in housing markets no longer absolutely keeps blacks out, its presence still discourages blacks from seeking homes in white areas (Courant 1978).[14] But perhaps the most important explanation is that blacks are discouraged from seeking homes because of neither realtor practices nor benign ethnic clustering, but rather because of a simple desire to avoid a neighborhood where one will be wholly unwelcome, or worse, will encounter outright hostility from white neighbors. Consider that some 90 percent of black respondents in the 1992 Detroit Area Survey who said they would not move into an all-white area gave as their reason that whites wouldn't welcome them (Farley et al. 1994). In a sense, such black avoidance—like white avoidance of racially mixed neighborhoods—shares elements of the other leading theories. It shares with benign ethnic clustering the notion that there are not insurmountable *marketplace* barriers (in the form of discriminatory practices by realtors, landlords, and lenders) that prevent blacks from moving into white neighborhoods. But it also shares with discrimination the notion that what explains black absence in white neighborhoods is hardly benign. If a black person chooses not to live in a neighborhood because it is well known that the whites there dislike living next door to blacks and will never be friendly or may even be hostile, in what sense is that morally unobjectionable? Such attitudes on the part of whites may be legal, and even constitutionally protected, but that does not make them unworthy of our concern.

There is one other observation to make here, which ties the race-based neighborhood stereotyping hypothesis to this black avoidance hypothesis. The core proposition of the black avoidance hypothesis is that blacks assume white residents of all-white communities will in fact be hostile to blacks and so do not attempt to move into such neighborhoods. But if the race-based neighborhood hypothesis is true, and whites are not categorically opposed to living among blacks, this assumption may be inaccurate. There may be some white neighborhoods, for example, that unbeknownst to blacks are fairly open to blacks' moving there. Of course, it is important not to overstate the case—especially since prejudice is likely to be highest in all-white communities (as opposed to mixed communities). In any event, given our sorry racial history and ongoing tensions, it is not surprising that blacks are hesitant to be such pioneers.

Correlates of Racial Stability

The previous chapter presented a hypothesis for explaining white behavior in the face of racial integration. The bulk of the rest of this book focuses on a series of empirical tests of this basic hypothesis. To be sure, all of the tests are imperfect, but together I believe that they build a strong case for the importance of race-based neighborhood stereotyping. This chapter starts us on this empirical journey with a neighborhood-level analysis of when racial transition occurs. As demonstrated in Chapter 2, rates of racial change are quite variable, and contrary to the accepted wisdom, not all racially integrated neighborhoods are necessarily on a path to becoming largely black communities.

What Makes Integrated Neighborhoods Stable?

Prior researchers examining the correlates of neighborhood racial stability have questioned the popular and resilient notion that racial transition is inevitable. To this end, they have posited several different neighborhood-level factors (other than simply the proportion of blacks) that correlate with relative racial stability.

First, consistent with the view that simple prejudice drives transition, some posit that racial attitudes in the broader community should predict racial stability (see, for example, Schnare and McRae 1978). In metropolitan areas where whites are more prejudiced, whites will be more apt to avoid integrated communities, and thus these communities will shift more rapidly to largely black. Similarly, others hypothesize that the level of prejudice among whites in a given racially integrated neighborhood will be positively correlated with the pace of white loss (Schelling 1971; Aldrich 1975; Galster 1990; Galster and Keeney 1993). The problem with this argument, however, is that if (as argued in this book) entry decisions ultimately determine the rate of white loss, then the attitudes of those whites currently living in a community will be less critical than those of white households living in the broader community.

Another neighborhood-level factor that has been emphasized—one that is clearly linked to the notion that class differences drive transition—is the relative incomes of blacks and whites in a community. According to this view, integrated neighborhoods where the minorities have incomes and education similar to those of the white population are likely to be more stable. Similarly, higher status areas—with more expensive homes and higher homeownership rates—are predicted to be more stable too, since they are less likely to be threatened by lower-income minorities in the first place.

As noted in Chapter 3, researchers have also offered three other potential correlates of relative racial stability: the degree of solidarity of the white population; larger demographic forces such as the relative growth rates of the black and white populations within the metropolitan area; and housing market discrimination. The former two possibilities are tested here, at least with proxy variables. Unfortunately, however, this study has no access to information about the extent of housing market discrimination and thus we cannot test the extent to which it affects racial change. But certainly, substantial evidence shows that housing market discrimination still occurs and, as discussed already, the evidence is clear that realtor behavior shaped the pace of racial change in earlier racially integrated communities.

As for the race-based neighborhood stereotyping hypothesis, it predicts by contrast that the size of the black population in an integrated community and its particular characteristics are probably less relevant to the future course of change than are the tract's past history of change, the location of the tract within the metropolitan area, and the presence of large, stabilizing institutions such as universities or military bases. The key is that any factors that weaken the chain of negative assumptions that whites hold about the future of racially integrated neighborhoods are likely to be correlated with greater racial stability. Finally, the extent of owner-occupied housing is predicted to be *negatively* correlated with stability, because homeowners are likely to be more concerned about future neighborhood strength.

The remainder of this chapter is dedicated to studying the extent to which the empirical evidence supports these various hypotheses. The first part reviews the evidence offered by past studies of racial change; the second presents an original empirical analysis of the factors linked to the greater stability that characterized certain integrated neighborhoods during the 1980s.

Past Studies of Racial Change

Early studies investigating the characteristics of stable, racially mixed neighborhoods focus on just a few areas (Caplan and Wolf 1960; Grier and Grier 1960; Mayer 1960; Rapkin and Grigsby 1960). The case studies done under the auspices of the Commission on Race and Housing are perhaps the most well known. Dating from the 1950s, these studies conclude that contrary to the pure prejudice view, the pace of racial change is not explained by underlying racial attitudes. Instead, the rate of change appears more related to housing market conditions and to the relative economic standing of the black and white populations.[1] They also find that the pace of change can be shaped greatly by institutional forces—accelerated by realtors and lenders and moderated by community organizations and property managers.[2] And several studies noted the importance of local schools in the decisions of white households (Mayer 1960).

A more recent and theoretically richer analysis of racial change is that authored by Taub, Taylor, and Dunham (1984). Studying eight neighborhoods in Chicago, they find that contextual factors can greatly influence the stability of racial mixing. In particular, they attribute the stability they see in three of their mixed neighborhoods to the combination of strong housing markets, attractive external amenities, the relative prosperity of the incoming black residents, and the presence of active community associations and durable institutional presences (the University of Chicago, for instance). In short, their results appear consistent with both the social class theory of neighborhood change and the notion of race-based neighborhood stereotyping.

In his examination of the Dorchester, Mattapan, and Roxbury neighborhoods in Boston during the 1960s and 1970s, Gamm (1999) too focuses on the important role of institutions—in particular religious institutions. He argues powerfully that the strong geographic ties of the Catholic Church may explain why the white Catholic neighborhoods remained so much more stable than the Jewish areas in the face of integration. Consider membership rules, for instance. Because Catholic churches define membership by strict physical boundaries, they were thus able to serve as a reassuring institutional anchor, a role that synagogues—much less tied to actual geographic communities—could not play. Thus, he argues that white Catholics were more committed to their neighborhoods, which as a result, transitioned more slowly.[3]

Another interesting set of case studies focuses on communities that have self-consciously worked to maintain their diverse racial mix (Husock 1989; Saltman 1990; Keating 1994; Nyden, Maly, and Lukehart 1997). These studies generally suggest that government intervention—and more critically, the actions of local community-based organizations—can stabilize racially changing neighborhoods. Community context, in other words, can make an enormous difference to the pace of racial change, by altering the behavior of real estate agents and softening white attitudes about racially changing communities. But I take issue with the implicit message of these studies—that without such explicit and ongoing efforts to support racial integration, the maintenance of stably diverse communities is virtually impossible.

All of these sets of case studies offer richly detailed information about each neighborhood and the factors that control its pace of change. The problem, of course, is that such case studies make generalizations somewhat difficult. Some researchers have therefore used census data to undertake broader, statistical analyses of the correlates of community racial change. The debate at the heart of these studies is whether the tipping model is correct when it posits that the pace of racial change in a community is determined solely by the size of its black population and the racial composition of neighboring areas. Could other, non-racial community characteristics play a part in either accelerating or moderating the process? If so, which factors are relevant? Socioeconomic status is the most frequently advanced alternative, but additional factors are tested as well. Unfortunately, these studies do not provide clear answers to these questions.

In general, these various studies make clear that at least until the 1970s, neighborhoods that had higher proportions of blacks were substantially more likely to experience a relative gain in black population (Taeuber and Taeuber 1965; Steinnes 1977; Schwab and Marsh 1980; Logan and Stearns 1981; Logan and Schneider 1984; White 1984; Lee 1985; Galster 1990b; Denton and Massey 1991; Galster and Keeney 1993). Moreover, a neighborhood's distance from the central black ghetto is a consistent predictor of racial change. As noted, both of these findings are often interpreted as evidence for the salience of racial prejudice in driving racial change. Whites, that is, do not want to live with or near blacks. But while the fact that distance to the central area of black residence matters may be consistent with the pure prejudice model, it is also consistent—and indeed perhaps more consistent—with race-based neighborhood stereotyping. For it is not so much that whites mind living in neighborhoods that are next door, and therefore nearer, to black ones. It is that they are fearful that such proximity puts their area at great risk of being incorporated into the adjacent largely black community.

And what about racial attitudes, which the pure prejudice model also predicts should matter? That is, in communities where the white population is more prejudiced, does the white population decline more rapidly? Since data on racial attitudes at the neighborhood level are difficult to come by, few test this proposition. One notable exception is Galster's study of Cleveland during the 1980s (1990b). Using a proxy variable for white racial attitudes, the author finds that tracts predicted to have stronger "segregationist sentiments" are likely to have much larger white losses, given the same black percentage in 1970—a discovery that supports the notion that prejudice drives much of racial change. Yet although this represents an innovative way to measure the importance of racial attitudes, the proxy variable used is an imperfect predictor of racial attitudes.[4] Thus we should not place too much weight on this result.

As for the importance of class, and in particular, class differences between blacks and whites, the evidence is quite weak. Four of the six studies that test for the relevance of the income of the white population find that it does not matter (Logan and Stearns 1981; Logan and Schneider 1984; White 1984; Galster and Keeney 1993), while a fifth finds that tracts with higher status whites are *more* likely to gain black population (Steinnes 1977).[5] But the sixth, the largest study to date of racial change, reports that mixed tracts of lower status were in fact significantly more likely to gain black residents between 1970 and 1980 (Lee and Wood 1991).

As for other correlates of racial change, two studies explore the relevance of the level of cohesiveness of a given neighborhood's white population, using proxy measures such as the share of white ethnics and population turnover. Both studies find that such cohesiveness is an important predictor of racial change (Logan and Stearns 1981; Logan and Schneider 1984). Again, the argument is that communities with a strong core of long-term residents are less likely to experience rapid racial change because the white population is more comfortable remaining there and more effective in resisting further racial change. (Interestingly, ethnicity is not found to be as important a factor in more affluent suburbs, perhaps because the white population there has other mechanisms through which they can protect their communities, such as expensive housing, strict zoning controls, and/or formal civic associations.)

The evidence is more mixed regarding the importance of the relative growth rates of the black and white populations in explaining the variation across cities. White (1984) examines ten cities during the 1940s, 1950s, and 1960s and finds that whether or not a city's neighborhoods increase proportionally in black residents (and how fast such transition proceeds) is largely dependent on the relative rate of increase of the black and white populations in the city as a whole. But it is not clear whether this pattern continued into the 1970s. In one analysis of this decade, the black-white growth differential appears to matter (Denton and Massey 1991), while in another, it appears irrelevant (Lee 1985).[6] Notably, Denton and Massey (1991) also find that white loss is correlated with the Hispanic-white growth differentials in the metropolitan area.

Another factor that is commonly raised in policy debates as a possible threat to neighborhood racial stability is the existence of subsidized housing. One study explicitly examines this claim by considering the case of Yonkers, New York (Galster and Keeney 1993). The authors find that the number of family-occupied subsidized units located in a tract in 1970 as well as the number built between 1971 and 1980 are both correlated with racial change between 1970 and 1980. The scale of subsidized housing appears to matter considerably more than its mere presence or absence. The relevance of subsidized housing may be explained either by the class theory of racial change—

whites are averse to living in integrated communities of lower status—or by the notion of race-based, neighborhood stereotyping. For clearly public housing in this country connotes more than simply poor neighbors.

In summary, the general conclusion here is that the initial black population share is an important predictor of future racial change (or at least it was in the 1960s and 1970s). But these studies also make clear that simply knowing the black population share is not sufficient to predict the subsequent course of change. Contextual factors in a neighborhood—social, economic, and historical—play a significant part as well, and an increasingly prominent one, it seems. But class does not appear to matter much, and there is little consensus as to which other neighborhood characteristics are relevant and why.

There are many reasons, however, to think that these studies—effective as they are in their own terms—might not adequately describe the contemporary urban and suburban landscapes. Most obviously, there is the simple issue of time—the most up-to-date study in the field focuses on the 1970s. The data used in this present study, in contrast, cover the 1980s and early 1990s. The evidence suggests that racial integration was more stable during the 1980s than it was during earlier decades. As discussed in the previous chapter, this might be because the dynamics underlying racial change have shifted. Thus, what explained racial change in the 1950s and even the 1970s may be simply not accurate today. In particular, contextual factors other than simple racial composition may have far more importance.

Moreover, with perhaps two exceptions, none of these studies examines neighborhood racial change within suburban communities.[7] Instead they focus exclusively on neighborhoods located within central cities. Yet much of today's racial mixing takes place outside of central city areas. This study therefore includes both urban and suburban neighborhoods. Furthermore, it also covers a broad geographic area—thirty-four metropolitan areas nationwide. (Many of these earlier studies focus on just one metropolitan area.)

Finally, due to data limitations, the studies described earlier omit many variables that are crucial to testing the chief alternative theories. None of these studies, for instance, examines how *changes* in neighborhood conditions influence racial change, though these are arguably more important to mobility decisions than actual conditions themselves. Nor (with the exception of a few case studies) do they have the data to examine how the status of incoming blacks influences the rate of change. The analysis that follows uses data that permit such considerations.

Data Description

In examining neighborhood racial change, this study uses census tracts to approximate neighborhoods and focuses on the decade between 1980 and 1990. As in Chapter 2, most of the data comes from the Urban Institute's Underclass Data Base (UDB), which includes social, demographic, economic, and housing variables for census tracts in the United States from the 1970, 1980, and 1990 censuses. The analysis is generally limited to the thirty-four metropolitan areas with total populations over one million in 1990, and in which blacks represented at least 5 percent of the total population and Hispanics less than 30 percent.[8] The focus is on tracts that were racially integrated in 1980.

Correlates of Racial Change in the 1980s

In this section, I estimate a regression in which the change in the percentage of non-Hispanic whites in a tract between 1980 and 1990 is taken to be a function of racial composition in 1980 as well as several other 1980 neighborhood characteristics. The idea is to learn what factors are correlated with greater and lesser racial change and therefore to explain the variation. Consistent with many prior studies, a neighborhood is included in the main analysis if it was between 10 and 90 percent black in 1980 and its non-Hispanic white population represented at least 10 percent of the total population. This somewhat larger sample is used for the regression models (rather than the group of tracts that were between 10 and 50 percent black) for consistency with the literature and to provide a somewhat broader picture of racial change. (The results are virtually identical when considering the smaller group of integrated tracts.)

The dependent variable—the variable to be explained—is the difference between the proportion of non-Hispanic whites in 1980 and that in 1990. Despite some potential limitations (outlined in Chapter 2), this measure of racial change is easy to interpret, consistent with past empirical literature, and most consistent with theories of racial change.[9] Significantly, a regression model was also estimated using the *percent* loss in the percentage of non-Hispanic whites as a dependent variable (as opposed to the absolute loss), and the basic conclusions were the same.[10]

The independent variables—the variables offered to help explain the pace of racial change—may be grouped into four basic categories: racial and ethnic composition; socioeconomic status; tract demographics; and metropolitan area characteristics. In terms of racial composition, the model includes percent black, percent non-black minority, and quadratic terms for each of these (that is, percent black and percent non-black minority squared) to allow for the possibility that additional declines in the white population are increasingly unlikely as that population shrinks. In addition, I include the growth in the black population between 1970 and 1980 (the difference between the percent black present in 1980 and that present in 1970) to reflect recent trends in the black population.

As for socioeconomic status, I include both measures of the overall status of the census tract (poverty rate and percent of workers in managerial or professional occupations) and measures of the status of the black population (the percent of black families earning more than $25,000 and the percent of black residents over age twenty-five who have completed at least one year of college). Two housing stock variables—the homeownership rate and the percent of buildings built prior to 1939—are also included as a measure of neighborhood status. Clearly, many of these variables are related. But the simple correlations are not that large—they are all below 0.5 with the exception of that between the proportion of black families earning more than $25,000 and the proportion of workers in professional occupations, which is –0.65. But I include them both since there are sound theoretical reasons to assume that these variables would have different effects on the rate of white loss. And in any case, including both variables in the regression does not seem to distort the results much. (The core results stay much the same when either is omitted.)

Tract demographics are included, largely to account for different mobility patterns. The percentage of white households with children is included, as is the percentage of elderly whites, for instance. The percentage of single-family homes is included as a measure of density, and the percentage of recent movers to the neighborhood is included as a measure of social solidarity. (Presumably those moving into a neighborhood more recently will feel less attached to their neighbors.) Finally, I include the growth in the number of households as a measure of the demand for housing in the neighborhood.

The last category of variables encompasses those measured at the metropolitan area level. Here I include regional controls to capture broader demographics, an index of black-white segregation in the metropolitan area, the percent of minorities present in the metropolitan area, and the difference in the rate of population growth between blacks and whites during the 1980s.[11]

Table 4.1 presents the estimated regression coefficients.[12] A positive

Table 4.1 Regression of loss in percent non-Hispanic white, 1980–1990

	Coefficient	Standard error
Intercept	0.15	3.7
% Black	0.008	0.06
% Black squared	−.003*	0.001
% Other	.416*	0.074
% Other squared	−.006*	0.001
% Black × % other	−.006*	0.001
Change in black, 1970–1980	.196*	0.015
Tract socioeconomic status		
% Professional	−.342*	.026
Poverty rate	−.02	.03
% Blacks with some college	.176*	.02
% Blacks earning > $25,000	.068*	.016
Homeownership rate	.05*	.019
% Old buildings	−.017	.011
Tract level control variables		
% White households with children	−.111*	.021
% Whites over 65	.097*	.027
% Single family homes	−.082*	.026
% Growth in number of households	−.013*	.002
% Recent movers	−.003	.022
MSA-level control variables		
Northeast	−.062	1.13
South	3.71*	1.14
Midwest	3.53*	1.25
Black-white growth difference	−.018*	.006
Segregation index	.16*	.04
% Black	.098*	.048
N/R-squared		2,647/.33

Note: All neighborhood variables reflect conditions in 1980.

* Coefficients significantly different from zero at the 5 percent level of significance.

coefficient indicates that a given variable is positively associated with white loss. The results here, for instance, suggest that the loss of non-Hispanic whites is greater in neighborhoods in which the proportion of white residents over age sixty-five is larger. Statistically significant coefficients are noted with asterisks. The key result here is that the share of blacks present in 1980 appears unrelated to the subsequent decline in the non-Hispanic white population. (The coefficient on *percent black squared* is meanwhile negative and statistically significant, indicating that marginal declines in the white population become less likely as the overall white population declines.)

By including only the percentage black and percentage black squared as explanatory variables, I constrain the shape of the relationship between the initial black population and subsequent white population loss. An arguably better (or certainly less constrained) alternative way of testing this relationship is to allow it to differ for different levels of black representation. Perhaps a small change in the proportion of blacks matters a lot when the black population is between 20 and 40 percent, for instance, but very little when it falls above or below this level. To test for such differences, I used a spline regression, which allows the slope of the relationship between the initial black population and subsequent white loss to differ for each decile of the black population (0–10 percent black, 10–20 percent black, 20–30 percent black, and so on).[13] These results confirmed that there is no statistically significant relationship between the percentage of black residents and the subsequent loss of whites.[14]

Interestingly, the share of non-black minorities in a tract (% Other) does appear relevant, with the proportion of non-Hispanic whites more likely to decline if the initial proportion of non-black minorities is higher. The negative coefficient on the quadratic term suggests that the effect on white population loss declines as the minority share increases, however, and the magnitude of the total effect is not all that large—the estimated loss in white population is 3.5 percentage points higher in a tract that is 30 percent non-black minority, compared to one that has no non-black minority residents (assuming a black proportion of 20 percent).

Significantly, this finding does not imply that whites are more averse to living among Hispanics and Asians. The loss in non-Hispanic white population measured here is a *net* loss—it may result from growing minority populations as well as dwindling white ones. And given the rapid growth of the Hispanic and Asian population over the 1980s, (in particular, the rapid influx of Hispanic and Asian immigrants who may find it beneficial to initially live among those who share their language and culture), it seems likely that the white loss in the tracts with larger Hispanic and Asian representation is driven by a relative expansion in the non-black minority population (Ellen 1999). Moreover, there are methodological reasons for the difference. First, while this regression model controls for past growth in the black population, it is not able to control for past growth in the non-black minority population.[15] Second, the sample here excludes tracts that are less than 10 percent black, but it does not exclude tracts that are less than 10 percent Asian and Latino. As shown in Chapter 2, there is a significant difference in the magnitude of white loss between tracts that are less than 10 percent black and those that are more.

As for the class model of racial change, the results provide little support. On the one hand, tracts with a greater proportion of workers in professional occupations tend to be more stable. In particular, if the share of professional workers in the tract is 10 percentage points higher, the change in the non-Hispanic white population is predicted to be 3.4 percentage points lower. On the other hand, tracts with newer housing and higher homeownership rates—also measures of higher status—appear *less* racially stable, while the coefficient on the poverty rate is statistically insignificant.

Further, the coefficients on both measures of black status (the share of black residents who have attended college and the share of black families with incomes of at least $25,000) are both positive and significant, indicating that mixed tracts with a more educated and prosperous black community are actually *more* likely to lose white population.[16] Contrary to the common claim, then, the lower status of the black population is not what triggers racial transition. If anything, whites are in fact more averse to living among blacks of higher social status than among those of lower status.

There are at least two possible interpretations. It might be that whites in fact feel more threatened by minorities who are more affluent. Or, since a census tract is not a perfect representation of a neighborhood, it is possible that when blacks are of significantly lower status than whites, they are more often living "on the other side of the tracks" from their more affluent white neighbors and thus perceived to be in a different community.

As for the hypotheses about the factors that might moderate racial change, there is little supportive evidence here. Consider first the argument made that homeownership should be positively correlated with stability, since homeowners move so much less often than renters. The results here suggest that tracts with more homeowners are in fact *more* likely to lose white population. As for the black-white differential in population growth in the metropolitan area as a whole (Black-white growth difference), it is found to be *negatively* related to white loss. Contrary to the standard hypothesis, that is, the loss in the non-Hispanic white population share is likely to be *smaller* in metropolitan areas in which the black population is growing relatively faster than the white population. The effect is admittedly quite small—the non-Hispanic white loss is predicted to be 0.18 percentage points lower in tracts located in a metropolitan area in which the black-white growth differential is ten percentage points higher—but it certainly undermines the relevance of the relative population growth hypothesis in the current world.[17]

There is also little evidence here to suggest that community solidarity slows the pace of racial change. In particular, the share of households in a tract that have moved into their homes within the last five years (% Recent movers) does not appear to influence racial stability. And the other ostensible measure of community commitment—the homeownership rate—is correlated with greater white losses.

In summary, these data refute the tipping model and offer little support for any of the other hypotheses that are commonly proposed as factors moderating the pace of change. During the 1980s, that is, racially integrated tracts were no more likely to lose white population if the initial black proportion was higher, if the poverty rate was higher, if the proportion of recent movers was higher, or if the black population in the metropolitan area overall was growing more rapidly. Moreover, integrated tracts are more likely to lose whites if the black population moving in is more affluent and more educated. The results do seem, however, to bolster the notion of race-based neighborhood stereotyping, or at the very least, they are consistent with it.

First, the overwhelming importance of past growth in the black population in predicting future change suggests that expectations about future black growth might be the critical factor in driving racial change. For people are apt to believe that communities that have gained minorities rapidly in the past are likely to gain them more rapidly in the future. Indeed, the high level of statistical significance of the coefficient on black growth over the 1970s (t-statistic = 13.1) may mean that past studies examining racial change suffer from omitted variable bias, and it may partly explain why these studies tend to find the initial black percentage to be more relevant in predicting future change than the results here suggest. Specifically, since growth in the black population between 1970 and 1980 is positively correlated with percent black in 1980, omitting the past change variable from the model will lead us to overestimate the degree to which the initial percent black is related to subsequent change.

Second, the fact that white loss is predicted to be greater when the homeownership rate in the census tract is higher is also consistent with the notion of neighborhood stereotyping. For given their financial investment in the community, homeowners are more likely to be sensitive to changes in the environment that might influence their future home values. Moreover, the greater transaction costs and time involved in moving for homeowners is likely to lead them to place more weight on what they think the future composition of the neighborhood will be. So they are probably more likely to resist a moderately integrated neighborhood if they believe that the number of minority residents is growing. Significantly, this result also casts some doubt on the importance of pure prejudice. For if whites simply dislike living near to blacks, then white renters—who face lower moving costs— would be expected to move away more rapidly than owners.

Third, the fact that white loss is predicted to be lower when the number of total households in a neighborhood—both black and white—is growing more rapidly also supports the importance of concerns about neighborhood strength. For in a neighborhood with a strong and growing housing market, white households are less likely to be concerned about community decline.

Fourth, both the degree of racial segregation and the size of the black population in the metropolitan area emerge as important intervening variables in determining how households view racial mixing. Specifically, the coefficient on the segregation index is positive and significant, as is the coefficient on the total black population, indicating that integrated tracts located in metropolitan areas with larger and more segregated black populations are prone to be less stable. The loss of non-Hispanic white residents is predicted to be 6 percentage points higher in a neighborhood located in hyper-segregated Detroit, for instance, than in a neighborhood with the same characteristics in Norfolk, Virginia, the least segregated metropolitan area in the sample. And when the proportion of black residents in the metropolitan area is ten percentage points higher, the loss in the percentage of non-Hispanic white inhabitants is predicted to be roughly one percentage point higher.

These results are once again consistent with race-based neighborhood stereotyping. In metropolitan areas with large black populations, whites are more likely to fear that minorities will outnumber them in a particular community. For whites are likely to feel more threatened by blacks in a more segregated environment, where people have less faith in the stability of mixed areas. (Of course, this result is also consistent with the pure prejudice alternative, since racial prejudice is likely to be correlated with the degree of segregation in a metropolitan area.)

At the national level, unfortunately, the data set does not include any measure of distance to other areas of black concentration. The density of development might be considered a proxy, however, given the typical pattern of development of our metropolitan areas—with blacks living in more dense, central-city neighborhoods and whites tending to reside in more outlying, dispersed suburban areas. And the negative and statistically significant coefficient on the proportion of single-family homes suggests that the loss of whites tends to be somewhat lower in tracts that contain a slightly higher share of single-family homes. This greater stability may occur because these tracts are farther from the central area of black residence. It is also possible that white residents are more comfortable with racial mixing when they are living in more dispersed environments and thus have less frequent interaction with those of different races.

At first glance, the fact that mixed communities with a greater proportion of white households with children appear more stable seems to run counter to the notion of race-based neighborhood stereotyping. But in fact it is not. For mixed tracts that attract large numbers of white households with children are probably precisely those with other attributes appealing to whites. If large numbers of white households with children have opted to live in a particular racially mixed community, this is probably a very good indication that the neighborhood is viewed by whites as attractive and secure. This may be because it is far from other communities with minority residents or because it contains a large, durable institution such as a university, military base, or hospital that promises to maintain housing prices.

One final point to mention is that the coefficients on two of the region dummies (South and Midwest) are positive and statistically significant, indicating that more non-Hispanic whites leave mixed tracts in the South and Midwest than in the West (the omitted category). The greater apparent stability of racial mixing in the West is consistent with prior studies and may perhaps be explained by the fact that Western cities are relatively new, and they simply did not experience the same kind of racial competition for housing and neighborhoods during the 1940s, 1950s, and 1960s as their counterparts in the rest of the country. Thus, people living there do not have the same expectations about the future course of racially mixed neighborhoods. The distinctiveness of the West may also be rooted in regional economic strength or even in governance issues, such as the greater power of annexation in the West and Southwest. (The fact that neighborhoods in the Northeast do not appear any less stable than neighborhoods in the West runs contrary to earlier analyses of the 1970s and is a function of the sample of metropolitan areas chosen for the analysis. When considering the full sample of metropolitan areas, the magnitude of white loss is generally greater in the neighborhoods located in the Northeast than in those in the West.)[18]

Changing Prospects for Racial Integration

So far, this discussion has focused on analyzing the nature of racial change in the 1980s, and in particular, on identifying the characteristics of racially integrated neighborhoods that are correlated with greater and lesser rates of white loss. Can this analysis also reveal lessons about changes over time? Certainly the lack of significance of the initial black proportion in 1980 is a striking departure from studies focusing on earlier decades, virtually all of which have found the initial black proportion to be a significant predictor of future change. Does this reflect an underlying difference between the 1980s and previous decades? Is racial integration more viable, that is, in the contemporary world? Methodological differences prevent us from directly comparing these results to those of earlier studies.[19] And unfortunately, data limitations prohibit estimating the identical regression for the 1970s as I did for the 1980s.

A comparison of the 1970s and 1980s can be produced, however, by constructing a somewhat simpler regression and estimating it for both decades.[20] There are several key differences from the model above. First, instead of considering the loss in the percentage of non-Hispanic white residents, I consider the loss in the percentage of white residents, since I do not have a sound estimate of the Hispanic population in 1970. Second, the set of independent variables available is smaller—most notably, I have no measure of the change in the black population between 1960 and 1970, so past growth in the black population is omitted from the new model.[21]

Table 4.2 compares the coefficients on the racial composition variables for the regression estimated for the two different decades. As shown, the coefficient on the initial proportion of black residents is positive and significantly different from zero in 1970 but not in 1980.[22] During the 1970s, that is, the proportion of whites declined more rapidly in census tracts in which the proportion black was larger in 1970. And this was true even after various measures of socioeconomic status and the housing market were taken into account. In particular, the proportion of white inhabitants in a census tract was estimated to decline by 2.4 percentage points more in a tract that was 30 percent black as compared to a tract that was 10 percent black.

By contrast, the coefficient on the proportion of blacks in the 1980–1990 model is not statistically different from zero. In other words,

Table 4.2 Selected coefficients from regression of loss in white population: comparing the 1970s and the 1980s

	Dependent variable = 1970–1980 loss in % white	Dependent variable = 1980–1990 loss in % white
% Black at outset of decade	.355*	−.026
% Black at outset, squared	−.0058	−.002*
N	2,832	3,086

Note: Regression also includes several control variables to characterize the census tract at the outset of the decade: poverty rate, proportion of workers in professional and managerial occupations, the proportion of blacks with middle class incomes, the proportion of white households with children, the proportion of whites who are at least 65, the homeownership rate, the proportion of buildings built prior to 1939, the proportion of people living in group homes, the proportion of housing units that are single-family detached homes. In addition, the overall growth in households over the decade is included as is a dummy variables for each metropolitan area in the sample.

*Coefficients significantly different from zero at the 5 percent level of confidence.

there does seem to be a notable difference between the 1970s and 1980s. What explains this difference is unclear. It may be that white racial attitudes have softened and that white households in the 1980s were less prejudiced than they were one decade earlier. It may be that the stereotypes that they held about racially integrated communities were less strong in the 1980s. Or finally, it may be that the nature of neighborhood preferences has undergone a qualitative shift. In the 1970s, white attitudes toward racially integrated neighborhoods may have been best described by tipping models that emphasized white prejudice. In the 1980s, by contrast, white household behavior may have been better described by the race-based neighborhood stereotyping hypothesis, and thus the relationship between racial composition and subsequent racial change was more complex.

A Look at Washington, D.C.

Looking at a selected metropolitan area in somewhat greater depth helps to give a fuller picture of the stability of racial mixing that occurred in the 1980s. One advantage of considering a single metropolitan area is that it permits the use of maps, which powerfully show the spatial distribution of the population. It also allows the use of data that simply cannot be collected for a broader sample. Finally, it permits the consideration of specific history and unique circumstances difficult to consider for a broader set of areas.

This section thus provides a sketch of racial integration in the Washington, D.C. metropolitan area. The Washington area differs from most other large metropolitan areas in many respects. First, among metropolitan areas of over one million people, it was surpassed only by New Orleans and Norfolk, Virginia, in its proportion of black residents in 1990 (which was 26.6 percent). Second, Washington's black population is relatively affluent. In 1989, Washington, D.C., was one of just ten metropolitan areas in which the per capita income for blacks was over $14,000. In the country as a whole, by contrast, per capita income for blacks was just $8,859 (U.S. Bureau of the Census 1990). Finally, because of its historically black middle class, Washington, D.C. has a substantial black suburban population; its suburban black population of 619,000 in 1990 was by far the largest in the country (O'Hare and Frey 1992). These unique features (a large black middle-class population and the existence of largely black, middle-class suburban communities) together suggest that the dynamics of racial integration may be different in Washington than in other large metropolitan areas. Affirmative black preferences, for instance, may play a more significant role in driving segregation there than in other metropolitan areas. Still, the story of Washington is likely to be relevant for other metropolitan areas and may indeed provide insights into the nature of neighborhood change to be expected in other metropolitan areas as the black middle class grows and moves to the suburbs.

The Washington metropolitan area is made up of five primary counties: the District of Columbia, Montgomery County and Prince Georges County in Maryland, and Arlington and Fairfax counties in Virginia. (More outlying counties include Calvert and Charles counties in Maryland, and Loudoun and Prince William counties in Virginia.) This analysis considers the full metropolitan area but focuses on three counties: the District of Columbia, Montgomery County, and Prince Georges County, which has the largest number of blacks of the surrounding counties. The maps in this chapter show the 1980 and 1990 black population concentration in these three counties.

The first map (Figure 4.1) shows the racial composition of District of Columbia neighborhoods in 1980.[23] As indicated, the darkly shaded tracts represent those in which the black population represents a majority, the lightly shaded areas indicate those with a black population share of between 10 and 50 percent, while the un-shaded areas are those that are predominantly white. Like many cities, the racial division is quite sharp, with the northwestern quadrant largely white and the rest of the city largely black. Still, there is a band of integrated communities down the middle. And as indicated in Figure 4.2, a map showing the distribution of black population in 1990, most of these areas remained integrated over the ten-year time span. (Indeed, the tracts surrounding Capitol Hill actually became more white over the ten-year period.)

As discussed at length in Chapter 2, census tracts are not perfect representations of neighborhoods. It is possible, therefore, that what appears to be a racially integrated census tract is instead a white-segregated and a black-segregated neighborhood that are side by side. By looking at block-group data, it is possible to gain some insight into this issue by learning whether the block-groups within racially integrated census tracts are themselves racially integrated. In the District

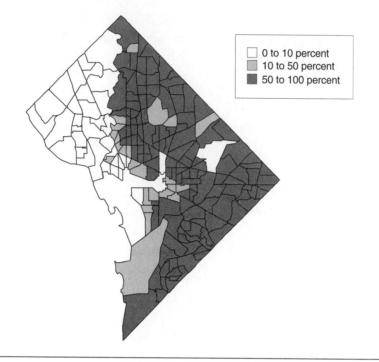

0 to 10 percent
10 to 50 percent
50 to 100 percent

Figure 4.1 Washington, D.C., percent black, 1980

of Columbia in 1990, there were twenty-eight racially integrated census tracts (measured by 1990 boundaries), sixteen of which could be broken down into their constituent block-groups. Of the underlying block-groups, 66 percent were integrated, 23 percent were predominantly white, and 11 percent were predominantly black. In Montgomery County, a similar analysis of underlying block-groups showed that 75 percent were integrated, 24 percent were predominantly white, and 1 percent were predominantly black.

It is difficult to interpret these figures. Clearly, one expects the level of integration to be less at finer geographic levels. After all, you cannot expect every block to perfectly reflect the racial composition of the larger community. Moreover, this simple methodology is obviously flawed—many of the integrated tracts examined here are only moderately integrated, say 10–20 percent black, so it is not surprising that their subcomponents are often predominantly white. In a tract that is 12 percent black overall, for instance, it is hardly surprising to

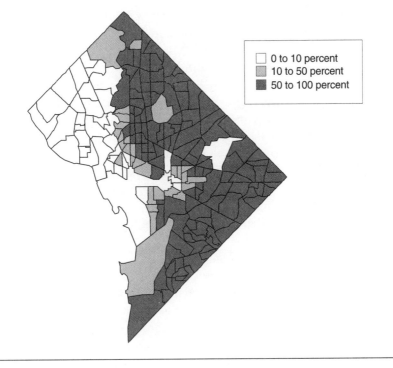

Figure 4.2 Washington, D.C., percent black, 1990

find a block-group that is under 10 percent black. Finally, the data do not indicate whether the integrated tracts are in fact composed of largely black blocks adjacent to largely white ones. Indeed, in only two cases does an integrated tract include both largely white and largely black block-groups.[24] The point is that there is racial mixing, even though it is lesser at the block level than at the tract level. But these results also suggest that further analysis of actual block data would be interesting and worthwhile.

Getting back to the map of the District of Columbia, can we learn anything further about the nature of racial integration in this city? The two primary clusters of integration include the Adams Morgan/ Dupont Circle area in northwest Washington, and the neighborhoods surrounding Capitol Hill. The Adams Morgan/Dupont Circle area might be classified as a "young, rental" integrated community. The homeownership rate in these census tracts was only 20 percent in 1980, compared with a metropolitan area average of nearly 60 percent. Further, less than 6 percent of the white households living in these tracts had children in 1980 compared with a metropolitan average of over 33 percent.

As for the other key area—Capitol Hill—the stability of its integration is perhaps best explained by the presence of the U.S. Capitol building together with several other major government buildings. Clearly, Congress is not moving anywhere in the conceivable future, and it promises to generate a strong supply of staffers who are interested in living nearby. And while the continued presence of the surrounding government buildings is somewhat less certain, they too probably help bolster the housing market. Significantly, both Capitol Hill and Dupont Circle have attractive, historic townhouses and apartment buildings that have undoubtedly helped to draw white households.

The other racially mixed neighborhoods in the city include four areas surrounding military bases, universities, or hospitals—Walter Reade Army Medical Center, Fort McNair, Bolling Air Force Base, and Catholic University. A key question, of course, is whether it is merely these institutions themselves that are integrated rather than the neighborhood surrounding them. Or more misleading still, whether segregated white (or black) institutions can give the illusion of integration by being located in a community populated largely by blacks (or whites).

By looking at the share of residents living in institutions or group quarters at the block-group level, it is possible to gain some insight into these questions.[25] The data indicate that the neighborhood surrounding Catholic University is in reality quite segregated. The apparent diversity simply results from an overwhelmingly white institution being situated in an overwhelmingly black neighborhood. The situation at the Walter Reade Army Medical Center appears instead to be that the institution itself is integrated but has generated little integration in its surroundings.[26] Fort McNair and Bolling Air Force Base represent the third case; that is, they seem to have fostered some racial mixing in the communities surrounding them. Admittedly, in the area surrounding Fort McNair, some of this racial mixing might stem not from the presence of the base but rather from the large-scale urban renewal efforts that were undertaken there in the 1950s: during that decade, massive amounts of public funds were spent in the area to clear land, upgrade public services, and clear the way for the development of modern and upscale apartment complexes.

In summary, stable racial integration appears most viable in the District of Columbia in neighborhoods that are home to large-scale institutions such as government buildings and military bases, or that are populated by young and childless renters. This seems clearly consistent with the notion of race-based, neighborhood stereotyping.

Next consider the surrounding suburbs. The maps of Montgomery County (Figures 4.3 and 4.4) suggest that racial mixing is quite stable. Indeed, not one of the forty-two tracts that were racially integrated in 1980 became predominantly black by 1990. And the stability of these tracts cannot be so simply explained. What does seem true is that the integrated areas are clustered in prospering areas. They seem, in particular, to be clustered in two key areas—the Silver Spring/Wheaton area just outside the city line—an area that is served by the convenient Red Line metro—and the communities surrounding the rapidly growing I-270 corridor near Gaithersburg.

The story in Prince Georges County (Figures 4.5 and 4.6) is quite distinct. For here it appears that integration *is* merely a step on the way to a neighborhood's becoming virtually all black. As shown in

Figure 4.3 Montgomery County, percent black, 1980

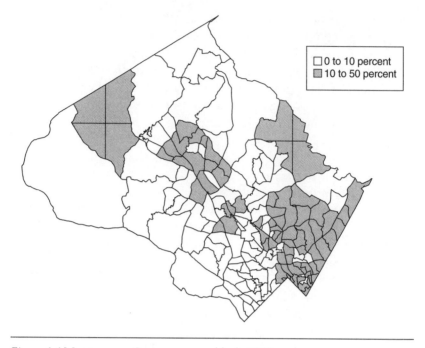

□ 0 to 10 percent
■ 10 to 50 percent

Figure 4.4 Montgomery County, percent black, 1990

Table 4.3, nearly 40 percent of eighty-one tracts in the county that were integrated in 1980 became predominantly black by 1990. This compares to just under 16 percent in the District of Columbia and none in Montgomery County. The map also makes clear that those integrated tracts located closest to predominantly black tracts are most likely to gain black population.

One point to stress is that it does not appear that Montgomery County is destined to follow in the footsteps of its Maryland neighbor. For we can compare the situation of Prince Georges County in 1970 with that of Montgomery County in 1990. In both cases, the proportion of the county population that was black was between 12 and 14 percent. Yet Prince Georges County was far more segregated. Consider that just 20 percent of the census tracts in Prince Georges County qualified as racially integrated in 1970, compared to 46 percent of Montgomery County's tracts in 1990.

What explains the difference between these areas and above all, the greater instability of Prince Georges County? Could the various fac-

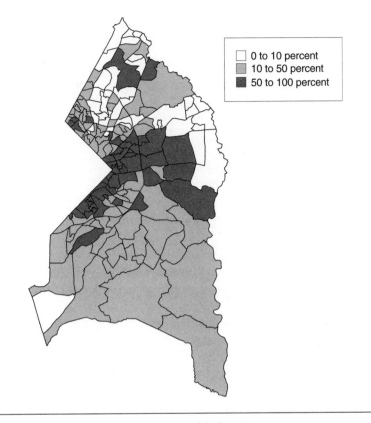

Figure 4.5 Prince Georges County, percent black, 1980

tors hypothesized above by the race-based neighborhood stereotyping hypothesis explain the difference? What about the pure prejudice and class difference theories? To test these hypotheses, the regression presented earlier is estimated for the Washington, D.C., metropolitan area, with a dummy variable for Prince Georges County.

The regression here also includes an additional variable not available in the broader national sample: distance to the central area of black residence. As explained above, the race-based neighborhood stereotyping hypothesis would predict that racially integrated areas should be more stable when located farther from other predominantly black areas. And certainly, it seems likely that such a variable would help to explain the greater instability of Prince Georges County. For Prince Georges County abuts the southeast and northeast quadrants

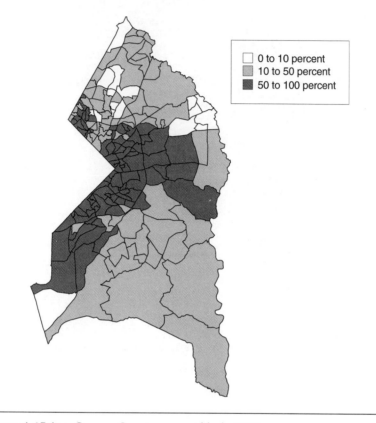

☐	0 to 10 percent
▦	10 to 50 percent
■	50 to 100 percent

Figure 4.6 Prince Georges County, percent black, 1990

of Washington, D.C., which are both predominantly black and include the most distressed, inner-city neighborhoods in the District of Columbia. Montgomery County, by contrast, lies above the most affluent and white communities in the District of Columbia. To try to capture this difference, I estimated the central point of the black population in 1980 using the internal latitude and longitude points of each census tract.[27] In particular, weighted means of the latitude and longitude points were calculated, using the number of black residents living in the tract as weights. The resulting central point is found slightly east of Capitol Hill.[28] The distance from this central point is then calculated for each tract in the metropolitan area.

The results confirm that distance to the black population center is critical. When comparing transitional and stable integrated tracts

Table 4.3 Distribution of neighborhoods by 1990 racial composition (tracts that were racially integrated in 1980, Washington, D.C., metropolitan area)

Area	Less than 10% black (%)	10–50% black (%)	At least 50% black (%)	Total, all tracts (%)	Number of tracts
Washington, D.C., metropolitan area	6.1	78.3	15.6	100.0	212
Montgomery County	7.1	92.9	0.0	100.0	42
Prince Georges County	2.5	58.0	39.5	100.0	81

Table 4.4 Selected coefficients from regression of non-Hispanic white loss, Washington, D.C., metropolitan area (dependent variable = 1980–1990 loss in % non-Hispanic white)

	Coefficient	Standard error
% Black	−0.42	0.25
% Black squared	0.002	0.002
Change in % black, 1970–1980	0.06	0.064
Distance from blk center	−39.2*	14.9
Prince Georges County (dummy var.)	9.2*	2.3
N	221	
R-squared	0.51	

Note: Regression also includes several control variables to characterize the census tract at the outset of the decade: the percentage of non-black minorities present, the poverty rate, proportion of workers in professional and managerial occupations, the proportion of blacks with middle class incomes, the proportion of blacks with college educations, the proportion of white households with children, the proportion of whites who are at least 65, the homeownership rate, the proportion of buildings built prior to 1939, the proportion of people living in group homes, the proportion of housing units that are single-family detached homes, and the proportion of recent movers. In addition, the overall growth in households over the decade is included.

*Coefficient significantly different from zero at the 5 percent level of confidence.

within the suburban Washington, the average distance to the black population center is 11.5 miles for stable tracts, and only 8.4 miles for transitional tracts, a difference statistically significant at the 1 percent level of confidence.

As shown in Table 4.4, this result holds up in a multivariate analysis as well. In particular, even after controlling for its racial, socioeconomic, and demographic mix, a census tract that is one-tenth of a degree (approximately six miles) closer to the central point is expected to lose 3.9 more percentage points of its non-Hispanic white population share.

Significantly, however, distance to the center of the black population does not explain fully the story of Prince Georges County. The coefficient on the Prince Georges County dummy variable remains large and highly significant even after this distance factor is accounted for. On average, the loss of non-Hispanic whites in a mixed tract in Prince Georges County was over 9 percentage points greater than in an otherwise identical tract located elsewhere in the metropolitan area. Something else, in addition to distance, and in addition to the many other socioeconomic and demographic factors included in this regression model, must explain this difference.

The notion of race-based neighborhood stereotyping, together with some knowledge of the Washington area, provide a few clues and suggest some other factors that may contribute to the difference. One key, for instance, might be the relative size of the black population in the county as a whole. The other suburban counties remain overwhelmingly white and thus, in contrast to Prince Georges County, there is little expectation that their integrated neighborhoods are on the way to becoming largely black. (Prince Georges County was over half black by 1990.) Perhaps even more important is the growth rate of the black population. The black population in the county rose by 170 percent during the 1970s and by another 49 percent during the 1980s. The non-black population, meanwhile, fell by 37 percent over the two decades (U.S. Bureau of the Census 1970, 1980, and 1990).

To some extent, the continued growth in black population in Prince Georges County reflects black preferences. Even as early as 1970, Prince Georges County was widely understood to be the "black" suburb: the number of blacks in the county was more than four times that of Montgomery County and six times that of the major Virginia suburbs (Gale 1987, p. 113). Blacks seeking suburban lifestyles have gravitated there—resisting the other, largely white suburban options that seemed far less welcoming. As one county resident put it, "We always wanted to make sure our child had many African-American children to play with, not just one or two" (Dent 1992, p. 18). And as blacks moved in to the county, whites tended to stay away.[29]

But the instability of racial integration in Prince Georges County is not simply due to black preferences for ethnic clustering. Whites have also clearly withdrawn from the county. And there is at least some evidence to suggest that worries about neighborhood strength may have played a role. Schools in particular seem to be a critical part of the story of Washington. With county-based school districts, counties take on far more importance in the Washington metropolitan area than in many other metropolitan areas. And there is evidence that by the early 1980s residents—both black and white—were concerned about the quality of schools in Prince Georges County. Consider that in 1983, one-third of respondents in Prince Georges County told the *Washington Post* that the local public schools were "poor" or "very poor" (Gale 1987, p. 130). And roughly one-third also said that the schools had deteriorated in the past five years (Meyer 1983).

To some extent, these figures probably reflect white residents' concerns about the changing racial balance of schools in Prince Georges County. During the 1970s, the number of blacks attending public schools in the county nearly doubled, and by 1980, blacks made up half of the county's public school enrollment (Gale 1987, p. 131). Thus, the declining confidence in the schools may be a direct result of whites' discomfort with largely black schools. But objective indicators suggest that schools were lagging behind to some degree in Prince Georges County. In 1983, for example, high-school students in the county scored a combined verbal and math average of 848 on the SAT, some forty-five points below the national average. In the other core suburbs of Washington, D.C., meanwhile, average combined scores ranged from 908 (the city of Alexandria) to 968 (Montgomery County). The performance of Montgomery County schools was particularly notable. Of the seven high schools with the highest mean SAT scores in the metropolitan area, five were in Montgomery County (Feinberg 1983).

More generally, Montgomery County has also been undergoing a rapid development—over the 1970s, its population increased by 11 percent and during the 1980s, its population swelled by a full 30 percent. Such a steady growth seems likely to counter any concerns that white households might have about declining property values in the face of growing minority populations. The growth in Prince Georges County, by comparison, was quite modest. The population was steady there during the 1970s and grew by less than 10 percent during the 1980s.

As for crime, the official statistics suggest that crime was substantially higher in Prince Georges County in 1980 than it was in other Washington suburbs. FBI records suggest that the number of reported crimes per capita in 1980 in Prince Georges County was 49 percent higher than the number in Fairfax County and 26 percent higher than in Montgomery County (U.S. Federal Bureau of Investigation 1980). And crime rates grew more rapidly in Prince Georges County as well—between 1970 and 1980 the number of reported crimes rose more rapidly there than they did in either Montgomery or Fairfax counties (U.S. Federal Bureau of Investigation 1980, and 1990). Finally, white residents of the county and the metropolitan area may well have viewed these disparities as even more extreme. According to one 1983 survey of approximately one thousand Prince Georges County residents, whites were more worried about rising crime rates than were blacks (Wynter 1983).

In summary, in a single metropolitan area, we see considerable diversity in the fate of racial integration. In one county (Prince Georges), black population continues to rise steadily, driving neighborhood racial change. Elsewhere in the metropolitan area (and in particular in the newly integrated suburbs in Montgomery County), racial mixing appears to be fairly stable. While some of the difference lies in the distance to the central area of black residence, much of it is clearly rooted in the particular history of Prince Georges County and in its early labeling as the "black" suburb in Washington. Another relevant difference may be the lesser confidence that whites (and to a lesser degree blacks) have in the structural strength (that is, the schools, safety levels, and property values) of Prince Georges County neighborhoods.

This chapter has begun an investigation of the roots of the variation in the pace of racial change across neighborhoods. Contrary to the conventional wisdom and the conclusions of much past research, the findings here suggest that the initial percentage of black residents is not a good predictor of the future course of change in racially mixed neighborhoods. What is relevant instead appears to be many of the factors predicted by the race-based neighborhood stereotyping hypothesis: the past history of change in the neighborhood; its distance to the center of black concentration; the homeownership rate; the overall strength of the neighborhood housing market; and the level of segregation and size of the black population in the metropolitan area as a whole. The next chapter digs a little deeper into racial change by examining how neighborhood characteristics influence the satisfaction levels of individual households.

CHAPTER FIVE

Racial Composition and Neighborhood Satisfaction

The previous chapter provided an overview of the correlates of racial change. It studied, that is, what kinds of racially integrated neighborhoods tend to remain stable over time. But such aggregate-level data analysis is difficult to interpret. The remaining empirical chapters offer an analysis of individual households and thus offer more insight into the underlying dynamics of racial change. It is, after all, the choices of individual households to move into and out of certain residential neighborhoods that ultimately determine neighborhood change and stability. This chapter begins to explain this process. But rather than examining the actual decisions that people make to leave and enter different neighborhoods (the subjects of Chapters 6 and 7), this chapter explores how those who live in racially integrated neighborhoods feel about the quality of life in their communities.

While such reports of neighborhood quality are arguably not as telling as actual residential choices and moves, we can certainly learn something from them about the viability of integration. If, for instance, households living in racially mixed communities uniformly report discontent, then the prospects for stable integration are certainly dim, since it is unlikely that these residents will choose, at least in the long run, to remain in such communities.

Predictions about Neighborhood Satisfaction

Chapter 3 outlines three chief alternative views of the motivations underlying attitudes toward racial mixing: pure prejudice, class differences, and race-based neighborhood stereotyping. Each of these generates different predictions about the ways in which racial composition is likely to affect the neighborhood satisfaction levels of black and white households. Theories emphasizing prejudice generally predict that the satisfaction of whites will be directly linked to the level of black representation in a community: the more blacks in a neighborhood, the less whites are satisfied (O'Brien and Clough 1983; Stipak and Hensler 1983; St. John and Bates 1990; Harris 1997c). As for black households, the assumption is that they will generally prefer communities with a *greater* share of black residents, at least up to about 50 percent black. As explained in the previous chapter, we may not in fact see such perfect relationships, since prejudice levels vary across households, and households may to some degree sort themselves according to racial preferences. The most racially tolerant white households, that is, will be those living in racially integrated communities, while the most prejudiced will be those in the predominantly white areas.

The class-based model, by contrast, predicts that people ultimately do not care much about race. Both blacks and whites should prefer neighborhoods in which the poverty rate is lower and income levels are higher. But once these measures of neighborhood socioeconomic status are taken into account, racial composition should be largely irrelevant.

As for race-based neighborhood stereotyping, the hypothesis suggests that white households fear racial integration because, first, they believe that all racially integrated communities are on their way to becoming largely black communities. And second, they automatically associate such largely black communities with neighborhood decline. Black households may also hold similar beliefs about predominantly black communities, but they are likely to be less strong.

Thus, in terms of satisfaction, the theory predicts that present racial composition should have little impact on neighborhood satisfaction levels. What is likely to be more critical to household satisfaction are recent *trends* in racial composition. Specifically, white households are likely to feel more uneasy in communities in which the black population, even if relatively small, has been growing. For it is these communities that white households fear will become largely black. And this should hold especially for households who are more invested in community quality, such as homeowners and households with children.

These predictions are distinct from those of the alternative theories. According to the class differences model, a growing black population should have little effect on black or white satisfaction levels if the economic status of the community's residents remains the same. As for pure prejudice, levels of racial mixing should theoretically matter more than changes. And even in the unlikely event that households have sorted themselves perfectly according to racial tolerance (and thus only changes in racial composition should affect satisfaction), we still wouldn't expect to see any differences between homeowners and renters.

The theory also suggests that households—and white households in particular—should report higher levels of crime and lower levels of services in racially changing (as compared to racially stable) communities. Whether or not these stereotypes are true—whether the quality of life is in fact lower in racially changing neighborhoods—is not clear. As discussed, both public and private institutions may treat racially mixed and largely black communities differently than predominantly white areas—opening fewer stores, assigning fewer patrols, and so on. It is possible too that current income levels simply do not capture the full extent of the social and economic differences between blacks and whites. Even after controlling for income and poverty levels, that is, largely black areas may be relatively deprived economically compared with their largely white counterparts. But even if the stereotypes are partly true, the theory implies that white households are likely to exaggerate to some degree the extent of community decline that accompanies racial change and therefore report greater dissatisfaction than black households.

Prior Evidence on Neighborhood Satisfaction

Before moving on to the empirical analysis, it is useful to review what prior evidence tells us about the determinants of neighborhood satisfaction and the particular role of race. There are two main approaches.[1] The first is to survey residents and ask them how they view neighborhoods of differing racial mixes. As discussed in the following chapters, much of the evidence we have concerning attitudes toward racial composition in fact comes from just such surveys. The results tend to suggest that whites prefer neighborhoods that are largely white, and that blacks prefer communities with roughly equal numbers of blacks and whites (Shlay and DiGregorio 1985; St. John and Bates 1990; Clark 1992; Farley et al. 1993).

Yet there are many reasons to doubt the accuracy of such surveys. Some have questioned whether surveys of racial preferences may understate people's level of racial prejudice (Schuman et al. 1997; Clark 1992). For respondents—and white respondents in particular—may be uneasy about reporting racially biased views. A white individual may dislike blacks and feel discomfort in integrated neighborhoods, but she may not admit these true feelings for fear of being viewed as racist. While worries about such socially modified responses are reasonable, it is also possible that these surveys actually *overstate* people's concern with race. For when asked about a 50 percent black community, white households are not likely to envision a community just like their own but 50 percent black. Rather, consistent with the stereotyping hypothesis, they are likely to imagine a community that has troubled schools, inadequate municipal services, and dangerous street corners. Thus, these surveys seem hardly to offer an assessment of the independent contribution of racial composition to neighborhood satisfaction.

The second, and preferable, approach is to survey members of households in neighborhoods of differing racial mixes and ask them how they feel about the quality of services and life more generally in their communities. Using information about the objective characteristics of the neighborhood, one can then analyze the extent to which individual neighborhood attributes contribute to their levels of satisfaction. And most relevant for our purposes, one is able to test the extent to which racial composition shapes neighborhood satisfaction levels, after controlling for other neighborhood conditions.

Few studies have in fact undertaken such analyses. Generally, the results are similar to those of racial preference surveys. They conclude, that is, that racial composition is an important determinant of neighborhood satisfaction, at least for white households. Controlling for neighborhood socioeconomic status, whites report lower satisfaction levels in neighborhoods with larger shares of black residents (O'Brien and Clough 1982; Stipak and Hensler 1983; Boehm and Ihlanfeldt 1991; Galster 1987a; Harris 1997c). For blacks, the results are less clear. Three studies suggest that blacks are largely indifferent to racial composition, while a fourth suggests that black households share views similar to those of whites and are less satisfied in neighborhoods with greater numbers of blacks (Stipak and Hensler 1983).

But it is not clear that these conclusions would still hold today, for most of these studies rely on data from the 1970s. Indeed, one of the two studies that consider more recent data finds evidence of considerable change (Harris 1997c).[2] In particular, the study examines two different data sets to learn whether the influence of racial composition on satisfaction levels has changed over the past few decades. First, it examines a national survey of 1,081 white households in 1975 and finds that racial composition is a highly significant determinant of neighborhood satisfaction, even after income level, perceived crime, and perceived deterioration are taken into account.[3]

Interestingly, however, when analyzing a more recent sample of white households—a sample of 2,000 households in the Chicago metropolitan area in the early 1990s, the study finds that there is no longer a relationship between neighborhood racial composition and white household satisfaction once income level and perceptions of crime have been taken into account. The comparison here is not perfect, of course. The study compares results from a national sample to a sample of households living in the Chicago metropolitan area. But if anything, such a comparison is likely to understate the extent to which racial attitudes have changed. For Chicago is among the most racially segregated metropolitan areas in the country, and thus its white residents are likely to be more resistant on average to racial integration than are residents in other parts of the United States.

Another reason to question the relevance of these earlier results is that most of these studies analyze surveys undertaken in single metropolitan areas. The extent to which these results are more broadly applicable is not clear. Indeed, most of the evidence comes from metropolitan areas in the Midwest, the region where racial segregation tends to be the most pronounced and integration tends to be the least stable (O'Brien and Clough 1982; Stipak and Hensler 1983; Galster 1987a).

The analysis that follows offers a chance to use a national data set to explore whether the relationship between racial composition and neighborhood satisfaction has indeed changed in recent years. Unlike these previous studies, it also offers a chance to study how racial change affects households' attitudes toward their communities. Third, unlike these prior studies, different groups of households are considered separately—renters and homeowners, and households with and without children. For it seems likely that racial composition will influence these households in distinct ways. Finally, it also offers a chance to explore how racial composition affects not only the overall assessment of a neighborhood's quality but also households' perceptions about specific aspects of the neighborhood—in particular, crime levels and school quality.

Data and Methods

The empirical analysis in this chapter explores how neighborhood conditions influence neighborhood satisfaction levels. As explained, the ideal way to address this question is to examine data that include information both about individual households and about the neighborhoods that they live in. But this combination is hard to come by, especially in a national sample of households. This study was fortunate to have access to such a data set, through a special arrangement with the U.S. Census Bureau.

Specifically, it uses the bureau's internal files of the American Housing Survey (AHS), a biannual survey of about 50,000 housing units nationwide that collects information about the members of the household, about their opinions regarding the neighborhood, and about the characteristics and quality of the housing unit.[4] Unlike the public use files, the internal AHS files also include the census tract in which each house is located.[5] With this geographic identifier included, a whole range of neighborhood characteristics taken from the decennial census—including racial composition, demographic information, economic variables, and housing conditions—can be linked to the AHS.[6] For this study, the AHS is linked to a set of 1980 and 1990 census tract variables obtained from the Urban Institute's Underclass Data Base (UDB) described in earlier chapters. Since both 1980 and 1990 variables are included, it is possible to explore not only how neighborhood characteristics at a given point in time influence household preferences, but also how *changes* in these contextual attributes play a part.

Figure 5.1 describes the data set used. The aim is to model a household's satisfaction with its neighborhood as a function of household information, objective neighborhood conditions, and recent changes in those conditions. The neighborhood satisfaction rating and the characteristics of the household are taken from the 1989 AHS, and the neighborhood characteristics are selected from the 1990 decennial census (via the UDB). Recent changes in neighborhood conditions are meanwhile captured by shifts in neighborhood characteristics between 1980 and 1990. Once again, the analysis is limited to households living in one of the thirty-four large metropolitan areas listed in Chapter 2.

The AHS provides a convenient measure of the neighborhood satisfaction levels of individual households. In particular, the survey's enumerators ask households to rate their neighborhoods on a scale of 1 to 10. This rating can then be interpreted as a measure of household satisfaction with its neighborhood or the amount of utility that the household derives from its neighborhood.[7] Households typically rate their neighborhoods fairly highly—the mean rating in 1989 was 8.1, with a standard deviation of 2.1.

Table 5.1 compares the neighborhood attitudes of black and white households living in largely white, integrated, and largely black communities. As shown, whites consistently rate as lower quality those neighborhoods with greater proportions of blacks. But the satisfaction levels of black households show an almost identical decline.

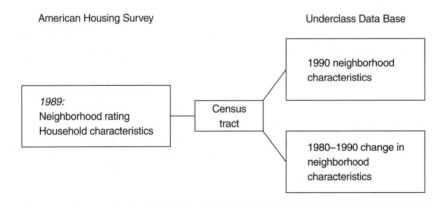

Figure 5.1 Data set description for Neighborhood Satisfaction Analysis

Table 5.1 Average neighborhood rating (1–10) given to neighborhoods of differing racial compositions

Race of respondents	Predominantly white tracts	Racially integrated tracts	Majority black tracts	Total households
Non-Hispanic whites	8.23	7.43	7.12	21,757
Blacks	8.08	7.60	6.90	3,218

Note: All differences in mean neighborhood ratings across neighborhood types are significantly different from zero at 5 percent level of confidence.

Thus, it hardly seems reasonable to interpret the white attitudes as evidence of any distaste for black neighbors.

The key question is what happens when we control for other, nonracial neighborhood characteristics. Does racial composition in fact independently contribute to neighborhood satisfaction for blacks or whites? In order to identify the independent contribution of racial mix, I estimate a regression model to show how various community characteristics influence the way in which residents rate their neighborhoods. Since the central task of this study is to explain patterns of change in racially mixed environments, the sample is limited to households living in integrated neighborhoods—census tracts, that is, that are between 10 and 50 percent black. (The identical models, however, were run on households living in all tracts, and the results were essentially the same.)

In addition to neighborhood characteristics, the regression also includes a set of household attributes, since certain types of households might have higher standards that lead them to view neighborhoods more critically. Households made up of older residents, for instance, might rate their neighborhoods more poorly because they compare them to the safe, socially cohesive neighborhoods that they remember. Alternatively, it is also possible that older residents are apt to rate their communities *higher* because they are more likely to have settled in what they consider their permanent home. Similarly, households with children might have higher standards of expected quality, as might those with higher incomes since they can afford a greater range of alternatives. Income is measured in the regression by two dummy variables that indicate if the household's income falls into the bottom or top quartiles of incomes in the sample ("bottom income" and "top income").[8] Finally, the length of time that the household has been living in its home aims to capture the fact that a recent in-mover to a neighborhood is presumably closer to her equilibrium and thus likely to rate her neighborhood more highly.

As for neighborhood characteristics in the model, they include, first, a dummy variable indicating if the neighborhood is in a central city (and thus served by a local government that may be fiscally weaker and less able to deliver adequate neighborhood services) and second, two measures of socioeconomic status—the poverty rate and the average family income of the tract in 1990. And since a household's satisfaction with its present circumstances are of course colored by the direction in which it sees the neighborhood to be changing, the difference between the poverty rate in 1990 and 1980 is added to the model. Finally, the share of blacks living in the tract in 1990 is included, as is the difference between the percentage of blacks present in 1990 and the percentage present one decade earlier.

To estimate the regression, the sample of households is stratified by race, tenure, and presence of children, since a key aim is to see how racial composition and changes in that composition affect these groups differently. Unfortunately, the sample of black households is not large enough to generate independent estimates for households with and without children, so we divide the sample into six distinct groups: white homeowners with children, white homeowners without children, white renters with children, white renters without children, black homeowners, and black renters.

As for the method of estimation, the best approach to analyzing such categorical survey response data is arguably to use what is known as an ordinal logit or probit model (see McKelvey and Zavoina 1975; Boehm and Ihlanfeldt 1991; Liao 1994). For the AHS neighborhood rating scale is better interpreted as a measure of ordinal, and not cardinal utility—the difference between a "4" rating and a "3" rating, that is, is not necessarily the same as that between a "9" and a "10." While the ordinary least squares model (OLS) assumes that these differences are identical, an ordered logit or probit model does not. It simply assumes that a "10" is greater than a "9" and a "4" is greater than a "3." The problem with these non-linear approaches, however, is that it is not clear how the estimated coefficients

Table 5.2 Selected coefficients from regression of 10-point neighborhood quality scale, non-Hispanic white households in integrated neighborhoods, by tenure and presence of children

	NHW owners with children		NHW owners, no children		NHW renters with children		NHW Renters, no children	
	Coeff.	Std. error	Coeff.	Std. error	Coeff.	Std. error	Coeff.	Std. error
Intercept	7.6***	0.705	7.7***	0.578	8.1***	1.272	6.5***	0.545
Central city	−0.672***	0.235	−0.37**	0.181	0.44	0.427	0.137	0.223
Mean income (000s)	0.018**	0.009	0.0003	0.008	0.0036	0.017	0.0086	0.007
Poverty rate	−0.05**	0.021	−0.082***	0.015	−0.119***	0.033	−0.075***	.013
Change in poverty, 1980–1990	0.057*	0.031	0.032	0.022	0.02	0.048	0.014	0.02
% Black	−0.016	0.013	0.01	0.009	0.032	0.024	−0.011	0.01
Change in % black, 1980–1990	−0.033**	0.015	−0.043***	0.01	−0.015	0.025	−0.001	0.012
R-squared	.237		.164		.179		.215	
N	247		530		161		450	

Notes: Regression also includes several household-level control variables, such as age of household head, length of tenure in housing unit, and two dummy variables indicating if the household's income is in the top or bottom quartile of the distribution. NHW = non-Hispanic white.

*, **, *** Statistically significant at the 10, 5, and 1 percent levels, respectively.

should be interpreted. Since the results from the OLS and the ordered logit estimations were largely identical, the easier-to-interpret coefficients from the OLS version are presented here.

Results

Table 5.2 shows these results for the white household samples. Recall that the dependent variable here is the neighborhood rating scale. Thus, a positive coefficient indicates a positive relationship with neighborhood satisfaction. For ease of presentation, the coefficients on the household characteristics are not shown. (In general, the household characteristics do not appear that critical. There is some evidence that older households and those who have more recently moved into their homes appear to rate the quality of their neighborhoods more highly, but the finding is not consistent. Interestingly, the only group for which income seems to matter is homeowners with children. This may indicate that white households only use higher incomes to purchase membership in better neighborhoods when they own their homes and have children.)

As for the neighborhood characteristics, the coefficient on the poverty rate is negative and significant in all four regressions, reflecting the unsurprising fact that people who live in neighborhoods with higher poverty believe that their communities are less desirable places to live. If the poverty rate is ten percentage points higher, households are on average likely to give their neighborhood a rating that is between 0.5 and 1.2 points lower. Curiously, the coefficient on the growth in the poverty rate is positive and marginally significant for white homeowners with children.[9]

As for the other measure of socioeconomic status, mean income, it appears to matter only to white homeowners with children. As hypothesized, it may be that this group is simply the most invested in neighborhood conditions and quality. The coefficient on the central city variable, meanwhile, is negative and statistically significant for the white household samples. On average, white households are predicted to rate their neighborhoods between .4 and .7 points lower if they live in the central city.

As for racial composition, the coefficient on the black population percentage is statistically insignificant in all of the white household samples, indicating that whites are indifferent to the magnitude of black presence in their neighborhood. Whether a neighborhood is 10 or 50 percent black, that is, whites are equally satisfied, controlling for other factors, especially the poverty rate. (Indeed, results from the full sample of households suggest that whether a neighborhood is 0 or 100 percent black, whites are equally satisfied once other factors are controlled for.) This finding seems to undermine to some degree prejudice-based theories of racial change. For unless households sort themselves perfectly by degree of racial prejudice, the pure prejudice theory would predict some relationship between racial composition and satisfaction.

And what about the class model of racial change? Clearly, the socioeconomic status of a community matters to both blacks and whites. But class does not explain the full effects of race. For while present racial composition appears irrelevant to white residents, past trends in this composition appear to matter, at least to those who are homeowners. White homeowners living in a neighborhood that is 50 percent black today but had no blacks a decade ago, for instance, rate their neighborhoods an average of two full points lower than those living in communities that have been 50 percent black for ten years.

Significantly, this result is consistent with the notion of race-based neighborhood stereotyping. For it suggests that what matters to white households is not necessarily the present racial mix of their neighborhood, but rather its future stability. It matters little, that is, whether their present neighborhood is 10 percent or 40 percent black; what is of concern to them instead is the uncertainty regarding its future status and in particular, whether the neighborhood might become majority black in the future.[10]

Moreover, the fact that white homeowners and not renters appear sensitive to this change underscores the importance of these expectations, since homeowners tend to live in their homes considerably longer than renters do. It also suggests that, as hypothesized by race-based neighborhood stereotyping, households may care less about racial composition per se than about the security of property values. There is little reason, after all, to think that homeowners are any more prejudiced than renters. A key characteristic that clearly does distinguish homeowners from renters, however, is their financial stake in the future of local property values.

Significantly, there is almost no difference here in the sensitivity of homeowners with and without children to changes in the racial mix.

But it is still possible that households with and without children will in fact behave differently in the face of racial mixing. They may, that is, give a neighborhood the same rating, but those with children may be faster to leave when their satisfaction levels decline.

What about black households? According to Table 5.3, the results for the non-racial variables are generally the same. Black households, like white households, consistently rate their neighborhoods lower when poverty rates are higher. Curiously, the one group of the six for whom present racial composition appears to matter is black renters, who are predicted to rate a neighborhood as 0.27 points lower for every 10 percentage point increase in the proportion of blacks. This surprising finding runs directly counter to the surveys of racial preference discussed earlier that suggest that blacks are most content in neighborhoods that are 50 percent black and 50 percent white.

In addition to asking households to report their overall rating of a neighborhood's quality, the AHS also questions households about their views regarding particular neighborhood attributes, such as local schools, crime, and other concerns such as shopping and transpor-

Table 5.3 Selected coefficients from regression of 10-point neighborhood quality scale, black households in integrated neighborhoods, by tenure

	Black homeowners		Black renters	
	Coeff.	Std. error	Coeff.	Std. error
Intercept	7.1***	1.170	8.6***	1.080
Central city	−0.208	0.361	−0.326	0.339
Mean income (000s)	−0.008	0.002	0.0081	0.016
Poverty rate	−0.093***	0.026	−0.049***	0.018
Change in poverty, 1980–1990	0.059	0.032	0.058***	0.021
% Black	0.026	0.014	−0.027**	0.014
Change in % black, 1980–1990	−0.022	0.014	−0.001	0.015
R-squared	.2		.157	
N	171		271	

Note: Regression also includes several household-level control variables, such as age of household head, length of tenure in housing unit, and two dummy variables indicating if the household's income is in the top or bottom quartile of the distribution, and a dummy variable indicating the presence of children in the home.

** and *** Significant at the 5 and 1 percent levels, respectively.

tation. Using the links to the census data, it is possible to test whether these views and concerns are sensitive to changing racial composition.

Here we consider attitudes toward schools and crime, starting with crime. In particular, the proportion of white and black residents describing crime as a "problem" in 1989 are compared in (1) racially integrated neighborhoods in 1990 in which the proportion of non-Hispanic whites declined by more than ten percentage points between 1980 and 1990, and (2) racially integrated areas in which the racial mix was stable or in which the white population increased between 1980 and 1990. As shown in Table 5.4, the differences are significant. Non-Hispanic white households surveyed by the AHS are more often bothered by crime when living in a *changing* racially integrated neighborhood as opposed to a stable one. This is not the case with black households, indicating that white households are using racial change as a signal of structural decline to a greater degree than blacks, and suggesting that white households might be exaggerating its importance. (Note that this is also true for the overall assessment of the community; the difference in average neighborhood rating between stable and transitional neighborhoods is statistically significant for white households and not for black households.)

And what about schools? Here I compare the proportion of white and black households describing schools as poor in the two types of neighborhoods. While a greater proportion of whites as well as blacks complain about schools in transitional as compared to stable integrated communities, the differences are not statistically significant.

Table 5.4 Comparing attitudes in stable and transitional integrated neighborhoods

	Non-Hispanic white households		Black households	
	Stable	Transitional	Stable	Transitional
Percent reporting crime as a problem	37.5*	44.9	35.2	32.1
Mean neighborhood rating (1–10 scale)	7.65*	7.07	7.37	7.47
N	637	755	219	227
Percent rating schools as poor	18.2	22.6	6.1	15.1
N	159	164	82	93

* Difference between responses in stable and transitional neighborhoods statistically significant at the 5 percent level.

The sample sizes here are considerably smaller since only households with children in school were asked about local school quality. Thus, it may be that the number of households is simply too small to perceive any effects.

In summary, these results are, at the very least, more consistent with the notion of race-based neighborhood stereotyping than with other theories of racial change. On the one hand, there is little evidence here that present racial composition influences neighborhood satisfaction, once socioeconomic status is taken into account. On the other hand, the socioeconomic status of a community fails to explain all the variation in satisfaction either, as class-based theories would have it. White households, or at least white homeowners, report lower levels of neighborhood satisfaction when the black population is growing. This may well be because these households fear that racially changing neighborhoods are on their way to becoming majority black and are experiencing the structural decline that they associate with such communities.

These results run contrary to most prior studies that suggest that present racial composition does affect the neighborhood satisfaction of whites. Since most prior studies utilize data from the 1960s and 1970s, it is tempting to conclude that whites have become more comfortable with living in racially integrated communities. Indeed, the results are consistent with another analysis that suggests such a shift (Harris 1997b). But this conclusion can only be tentative, since there are methodological and sample differences between this study and earlier analyses.

In the end, these survey responses are clearly imperfect measures of neighborhood satisfaction and neighborhood satisfaction does not in any case predict departure rates. Many dissatisfied residents may remain in their communities, and many highly satisfied residents may leave. Thus, to learn about the influences of racial composition on household behavior, we ultimately need to study the actual decisions of residents to leave their communities.

Race, Neighborhood, and the Decision to Move

The previous chapter analyzed how racial composition influences reports about neighborhood satisfaction. But while analysis of such neighborhood satisfaction is instructive, to truly understand the nature of racial change, one ultimately needs to gain insight into how racial composition influences the actual household decisions that underlie such change—the decisions, that is, to leave certain neighborhoods and move into new ones. This chapter examines one of these two key household decisions: the decision to move out. To what extent is racial composition indeed a factor in the decision by residents to leave their homes and communities? Does race influence all types of households in the same way? Are certain types of households, that is, less sensitive to racial composition and thus more likely than others to remain in a racially mixed environment? In attempting to answer these questions, particular attention is paid to testing the predictions generated by the hypothesis of race-based neighborhood stereotyping.

Why Do People Move?

Before considering the role of racial composition and neighborhood conditions more generally, it is useful to take a step back and explore why people move and how social scientists have modeled these decisions. In general, most sociologists and demographers view household mobility as a function of major life-cycle changes, such as births, deaths, and marriages, which in turn alter housing needs.[1] A household with young children, for instance, is more likely to move than one without, in order to accommodate the family's need for additional space. Economists, meanwhile, have tended to focus on household mobility as a response to employment opportunities.

More formally, the theoretical framework used by sociologists to investigate household mobility centers on thresholds of dissatisfaction (see Rossi 1955; Speare 1974; Speare, Goldstein, and Frey 1975). According to this model, households are bound to particular locations by jobs, social ties, and attachments to homes and neighborhoods. But over time this bond may weaken as a result of "changes in the needs of a household, changes in the social and physical amenities offered by a particular location, or changes in the standards used to evaluate these factors" (Speare, Goldstein, and Frey 1975, p. 175). When residential dissatisfaction or stress exceeds some set threshold, a household will decide to move. Implicit in this framework is the notion that generally "satisfied" households do not consider moving, even if they discover that they would be better off in a different location.

The basis of the economic theories of mobility is, naturally, utility maximization. Economists posit that a household aims to maximize its individual utility in making residential choices. Over time, however, a household is likely to drift out of equilibrium because of changes in its utility function (perhaps as the result of a job change), changes in the price of housing relative to other goods, or most relevant here, changes in the actual housing bundle consumed (say, for instance, a change in neighborhood racial mix). In a market with no adjustment costs, a household should move as soon as its demand for housing diverges from its consumption. But adjustment costs do exist—both in acquiring information about alternative homes and in moving itself. So a household is not expected to move the moment it finds itself out of equilibrium, but rather when the discounted sum of the expected utility losses from remaining in its present unit exceed the costs of moving. Put another way, the probability of moving is directly related to the degree of disequilibrium and inversely related to moving and search costs.

In short, both economists and sociologists view mobility decisions as a function of the degree of mismatch between a household's needs and its present residential location. There are key differences—economists pay more attention to the costs of moving, and in contrast to the conceptual framework used by sociologists, the economic model includes no set threshold level of disequilibrium or discomfort beyond which a household will automatically decide to move—but the general understanding of mobility decisions is similar. Most relevant for our purposes, neither economists nor sociologists pay much attention to the role of neighborhood factors in driving mobility decisions. As a result, little work, even of a theoretical nature, has been done to explore how—if at all—neighborhood attributes affect mobility. This is not to say that neighborhood factors have been ignored entirely— clearly, the models above do afford a potential role to neighborhood (for instance if neighborhoods change over time, households may drift out of equilibrium), and some research has explored it. And it is worth reviewing the relevant findings. The discussion that follows is divided into evidence from surveys of preferences about neighborhoods and evidence from studies of actual mobility.

Predictions about When People Move

The theory presented in Chapter 3 predicts that racial composition should be less central to the decision to leave a neighborhood than it is to the choice of which one to move into. For one thing, people already living in a community are likely to have considerable information about their neighborhood's quality and future prospects, and therefore their decision to move should be less dependent on racial considerations. Outsiders, by contrast, are more likely to rely on racial stereotypes. One researcher, for instance, has found that while outsiders view racially diverse neighborhoods as "dicey," "crime infested," and "drug-ridden," those living in the areas—both white and black—see their neighborhoods as "safe" and "family oriented" (Maly and Nyden 1996, p. 29). Further, to be provoked to move out of a neighborhood a household has to be first provoked to actually move and absorb the consequent costs. Its distaste for racial mixing, in other words, must at least exceed the costs of moving.

With this said, a dramatic *change* in racial composition might well affect exit decisions. Such change, however, is not likely to affect all households in all communities in the same way. First, residents who are more invested in their neighborhood's quality than others (consider again, homeowners and households with children) are likely to be more wary about neighborhood change and its impact. Second, residents who believe more strongly than others that a growing number of black neighbors will undermine their community's structural strength are expected to be more averse to racial mixing. Most of these residents are likely to be white, but blacks too might share these beliefs.

Third, it seems likely that residents of metropolitan areas in which neighborhood decline has typically accompanied minority growth in the past are probably more likely to make this connection in the present. Finally, the theory also predicts that people living in very secure neighborhoods—that is, in communities that are either seemingly shielded from additional minority growth by their location or past history or insulated in some way from declines in school quality, public safety, or real estate values—will be less fearful of racial mixing.

Evidence from Racial Preference Surveys

The most commonly cited evidence on race and household mobility behavior clearly comes from surveys of racial preferences. Given the difficulty of finding data that link individual households to their actual neighborhoods, these surveys of racial preferences are often all that researchers and observers have. And because many surveys have asked the same questions in repeated years, they also provide a useful insight into changes over time.

Over the last forty years, the Gallup Organization has surveyed a national sample of white households about their attitudes toward integration. In particular, their surveys have asked white respondents two key questions: whether they would move if blacks came to live next door to them, and whether they would move if blacks moved "in great numbers" to their neighborhood. In 1958, 44 percent of whites polled reported that they would move if a black family came to live next door. In 1978, the share had fallen to 13 percent, and by 1997, the proportion had dropped to just 1 percent. As to whether they would move if blacks moved "in great numbers" to their neighborhood, 18 percent said they would do so in 1997, down from 53 percent in 1978 and a remarkable 80 percent in 1958 (Gallup Poll Social Audit 1997).

The changes here are dramatic and sustained. Aside from demonstrating a growing tolerance among white households for residential integration, however, these figures are hard to interpret. What does "great numbers" mean? Two? One hundred? A majority? At what point, if any, do most white households grow uneasy with racial mixing? Far more detailed information about stated intentions to leave racially mixed neighborhoods comes from the Detroit Area Surveys undertaken in 1976 and 1992. These surveys showed respondents a series of cards representing neighborhoods of various racial compositions. For each type of neighborhood, white residents were asked whether they would feel comfortable living there, and if not, whether they would try to move out. The findings generally suggest considerable white withdrawal from mixed areas, with more whites declaring that they would move the greater the proportion of blacks within a given hypothetical neighborhood.[2] The figures do decline over time, however, with 41 percent of whites declaring they would move from a neighborhood that is 36 percent black in 1976 and only 29 percent declaring they would do so in 1992 (Farley et al. 1993).[3]

Because blacks are generally seen as the incomers, none of these surveys specifically asks blacks if they would move out of a neighborhood if it reached a particular racial mix. The surveys tend instead to ask blacks to identify their preferences for neighborhood racial mix and to specify which neighborhoods they would be willing to move into. These findings are discussed at greater length later, but in brief, the responses indicate that black households are largely indifferent to race, except for a reluctance on the part of some to move into all-white areas and of a smaller number of others to move into all-black areas. Given that exit decisions are likely to be less influenced by racial concerns, it seems safe to assume that very few blacks would try to move out of a neighborhood as a result of its racial mix.

In summary, while these surveys seem to indicate a growing willingness by whites to remain in integrated communities, they still suggest discomfort with high levels of integration. Yet the results of these surveys should be viewed with some scepticism. First, as shown below, there is often a gap between intentions to move and actual moves; that is, residents voicing a desire to move do not always end up doing so. Second, since the cards representing racial composition are shown to households in a sequence of increasing black concentration, they themselves tend to suggest a pattern of change rather than one of stability. Thus, the responding white households are likely to see the hypothetical mixed neighborhoods as not simply 20 or 30 percent black, but as increasingly black—and vulnerable to becoming majority black in the future. Third, it is not clear that white households in Detroit are representative of those in the country at large. In 1990, Detroit was the most racially segregated metropolitan area in the country (Cutler, Glaeser, and Vigdor 1999). White households in Detroit are thus likely to be more resistant to racial mixing than those living in other cities and metropolitan areas.[4]

Finally, since the racial change is hypothetical, these surveys can only reflect how households believe they would react rather than how they would actually react. Since white households in the Detroit area are overwhelmingly situated in predominantly white neighborhoods, residents of these households are likely to have had no experience with racial mixing in their particular communities so their responses are probably best judged as a reaction to stereotypes. Their answers reflect, that is, how they *imagine* it would feel to live in what they *imagine* to be the typical black neighborhood—a neighborhood that they see as having not only a larger share of black residents, but also lower incomes, more deteriorated housing, poorer schools, and higher crime—not what it would feel like to live in their own neighborhood with a different racial mix. And to the extent that these results indicate what white households believe to be true about racially integrated neighborhoods, they might be more useful barometers of the willingness of white households to move into racially mixed neighborhoods, decisions that will be considered in Chapter 7.

Indeed, a more detailed analysis of the 1992 Detroit survey suggests that such neighborhood stereotypes play an important role in explaining white resistance to integrated neighborhoods. For the survey also questioned the white respondents who said that they would leave a racially mixed area about their motives, and the most commonly stated reasons were falling property values and rising crime. A full 40 percent of the residents who said they would move gave property values as their reason. "I'd like to feel I'm not racist," said one respondent, "but . . . I'd be concerned that my property values would go down" (Farley et al. 1994, p. 760). Approximately 20 percent of white respondents meanwhile mentioned crime as their chief concern. One resident put it bluntly: "Because the neighborhood is turning black—I assume crime rates would rise" (pp. 760–761). The point is, if white attitudes are driving segregation, these attitudes do not seem to be purely about race itself—that is, about a dislike of blacks or a desire to live among other whites. Indeed, fewer than 10 percent of respondents said they would leave a mixed neighborhood because they would prefer to "be around people that are like myself" (p. 761).

In summary, there are reasons to be skeptical about these survey results as indicators of people's probability of moving in the face of racial mixing. And while the results of these surveys are often used to demonstrate the importance of racial preferences in driving racial change, careful analysis suggests that they may in fact be more supportive of race-based neighborhood stereotyping.

Studies of Actual Residential Mobility

Studies of actual residential moves offer more reliable clues to the importance of racial composition and neighborhood more generally. But while many studies of household mobility have been undertaken over the years, they provide little evidence on the role of racial composition—or more broadly, of neighborhood characteristics—in determining household mobility. In large part, this gap results from the paucity of data that tie households to small geographic units. As discussed above, however, theoretical reasons may have contributed as well, with researchers not viewing neighborhood factors as critical in the decision to move. Nonetheless, the existing literature does offer some insights.

The first conclusion to be drawn is that neighborhood generally does seem to matter. Studies consistently suggest that general neighborhood concerns play a part in mobility decisions. Measures of neighborhood satisfaction, for instance, are typically found to be correlated with moving decisions. There are two main types of studies. The first type (which might be called *ex post*) asks people to explain their reasons for moving *after* they have moved. The second type *(ex ante)* surveys households about their neighborhood and then assesses the usefulness of neighborhood satisfaction as a predictor of mobility.

In the *ex post* studies, households consistently report that neighborhood concerns were significant in motivating their moves (Stegman 1969; Greenberg and Boswell 1972; Birch et al. 1977). While the findings of *ex ante* studies of mobility are more mixed, there is evidence that neighborhood matters here too, with most studies finding that people are more likely to move when they are more dissatisfied with their neighborhood (see Boehm and Mark 1980; Shear 1983; Boehm and Ihlanfeldt 1986; Galster 1987a; Deane 1990; Bartik, Butler, and Liu 1992; South and Deane 1993). Interestingly, although few studies look separately at households by race, there is some evidence that the relationship between neighborhood satisfaction and mobility is weaker for blacks. Indeed, according to one analysis, black households are actually *less* likely to leave neighborhoods that they rate as "fair" as compared to those rated as "excellent." This surprising finding may reflect the difficulty that black households face in finding alternative housing in relatively desirable neighborhoods (South and Deane 1993).

One qualification to the conclusion that neighborhood matters is that although neighborhood satisfaction is typically correlated with the probability of moving, it appears to be a better predictor of the *desire* to move than it is of the actual fact of moving (see Speare et al. 1975; Deane 1990; Lee, Oropesa, and Kanan 1994). Moreover, there is evidence to suggest that neighborhood satisfaction is more critical to short-term rather than longer-term moving plans. When it comes to longer-term plans, life-cycle influences such as age and family composition seem to be dominant (McHugh, Gober, and Reid 1990).

Economic studies using more objective measures of the extent of mismatch between a household's needs and its actual neighborhood also conclude that neighborhood generally matters. In particular, several studies estimate predicted housing and neighborhood expenditures by using the parameters from a model of housing demand. A dollar value measuring the extent to which a household is out of equilibrium is then calculated by measuring the difference between predicted and actual housing expenditures (Goodman 1976; Hanushek and Quigley 1978; Weinberg, Friedman, and Mayo 1981). In general, these studies find that the expenditure gap is positively linked to mobility. What is missing from these analyses, however, is any information about what particular attributes of the housing unit or neighborhood underlie the disequilibrium.

Past research offers little guidance on this issue. While neighborhood concerns generally appear important, studies have rarely been able to identify particular features of neighborhoods (or changes in these features) that prompt households to move (see Fredland 1974; Weinberg 1979; Boehm and Ihlanfeldt 1986; Lee, Oropesa, and Kanan 1994; Harris 1997a). Lee, Oropesa, and Kanan (1994) identify some neighborhood attributes that are related to the *desire* to move, but neither their study nor the many others finds any particular objective measures of neighborhood quality to be linked to actual mobility. The one exception is the finding of one study that people are more likely to leave a neighborhood the lower its mean housing values (Boehm and Mark 1980). Part of the uncertainty results from so few studies having had the appropriate data even to test the importance of neighborhood concerns.

And what about racial composition? Does it play a role in either short-term or longer-term decisions to move? Is the phenomenon of "white flight," so widely reported in the popular media, a reality? And what about black households? Do their decisions about moving indicate a preference for mixed environments, as some have suggested? Unfortunately, past studies tell us very little in this regard.

One source of information about the importance of race comes from *ex post* surveys of movers. While these surveys suggest that neighborhood concerns are generally important in prompting moves, racial considerations appear to play only a minimal role. Several case studies of racially changing neighborhoods dating from the early 1960s, for instance, compare the racial attitudes of residents who opt to leave racially changing areas and those who remain and generally find no correlation between intensity of racial prejudice and moving (Wolf 1960; Fishman 1961). In particular, whites who voice stronger anti-black feelings are no more likely to leave a racially changing neighborhood than their more tolerant neighbors. Two other studies of moving decisions undertaken during the late 1970s confirm this lack of connection. The studies suggest that concern about the racial mix of the neighborhood is considerably less important to moving decisions than public safety, workplace accessibility, school quality, open space, distance from friends, and the affordability and cost of housing (Taylor 1981, p. 272). Yet while very few people state that racial mix plays a role, one study examines the actual origins and destinations of white residents and finds that the vast majority of those living in mixed areas move into neighborhoods that have lower concentrations of minorities (Birch et al. 1977).

It is possible, in other words, that race does play a critical role, but people, especially white people, are not comfortable admitting this. Thus, it seems critical to examine data on actual mobility behavior. Several researchers do so through ecological analyses—studies that attempt to explain variations in the mobility rate across different geographic units. The results are inconsistent: some studies suggest that white household turnover is higher than expected in racially mixed tracts, given the demographics of the households living there (Wilson 1983; Galster 1990c), while others find that the rates of housing turnover in these areas are no higher than normal (Molotch 1969; Guest and Zuiches 1974; Molotch 1972).[5] There is little evidence meanwhile that city-to-suburb migration is influenced by the racial composition of the central city as a whole. In particular, several studies have examined "white flight" to the suburbs and concluded that such flight is no more prevalent in cities with larger black populations (Bradford and Kelejian 1973; Guterbock 1976; Frey 1979; Marshall 1979; Goodman and Streitweiser 1983).

But even if these ecological analyses provided a more consistent story, they are ultimately unsatisfactory from a methodological standpoint. Because they do not utilize individual data, these studies can never precisely determine the causes of individual moves (King 1997). Moreover, because these studies typically rely on cross-sectional data, they generally have information on racial composition for a particular point in time and rates of mobility for the time period preceding that point, rather than following it.

A better way to study the role of racial composition in mobility decisions is to examine individual household moves and test the extent to which racial composition plays a part in these decisions, after controlling for all other factors. A handful of researchers have attempted such analyses. One study, for instance, examines a sample of households in St. Louis in the early 1970s and finds that white households are somewhat more likely to move if the non-white percentage in their community is higher (Boehm and Mark 1980). More recent studies of household behavior suggest otherwise, however. A survey of households in Nashville in 1987 (Lee, Oropesa, and Kanan 1994), for instance, as well as an analysis of a national sample of white households in the early 1980s, provide no evidence that racial composition plays any role in moving decisions (Harris 1997a).

Ultimately then, despite a continued belief that "white flight" is pervasive, there is in fact little empirical evidence to support its existence. In surveys of racial preferences, many white households report that racial mixing would prompt them to leave their communities, but further analysis suggests that these responses are more complicated than commonly assumed. Studies of actual mobility behavior, meanwhile, offer little evidence of white flight. While neighborhood concerns emerge as important in general, racial composition in itself does not seem to be a critical factor.

This chapter aims to provide an updated look at the determinants of household mobility, with a particular focus on the importance of racial composition and other neighborhood characteristics. Utilizing a unique, national data set that links individual households to the communities that they live in, the analysis below also has some methodological advantages. It provides an unusual opportunity to view how a national sample of actual, individual households responds to racial integration, controlling for other characteristics. And in contrast to these earlier studies, the analysis here considers the import of *changes* in racial composition on household mobility. For the race-based neighborhood stereotyping hypothesis implies that changes in racial mix should be a better predictor of mobility behavior than the actual mix itself. Indeed, the omission from these studies of the growth in the percentage of black residents, a variable that is undoubtedly positively linked to the proportion of blacks present in a tract, is likely to produce positive bias in the coefficient on the current percentage of blacks, which in turn casts some doubt on any evidence that the current proportion of blacks is linked to mobility.

Finally, the analysis addresses questions not generally posed in these earlier studies. In particular, it explores how the effects of racial composition may vary across different households and different communities. It considers, for instance, the behavior of black as well as white households. In addition, it looks separately at homeowners and renters, households with and without children, and suburban and central city residents. In this way, this analysis helps us to understand not only if racial composition influences moving decisions but how and why. (For instance, the one existing study that separates white households into those with children and those without finds that white households with children appear significantly more likely to move when they live in a racially integrated census tract, while those without children appear unaffected [Harris 1997a]. This finding is consistent with the idea of neighborhood racial stereotyping and suggests that white households may be particularly concerned about the effects of changing racial composition on school quality.)

Data and Methods

The empirical analysis in this chapter—which considers the extent to which neighborhood context prompts actual mobility decisions—once again uses a specially coded version of the American Housing Survey (AHS). This version includes the census tract in which each house is located and can thus be linked to a whole range of neighborhood characteristics taken from the 1980 and 1990 decennial censuses.[6]

Figure 6.1 describes the data set used. As before, the household information, the housing unit characteristics, and the subjective unit and neighborhood ratings are taken from the AHS, while the neighborhood characteristics are selected from the 1980 and 1990 decennial censuses (via the Underclass Data Base, or UDB). Household mobility is examined during two different periods: between 1985 and 1989, and between 1989 and 1993. When modeling decisions to move between 1985 and 1989, 1980 measures are used to represent neighborhood characteristics. When modeling mobility decisions

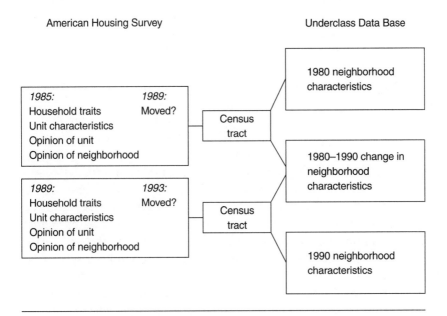

Figure 6.1 Data set description for Household Mobility Analysis

between 1989 and 1993, 1990 measures are used. In both cases, changes are represented by shifts occurring between 1980 and 1990. The analysis is once again limited to households living in the sample of thirty-four metropolitan areas.

Before moving on to describe the analysis of household mobility and the particular variables used, a few additional words should be said about the data. First, the AHS does not indicate where households resettle when they leave their present homes. Some households, therefore, might be moving next door, while others might be relocating to another metropolitan area. In neither case are neighborhood characteristics likely to play a dominant role in the household's decision, and the inclusion of such cases may cloud the importance of race in motivating moves from one neighborhood to another. A second and related issue is the failure of the AHS to identify the cause of the move. Some moves may have nothing to do whatsoever with the conditions of the neighborhood; they may be driven instead by job considerations or forces beyond the household's control. But while the AHS might understate the role of race in prompting the subset of residential moves in which a household moves from one neighborhood to another, it nonetheless provides a good estimate of how racial composition influences overall household mobility, which is what ultimately facilitates neighborhood change. After all, whether residents move out for new jobs or because they dislike their neighborhood, their departure still offers opportunities for new residents of different races to move in.

To test the importance of racial composition in motivating household moves, I estimate a multivariate regression that tries to capture the multiple factors influencing mobility decisions. In this way, we can be more confident that the racial composition of the tract is not a proxy for some other neighborhood characteristics or for characteristics of the households that tend to live in certain tracts. The regression estimates the probability that a household moves during a particular four-year period as a function of four main groups of control variables that may influence mobility decisions: household demographic traits, housing unit attributes, metropolitan area characteristics, and neighborhood characteristics. A positive and statistically significant coefficient indicates that the variable is positively correlated with the probability of moving. If the coefficient on "household size" is positive and statistically significant, for instance, this indicates that larger households are more likely than smaller households to move out of their homes.

The first category consists of the household variables. There is widespread agreement that family life-cycle variables are important determinants of intra-metropolitan mobility. As mentioned earlier, these demographic measures (age, marital status, household size, and presence of children) may be considered proxies for housing demand, or for the likelihood of experiencing *changes* in housing demand that would prompt a household to move.[7] These variables might also be viewed as proxies for moving costs. (A larger household, for instance, faces higher moving costs than does a smaller one.) In addition to these life-cycle variables, a measure of income is included, as well as the length of time the household has lived in its current unit, which certainly contributes to moving costs.

The second group of variables includes the structural characteristics of the dwelling unit. One variable, for instance, indicates whether the unit is a single-family home or apartment, since families living in single-family homes are likely to feel more permanently settled. The American dream, after all, is to own a detached single-family home. Second, for obvious reasons, I include a dummy variable noting if the unit is judged to be poor quality by the household. Finally, in the case of rental units, I include a variable indicating if the unit is publicly (as opposed to privately) owned. Given the paucity of decent affordable housing provided by the private market and the lengthy waiting lists to obtain subsidized apartments, households living in public housing are probably less likely to move.

The third category of variables includes metropolitan area characteristics—in particular, those that may contribute to rates of mobility within a given metropolitan statistical area (MSA). Thus, the model controls for MSA population growth, an index of black segregation (measured by the dissimilarity index), and the MSA-wide housing vacancy rate. The model also controls for region of the country to capture any regional effects in household mobility patterns.[8]

The central variables of interest to this study are of course the neighborhood characteristics. In terms of racial composition, the proportion of blacks and the proportion of non-black minorities in the tract (largely Hispanics and Asians) are both included, as well as measures of growth in these proportions between 1980 and 1990. To measure a tract's socioeconomic status, I use two absolute measures (the share of working residents in professional or managerial occupations and the poverty rate) and one measure of *relative* economic status (the ratio of a household's income to the mean income of the census tract). One measure of *change* in socioeconomic status is also included: the increase in the poverty rate between 1980 and 1990. Finally, the regression also includes the housing vacancy rate, the home ownership rate, a subjective assessment of the neighborhood environment, and a measure of household turnover.

Table 6.1 presents the means for the independent variables used for the 1985–1989 time period. Means are displayed for non-Hispanic white homeowners, non-Hispanic white renters, black homeowners, and black renters, since separate regressions are estimated for each of these sub-samples. As shown, the behavior of between 9,000 and 10,000 households is analyzed in each time period. Approximately 82 percent are non-Hispanic white and 62 percent are homeowners.

The table reveals some significant differences between owners and renters on the one hand and between black and non-Hispanic white households on the other. In general, black households have lower incomes and live in inferior housing compared to their non-Hispanic white counterparts. Specifically, controlling for tenure, black households are nearly twice as likely to be in the bottom income quartile, about five times more likely to live in public housing, and between 33 and 70 percent more likely to describe the quality of their housing unit as poor. Similarly, after controlling for race, renters have lower incomes than homeowners and are about three times more likely to describe their unit as poor.

As for the neighborhood variables, the differences between blacks and whites are striking. In general, blacks live in much less prosperous and structurally weaker communities. On average, for instance, black households live in neighborhoods with a proportion of professional workers that is one-third lower than the typical neighborhood of their white counterparts, with poverty rates nearly three times as high, and with considerably higher vacancy and lower home ownership rates. Subjective assessments confirm these disparities—black households are almost twice as likely as white households to rate their neighborhood as poor. The most significant difference between the communities in which the black respondents live and those of the non-Hispanic white respondents, however, is racial composition. The average black household lives in a neighborhood that is roughly two-thirds black;

Table 6.1 Means of variables used in analysis for 1985–1989

Variable	NHW owners	NHW renters	Black owners	Black renters
Moved	0.24	0.64	0.18	0.57
Household variables				
Age	51.30	43.50	51.70	41.40
Never married	0.07	0.27	0.08	0.32
Divorced	0.22	0.35	0.36	0.43
Children, 0–6 years old	0.15	0.15	0.17	0.25
Children, 6–17 years old	0.29	0.17	0.39	0.36
Household size	2.80	2.10	3.10	2.70
Length of tenure	14.30	5.20	14.40	5.40
Bottom income quartile	0.14	0.31	0.27	0.56
Top income quartile	0.37	0.12	0.23	0.04
Housing unit variables				
Single family home	0.90	0.24	0.89	0.22
Poor quality unit	0.06	0.16	0.08	0.27
Public housing	NA	0.04	NA	0.21
Metropolitan area variables				
Northeast	0.33	0.36	0.26	0.31
South	0.29	0.27	0.39	0.36
West	0.08	0.11	0.05	0.05
Population growth	151.00	125.00	89.00	115.00
Segregation index	73.00	72.00	73.00	74.00
MSA vacancy rate	1.69	6.37	1.73	6.42
Neighborhood variables				
Poor neighborhood	0.10	0.19	0.17	0.33
Percent black	4.70	6.80	66.00	63.50
1980–1990 change in % black	2.40	3.10	4.40	3.80
Percent other	5.20	8.10	5.10	7.80
1980–90 change in % other	3.10	4.40	1.70	2.10
Income ratio	1.12	0.74	1.10	0.66
Percent professional	30.10	30.50	20.60	19.40
Poverty rate	6.40	9.90	18.80	26.70
1980–1990 change in poverty rate	0.66	1.10	2.30	2.90
Percent new residents	47.80	54.40	44.20	52.80
Vacancy rate	4.80	5.90	6.70	8.30
Homeownership rate	72.60	49.00	59.50	34.10
N	5,438	2,720	725	1,001

Note: NHW = non-Hispanic white.

Table 6.2 Selected parameters from 1985–1989 mobility model (dependent variable = MOVE)

	Non-Hispanic white owners		Non-Hispanic white renters		Black owners		Black renters	
	Coeff.	Std. error	Coeff.	Std. error	Coeff.	Std. error	Coeff.	Std. error
Poor neighborhood	0.31***	0.1155	−0.133	0.132	0.385	0.286	0.035	0.176
Percent black	0.0038	0.0034	0.005	0.0039	0.0006	0.0052	−0.0018	0.0037
1980–1990 change in % black	0.02***	0.0051	0.0068	0.007	0.0069	0.012	0.0038	0.0082
Percent other	0.0085	0.0052	−0.003	0.0052	0.0015	0.015	−0.0018	0.0078
1980–1990 change in % other	−0.007	0.0078	−0.0072	0.0079	0.024	0.026	0.015	0.0155
Income ratio	0.145***	0.045	0.137	0.123	−0.5*	0.302	0.218	0.224
Percent professional	0.0077**	0.0032	0.0049	0.0044	0.014	0.015	−0.0184**	0.0093
Poverty rate	−0.0095	0.0093	0.0005	0.0091	0.0115	0.017	−0.0047	0.0086
1980–1990 change in poverty rate	−0.0027	0.009	0.0199*	0.01	−0.018	0.017	0.0044	0.0097
Percent new residents	0.012***	0.003	0.017***	0.0046	0.0028	0.01	0.0046	0.0071
Vacancy rate	0.0069	0.009	0.0048	0.012	0.051*	0.027	0.0143	0.014
Homeownership rate	0.002	0.0024	0.012***	0.003	−0.0043	0.007	0.0023	0.0053
N	5,438		2,720		725		1,001	

Source: Ellen (2000b).

Note: Regression also includes all the control variables listed in Table 6.1: household characteristics; housing unit attributes, and metropolitan area characteristics.

*, **, *** Significant at the 10, 5, and 1 percent levels, respectively.

the average white household lives in a community that is not much more than 5 percent black.

Many of these characteristics are of course correlated. When poverty rates are high, the proportion of professional workers tends to be lower and the share of minorities higher. When characteristics are too closely correlated, it is difficult, if not impossible, to dissect independent effects. If the poverty rate and the share of blacks were to move together perfectly, for instance, it would be impossible to distinguish between the effects of a larger black population and the effects of a higher poverty rate. An examination of the correlation coefficients between the neighborhood variables for the 1985 and 1989 samples does not suggest much of a problem. While some correlation is evident, only two coefficients in each year are above 0.5. The strongest correlation, however, is between the percentage black in the tract and its poverty rate, two variables that we of course would like to be able to interpret clearly. Unfortunately, there is little that we can do about this problem. Omitting the poverty rate from the regression would clearly bias the coefficient on the proportion of black residents and lead us to overstate the impact of race. Put simply, without controls for class, what appears to be an effect of race may indeed be an effect of class.

The basic estimation tool used to model mobility is logistic regression analysis, with the probability of a household moving between 1985 and 1989 or between 1989 and 1993 regressed on various neighborhood characteristics and other control variables. A number of different specifications were estimated, but for the sake of brevity, the chapter generally focuses on a single set of results.[9] (The key conclusions were largely the same.) As mentioned, the sample is stratified into four different groups: non-Hispanic white homeowners, non-Hispanic white renters, black homeowners, and black renters.

Results

Tables 6.2 and 6.3 present the neighborhood coefficients from the 1985–1989 and 1989–1993 mobility regressions. The estimated coefficients for the control variables are not shown, but they generally provide few surprises. The household and housing unit variables emerge as highly significant to mobility decisions, and their coefficients typically have the expected signs. The metropolitan area vari-

Table 6.3 Selected parameters from 1989–1993 mobility model (dependent variable = MOVE)

	Non-Hispanic white owners		Non-Hispanic white renters		Black owners		Black renters	
	Coeff.	Std. error	Coeff.	Std. error	Coeff.	Std. error	Coeff.	Std. error
Poor neighborhood	0.113	0.139	0.325**	0.136	0.222	0.271	0.08	0.183
Percent black	0.0019	0.0039	0.0016	0.0042	−0.0034	0.0056	−0.0019	0.004
1980–1990 change in % black	0.013*	0.0076	0.0037	0.0084	0.0096	0.011	0.017**	0.0079
Percent other	0.0089	0.0057	−0.0045	0.0056	−0.0099	0.014	0.01	0.0085
1980–1990 change in % other	−0.002	0.011	0.025**	0.011	−0.029	0.029	0.009	0.017
Income ratio	0.038	0.052	0.019	0.069	−0.46*	0.239	0.241	0.201
Percent professional	0.01***	0.0034	0.0032	0.004	−0.023*	0.014	0.0065	0.0082
Poverty rate	0.0052	0.01	0.0092	0.009	−0.005	0.017	0.011	0.0091
1980–1990 change in poverty rate	−0.0069	0.013	−0.0087	0.0013	−0.011	0.018	−0.012	0.012
Percent new residents	0.0045	0.0039	0.011**	0.0052	0.013	0.013	0.003	0.0078
Vacancy rate	0.002	0.0083	0	0.01	−0.022	0.025	0.005	0.013
Homeownership rate	0.0024	0.003	0.005	0.0034	−0.014	0.0085	0.0083	0.0053
N	5,179		2,514		744		982	

Source: Ellen (2000b).

Note: Regression also includes all the control variables listed in Table 6.1: household characteristics; housing unit attributes, and metropolitan area characteristics.

*, **, *** Significant at the 10, 5, and 1 percent levels, respectively.

ables, meanwhile, do not appear to strongly influence mobility, but the coefficients that are significant do have the expected signs. One interesting result to note is that black renters in more segregated metropolitan areas appear less likely to move, which perhaps reflects the more limited choices faced by blacks in such racially divided environments.

As for the central measures in this study—the neighborhood variables—they generally appear to play a role in moving decisions and are thus important to include in any model attempting to explain intra-urban mobility.[10] Interestingly, neighborhood variables appear less important to the moving decisions of black households, a finding that is consistent with some prior research and that probably reflects the more limited choices and higher search costs faced by minorities, rather than a reduced concern with neighborhood quality (South and Deane 1993).

Even so, not all aspects of the neighborhood context appear to have strong effects. There is little evidence here, for instance, that housing market conditions play much of a role and little evidence that either absolute socioeconomic status or changes in that status influence moving decisions.[11] Households living in distressed communities, that is, appear no more likely to move than their counterparts in more affluent areas. There is some evidence, however, that relative status matters. The coefficient on *income ratio* in the 1985–1989 white homeowner model is positive and significant, suggesting that white homeowners whose earnings are high relative to their neighbors are more likely to move away than those who earn relatively less. In particular, a 1985 white homeowner earning twice the neighborhood mean is approximately 2.5 percentage points more likely to move over the next four years than one earning exactly the mean. Black homeowners, meanwhile, appear *less* likely to move away when they earn more than their neighbors, perhaps again reflecting the more limited options open to black households, and/or their more limited incomes and wealth.

As for neighborhood quality, there is some evidence that judgments about such quality play a meaningful role in mobility decisions. In particular, the coefficient on the "neighborhood rated poor" dummy variable is positive and significant in two cases for white households, suggesting that white households are more likely to move away from neighborhoods that they believe are substandard. The probability of a typical white homeowner moving between 1985 and 1989 increases from 21.8 to 27.5 percent if he or she rates the neighborhood as poor.

As for the variables of central interest in this study, neither the coefficient on the proportion of blacks nor that on the proportion of non-black minorities in a tract is statistically significant, suggesting that current racial composition has little effect on the moving decisions of households. Even a white household, that is, appears to be no more likely to leave a neighborhood that is 40 percent black than one which is 5 percent black. As hypothesized, however, the growth in these minority populations—especially the black population—does appear to be important. Specifically, the probability of the typical white homeowner moving is between 2.0 and 3.5 percentage points higher when the black population has grown by ten percentage points over the decade.[12]

The class theory of racial change posits that changes in racial composition are merely a proxy for changes in class status. But there is little evidence here that class is what matters. First, the growth in the poverty rate is included in the regressions. Thus, a growing black population appears to have an effect on mobility even after controlling for the change in the poverty rate.

In another regression (not shown), I also explored whether the status of the black population, measured by both income and education, seemed to matter to white household decisions (Ellen 1996). Surprisingly, white homeowners appear to react in the same way to a growing and affluent black population as they do to a growing and poor black population.[13]

Similarly, I also tested whether the socioeconomic status of the white population mattered. For the class theory of racial change predicts that wealthier white households should be more averse to racial mixing than those of lesser means. But when separately analyzing white households earning more and less than the median income, no differences in the behavior of white households of different incomes were found.

If there is little support for the class model here, there is also little evidence to support the pure prejudice view of racial change. For the fact that change is relevant, and not the absolute level of the black population, runs counter to the common assumption that white households have a particular threshold level of blacks that they will tolerate. White households appear content to live with a wide range of black population shares—10, 20, even 50 percent. Consistent with the notion of neighborhood racial stereotyping, however, and echoing the neighborhood satisfaction results in the previous chapter, white homeowners do appear uncomfortable living in a neighborhood where the black population has been growing. In this situation, households are more likely to fear that these neighborhoods will become largely black and suffer the structural decline that they associate with largely black environments. If their neighborhood has instead had a consistent racial mix—of say, 20 percent black for ten years—and the schools remain solid and crime fairly moderate, these results suggest that most white residents will be fairly comfortable remaining in the community. (Current racial composition will also influence opinions about future composition, but recent growth is undoubtedly a better predictor.)

There are of course other interpretations of these results, some of which afford a more direct role to racial prejudice. Most centrally, households might react to racial change not because it connotes any broader changes in the community, but quite simply because it has raised the black population in the neighborhood to a level beyond that which is comfortable for them. After all, the lack of significance of the coefficient on percentage black is arguably an expected and natural result of the selection bias inherent in this data. As discussed in earlier chapters, households have chosen to live in their particular communities (or at least in the communities that existed when they moved in), and the preferences of white households living in 50 percent black areas are thus likely to be distinct from those of others living in areas that are only 2 percent black. To the extent that the households in this sample have already sorted themselves to some degree by racial preferences, there is less reason to expect that present racial composition should be related to mobility. Thus, one might argue that the only way to empirically observe sensitivity to race is through a *change* in racial composition, since this moves a neighborhood to a mix that was not initially chosen by its resident households.[14]

The problem with this interpretation is that it does not explain why the coefficient on black population growth should be significant in the case of white homeowners and never in the case of white renters. If anything, renters, for whom moving is much cheaper, would be expected to leave neighborhoods more quickly than homeowners if the racial mix becomes unacceptable to them. This difference across tenure groups is anticipated, however, by the race-based neighborhood stereotyping hypothesis, for to the extent that concerns about property values lie behind the aversion to a growth in the black population, homeowners are expected to be more sensitive to racial change. (Although the empirical evidence is mixed as to whether property values decline as a result of racial change, many people share this perception.) Part of the difference between homeowners and renters might also lie in the typically longer time periods that homeowners stay in a given community, which makes them naturally more invested in a community's long-term prospects.

The fact that the coefficient on the growth in the percentage of blacks is positive and significant for black renters over the 1989–1993 time period seems to offer additional support for neighborhood stereotyping. Certainly, it seems unlikely that this positive coefficient reflects any aversion on the part of black renters to living among an increasing number of black neighbors. But it does seem possible that black households, as well as white, fear the changes that they believe are associated with growing minority populations.

Finally, as discussed in the previous chapter, given mobility constraints and moving costs, it seems implausible that white households are sorted perfectly into different neighborhoods based on the intensity of their racial preferences.

While the results suggest that non-Hispanic white household mobility is influenced by an increase in the black population, and not the size of the population itself, it still may be true that households will react differently to a similarly sized increase when the actual proportion of blacks differs. In order to test for such an interaction, the growth in the black population was divided into four separate variables, depending on the proportion of blacks present in 1980. In general, the change in black population is positively correlated with white mobility only when the initial percentage of blacks is non-trivial (Ellen 1996). The implication is that white households respond to black population growth only when the black population threatens to become a substantial presence. This is once again consistent with the notion of race-based neighborhood stereotyping. For white households seem to associate community decline most strongly with areas that are composed largely of minorities; they do not have such strong stereotypes about neighborhoods with only a handful of minorities.

The final results presented here show the basic model estimated for homeowners with and without children. The aim is to test the proposition that households with children—both white and black—are more bothered by racial change than their childless counterparts since they are likely to worry that the quality of local schools will decline in the face of racial change. Table 6.4 shows the mobility model results for these sub-populations. For the sake of clarity and conciseness, coefficients for only two key variables are shown here—the dummy variable for "poor neighborhood," which is our best proxy for neighborhood quality and strength, and the growth in the black population.

The evidence appears fairly strong. The coefficient on the "poor neighborhood" variable is statistically significant only for white and black homeowners with children, suggesting that owners with children are indeed more sensitive to neighborhood quality than their childless counterparts. The growth in the black population, meanwhile, has a more powerful effect on the mobility of white homeowners with children than those without. In 1985, the coefficient on the growth in percentage of blacks is larger for white owners with children than those without (indicating a larger effect on the probability of moving), and in 1989, the coefficient is statistically significant *only*

Table 6.4 Key coefficients from Mobility regressions, Homeowners, by race and presence of children

Variable	1985		1989	
	Children	No children	Children	No children
Non-Hispanic white homeowners				
Poor neighborhood	.473**	.23	.131	.066
1980–1990 change in percent black	.031***	.016***	.043***	.0003
N	1,987	3,451	1,724	3,455
Black homeowners				
Poor neighborhood	−.145	.457	.99*	−.117
1980–1990 change in percent black	.034*	−.004	.012	.006
N	322	403	311	433

Source: Ellen (2000b).

Note: Regression again includes all the control variables listed in Table 6.1: household characteristics; housing unit attributes, and metropolitan area characteristics (with the exception of the children variables).

*, **, *** Significant at the 10, 5, and 1 percent levels, respectively.

in the case of white owners with children. Interestingly, there is even some evidence that black homeowners with children move more often when the black population is increasing, while their childless counterparts do not. Again, it seems fairly certain that departing black households are acting out of their fear of potential non-racial changes in their increasingly black community, rather than an unwillingness to live near other black households.

To further explore the roots of this "households with children" effect, and specifically to test if households with children are more averse to racial mixing because of their concerns about local school quality, the households with children in the 1989–1993 model were further divided into those with children in public school and those with children in private or parochial school. (This school information was not requested in 1985 and was available for only about 75 percent of the households with children in the 1989 survey.) Unfortunately, there were generally not enough black households with children in private school to examine the differences in how black households react to racial change in private versus public schools. But the results regarding the white households are quite telling. In particular, it appears that only those with children in public school are more likely to move in response to racial change. White households with children in private school, by contrast, appear unaffected by racial change. It seems, then, that concerns about school quality are a key factor underlying white households' uneasiness about racial change.

Some work was also done to further explore the role of housing price appreciation. In particular, if white homeowners fear racial change because of concerns about property values, growth in the black population should be less of a factor after controlling for recent appreciation. Unfortunately, the data available here were not very good. Since actual neighborhood housing prices were unavailable, the difference between the value reported by the owner in 1989 and that reported by the same owner in 1985 was used.[15] This variable was then included in a regression of the probability of moving between 1989 and 1993. Notably, including this variable had little effect on the basic results (and the coefficient on this price appreciation proxy was consistently insignificant). Indeed, there is no correlation between changes in reported housing values between 1985 and 1989 and changes in the proportion black in the census tract between 1980 and 1990.

But this result does not necessarily undermine the race-based neighborhood stereotyping theory. For one thing, these owners are by definition "insiders" who may use more sophisticated measures than racial change to gauge a neighborhood's prospects. For another, much of the growth in black population occurring in a neighborhood between 1980 and 1990 may have already occurred by 1985, or at least have been foreseen by the white residents.[16] Finally, there are some reasons to doubt the quality of the data: these self-reported housing values may not be very accurate, and the over-representation of non-movers in the sample may be clouding effects.[17] The point is, additional study into the role of price changes is clearly warranted.

Finally, in addition to stratifying the sample by tenure and race, I looked separately at households living in central city and suburban communities. The idea was to test whether white households living in suburban areas, which are presumably less at risk of being incorporated into nearby majority black neighborhoods, would be more open to racial mixing. There is some modest evidence to support this hypothesis. White renters living in central city neighborhoods, that is, were more likely to move between 1985 and 1989 in the face of racial change, while the rate of racial change had no apparent effect on the behavior of those living in the suburbs.

The lack of a stronger result here is perhaps not surprising, for such a simple dichotomy between suburbs and central cities is increasingly misplaced. As many have pointed out, suburbs are hardly monolithic. Many inner suburbs are deteriorating, suffer high rates of crime, and are if anything more fiscally stressed and vulnerable than their central cities, which have a larger commercial tax base (Orfield 1997). Thus, it may be that the residents of many suburban areas are more threatened by racial change than those living in central cities. (Consider, for example, the case of Prince Georges County, discussed in Chapter 4.)

In summary, these results suggest that households—both black and white—might be a good deal less concerned about their neighborhood's racial mix than is commonly believed and than is indicated by the often-cited surveys of racial preferences. Indeed, neither households' evaluations of their neighborhoods nor their probability of leaving them appear to be influenced by present racial composition. Changes in that composition, however—and implicitly, expectations about future composition, which are no doubt linked to a whole host of assumptions about the future neighborhood quality—do sometimes appear connected to neighborhood satisfaction and mobility. Specifically, white residents who are more invested in community quality and thus have more to lose from the changes they believe to be correlated with minority population growth (homeowners and households with children, for instance) appear more resistant to racial mixing. Indeed, there is evidence that black households with children worry about growing black populations as well.

In general, these findings are plainly supportive of the notion of race-based neighborhood stereotyping outlined in Chapter 3. To be sure, the analysis did not find that white households were any more resistant to racial change in declining housing markets, which is one of the hypotheses generated by the theory. But as discussed, the measure used to proxy such decline is somewhat suspect (and the sample potentially biased), so we should not place too much weight on the result.

The key point is this: as long as a racially integrated community remains stable, it appears that white and black households are willing to stay there. In other words, exit decisions or "white flight" do not typically cause instability in racially mixed neighborhoods. Whether such neighborhoods may ultimately be viable, then, depends on the willingness of households to move *into* racially mixed areas—which is precisely the focus of the next chapter.

CHAPTER SEVEN

Racial Composition and Neighborhood Choice

If households care less about the racial composition of their neighborhood per se than about its quality of life, then racial composition should be much more important to the decision whether to move into a neighborhood than it is to the decision as to whether to leave one. For as explained, people already living in a community are likely to have considerable information about its quality and future prospects and thus will tend to be less concerned about racial composition. Outsiders, by contrast, when choosing among many alternative communities, may find it easier to rely simply on such indicators as racial composition. In addition, outsiders have already decided to move somewhere and thus to bear the often substantial financial and psychological costs of moving, so very slight preferences for racial mix might lead white households to opt for white areas.

As to which types of households will move into integrated versus segregated communities, the hypothesis would suggest that white householders who opt to move into mixed areas are likely to have no children and rent their homes. They might also be younger since younger households are more likely to see themselves as only temporary residents. The expectations about black households are less clear. To the extent that black families share the same stereotypes about largely black communities, those opting for mixed areas (as opposed to largely black areas) might be more likely to have children and more likely to be homeowners. We might also expect those sharing neighborhoods with whites to be somewhat more affluent on average, given the difference in incomes between whites and blacks.

Past Studies of Neighborhood Choice

As with the study of the decision to move, the research exploring neighborhood choice may be divided into (1) analyses of survey data that detail peoples' stated preferences and intentions, and (2) analyses of actual household behavior. Unfortunately, it is quite difficult to model the choice of neighborhood and as a result, very few studies have analyzed actual neighborhood choice. Even fewer have considered how racial composition affects those decisions. Thus, most of the existing evidence concerning the link between preferences for racial composition and neighborhood choices comes from responses to social surveys.

Evidence from Surveys of Racial Preference

There are at least three ways that surveys can illuminate the importance of racial composition in neighborhood choices. First, a survey can ask households to report on their willingness to move into communities of different racial mixes. Second, it can ask them to state their actual preferences for neighborhood racial mix. (A white household, after all, might be willing to move into any neighborhood but would still prefer a predominantly white one.) The third approach is to ask households about the actual decision-making process, and in particular, to assess the extent to which race is a critical ingredient.

The 1976 and 1992 Detroit Area Surveys use the first method to analyze the neighborhood choices of whites (Farley et al. 1978; 1993). In particular, they show respondents a series of diagrams depicting neighborhoods of different racial mixes and ask them to imagine that they have found an attractive home that they could afford in all of the communities. They then ask if there is any neighborhood that they would not move into. The results of the 1976 and 1992 responses to this question are reported in Table 7.1.[1] The table also shows the responses to an identical question asked of white households living in Los Angeles in 1993 (Zubrinsky and Bobo 1996).

On the one hand, this table indicates that white racial attitudes appear to be softening with time. In 1992 and 1993, whites are consistently more willing to share neighborhoods with blacks than they

Table 7.1 Willingness of whites to move into neighborhoods, by percent black, selected survey results

% Black	Detroit, 1976 (%)	Detroit, 1992 (%)	Los Angeles, 1993 (%)
7	73	87	82
20	50	69	71
33	27	41	49
53	16	27	31

Source: Farley et al. 1978; Farley et al. 1993; Zubrinsky and Bobo 1996.

were in 1976. On the other hand, the willingness of whites to move into a neighborhood still declines as the share of blacks rises, and by the time a neighborhood reaches about 50 percent black, less than a third of whites say they are willing to move in.

Significantly, these figures suggest a great deal more resistance to racial mixing than was indicated by the statistics reported in the previous chapter regarding the intentions of white households to leave racially mixed areas. Consider that when confronted with a neighborhood that is one-third black, 59 percent of white respondents in 1992 said they would be unwilling to move in, while only 29 percent said they would try to move out. Thus as predicted, there does indeed appear to be a distinct difference in the degree to which race affects these two residential decisions. In fact, these survey results are likely to understate the distinction between exit and entry in the case of real-world decisions. For in these survey responses, those considering exit as well as entry decisions are reacting to merely hypothetical communities, and thus inevitably relying on stereotypes.

A final point to make here is that the neighborhood choices of whites do not appear to be solely the result of a desire to live among other whites. For the study of Los Angeles shows that whites are considerably more open to sharing neighborhoods with Latinos and Asians than with blacks. Consider that only 31 percent of white households express a willingness to move into a neighborhood that is just over half black (and just under half white). In comparison, 45 percent of whites are willing to move into a neighborhood that is just over half Latino, and 63 percent say they would move into one which is over half Asian (Zubrinsky and Bobo 1996). Clearly, a particular distaste for living in black neighborhoods plays a role in racial preferences, whether because of unique racial animus or because of distinctly negative images of largely black communities.

Of course, many of those whites who express a willingness to move into racially mixed areas will not actually do so when offered alternatives. Another approach is to ask households to state their preferences for different neighborhoods. A 1978 survey of white residents in Omaha asked such a question, and virtually none said they would *prefer* to live in a largely black area (Taylor 1981). Perhaps surprisingly, however, just 25 percent of whites expressed a preference for mostly white neighborhoods, and 25 percent said racial composition was entirely irrelevant to them. Indeed, there were actually not enough black residents in Omaha at the time of this survey (10 percent) to fully satisfy whites' professed desires for racial mixing.[2] In a more recent survey of white residents in suburban Cleveland, meanwhile, only 16 percent of whites chose mostly white as their preferred racial mix (Keating 1994, p. 64). Quite significantly, the Cleveland results suggest that blacks would have to represent over a third of the population and all live in neighborhoods with whites to satisfy *whites'* desires for racial mixing.[3]

The third approach is to probe households about their actual process of choosing neighborhoods. The 1978 Omaha survey, for instance, asked white respondents to identify their top three reasons for choosing their neighborhood, and only 1 percent of households volunteered race (Taylor 1981). Factors such as school quality, public safety, housing quality, housing cost, accessibility, and open space were all mentioned instead. Of course, it is likely that some white households were simply uncomfortable admitting that race is independently important to them. But these results do seem to suggest that a fairly small number of white households view racial composition as an *overriding* concern in choosing a neighborhood. Consistent with race-based neighborhood stereotyping, concerns about neighborhood quality seem to trump preferences for racial composition per se.

In a 1991 survey, white suburban residents of Cleveland also reported that concerns about neighborhood quality of life are often more important than purely racial concerns. And once again, schools and safety emerge as paramount. When whites were asked what it would take for them to move into a mostly minority neighborhood, the top three responses were "better education for their children," "guarantee of public safety," and a "belief that city services would be better" (Keating 1994, pp. 64–65).

In summary, the evidence suggests that white households tend to be reluctant to move into neighborhoods with substantial numbers of minorities. But in the case of many whites, much of their reluctance stems from fears about the future quality of services delivered in the neighborhood, rather than a simple dislike of non-whites. Moreover, these preferences for largely white neighborhoods do not appear strong or widespread enough to explain the degree of racial separation existing in contemporary metropolitan areas.

What about preferences of black households? Is it true, as some have suggested, that preferences of black households for largely black neighborhoods are a root cause of racial segregation (Kantrowitz 1979; Clark 1986; Patterson 1997)? Surveys exploring the willingness of blacks to enter different neighborhoods have found that blacks are in fact almost indifferent to racial mix. Table 7.2 shows the proportions of blacks who reported a willingness to move into various different neighborhoods in the 1976 and 1992 Detroit Area Surveys and the 1993 Los Angeles survey analyzed by Zubrinsky and Bobo. As shown, virtually all black households were willing to move into neighborhoods of any racial mix, with the exception of all-black and all-white. Approximately 70 percent say they would move into an all-black area, and between 31 and 38 percent say they would move into an all-white one. (Note that the lowest percentage of blacks indicated on the table is 7 percent, this is the percentage of blacks that would be present *after* the prospective black household moves in. So the survey is really asking whether a black household would be willing to be the very first black in a neighborhood.)

Given the pervasive and overt racial discrimination that made it difficult for blacks to enter white areas in the recent past, the hostility

Table 7.2 Willingness of blacks to move into neighborhoods, by percent black, selected survey results

% Black	Detroit, 1976 (%)	Detroit, 1992 (%)	Los Angeles, 1993 (%)
7	38	31	36
20	95	87	90
53	99	98	99
73	99	98	98
100	69	75	74

Source: Farley et al. 1978; Farley et al. 1993; Zubrinsky and Bobo 1996.

that typically welcomed them when they got there, as well as the (perhaps less overt) discrimination and racial threats that persist today, it is hard to know the extent to which the reluctance of blacks to enter all-white neighborhoods is a reflection of genuine preferences.[4] Indeed, further questioning of the black respondents in the 1992 Detroit survey indicates that fears of white hostility loom large in the choices of black households: approximately 90 percent of blacks who said they would not move into an all-white area said it was because the whites would not welcome them (Farley et al. 1994).

When probing blacks about their preferred neighborhoods, past surveys have generally found that they favor racially balanced areas. Thomas Pettigrew (1973), for instance, examines the results of eleven different surveys of racial attitudes undertaken between 1958 and 1969 and concludes that "black residents overwhelmingly favor" mixed neighborhoods over all-black areas. The Los Angeles and Detroit surveys generally confirm this. But there is also slight evidence that black households (at least those that are less educated and affluent) are somewhat less interested in racial integration today than they were twenty years ago (Farley et al. 1993).[5]

It is important not to make too much of these stated preferences, however. First, as shown above, nearly all blacks are willing to move into neighborhoods of all racial mixes, with the exception of all-white areas. Second, blacks' stated preferences for 50–50 neighborhoods is probably more a reflection of their desire for racial balance and harmony than any rigid attachment to this particular mix. Indeed, in the original Detroit Area Survey, when black households were asked why they preferred a 50–50 mix, most gave reasons having to do with a hope for racial harmony. "It might make it better to get along with white people," said one typical respondent (Farley et al. 1978).

Finally, the evidence suggests that these preferences are in reality not all that strong. For in evaluating the actual decision-making process of blacks, it appears that race hardly counts in their selection of neighborhoods. In the 1978 Omaha survey, only 5 percent of black respondents say that having mostly black neighbors was a "very important" factor in their choice of their current neighborhood, compared to 20 percent of whites (Taylor 1981). Significantly, the factors that emerge as more prominent are precisely those that whites value: housing quality and cost, public safety, and school quality. Thus, different preferences for non-racial neighborhood attributes do not seem to explain any of the racial separation found in our metropolitan areas.

Actual Neighborhood Choices

Do these surveys indeed predict the choices that households make? As discussed already, there are reasons to believe that they do not. Thus, it is critical to examine actual residential choices. While there may be some doubt about mobility decisions, the importance of neighborhood concerns in general seems self-evident in the case of housing choice. "Location, location, location," after all, is the all-too-familiar rule of thumb in choosing residential real estate. One study, for instance, has found that when faced with two equally priced homes, nearly three times as many people opt for a less desirable house in a good neighborhood as choose a very good house in a less desirable neighborhood (Lee, Oropesa, and Kanan 1994). Indeed, to my knowledge, every study that has explored the importance of neighborhood factors in residential choices has found them to be critical.

Unfortunately, it is considerably more difficult to model the decision to move into a particular neighborhood than it is to model the decision to leave one. When leaving is at issue, the dependent variable is bivariate: households can choose either to stay or to leave. But the options for moving in are numerous—a household can theoretically choose any neighborhood within its metropolitan area.[6] As a result, studies of neighborhood choice have generally utilized complex, multinomial logit models that are somewhat difficult to interpret. Indeed, because of the computational difficulty of the modeling, few studies have actually explored the choice of neighborhood; most have considered instead the choice of a larger geographic area, such as a city or county.

Gabriel and Rosenthal (1989), for instance, examine the county choices of white and black households in the Washington, D.C., metropolitan area during the 1980s and find that the propensity of a household to locate in a given county increases with the share of residents of its own race living there. Indeed, even when assuming that blacks have the same socioeconomic status as whites, their estimates still predict that blacks will be overwhelmingly concentrated in just two counties: the District of Columbia and Prince Georges County.

DiPasquale and Kahn (1999) consider the choice of a somewhat smaller geographic unit in Los Angeles County: Public Use Micro

Areas (PUMAs), which are aggregates of census tracts containing 100,000 people or more. Their study reaches beyond standard measures collected by the census and is therefore able to deploy a far richer definition of community quality. The study, for instance, includes mean test scores from local schools, air-quality data, homicide rates, and information on accessibility to the downtown area. But even after all of these factors are taken into account, the authors find that race and ethnicity remain a highly significant determinant of community (that is, PUMA) choice for households with children— black, white, and Hispanic.

A third study examines the choice of yet another geographic area— the elementary attendance area (Jud and Bennett 1986). Consistent with the results of these other studies, the racial composition of the overall population in the destination area appears significant—whites are less likely to move into neighborhoods with higher proportions of black residents. But interestingly, the percentage of black students in the local school is not a consideration once school quality (measured by average third-grade reading score) has been taken into account. Since the racial mix of the students appears relevant when school quality is omitted, they argue that a failure to properly consider the quality of local public schools may bias the racial composition variable, making it appear much more significant than it is.

The few studies that have examined household choice of actual census tracts are by now fairly dated. One analysis, for instance, uses a conditional logit model to examine residential location in the Pittsburgh metropolitan area in the late 1960s (Williams 1979). Using mean income in a census tract as the measure of neighborhood quality, the study finds that such quality is a highly significant factor in people's choice of where to live. It appears especially important to larger households and households with higher income, though there is of course a causality problem in interpreting the tendency of higher-income households to purchase "better" neighborhoods, since "better" neighborhoods are themselves defined by the presence of higher-income residents. The problem is lessened somewhat by the fact that mean income was measured prior to household income and that the households examined had all recently moved in.

Quigley (1985) uses a sub-sample of this same Pittsburgh data set to consider residential choices of renters. In this case, however, a much broader set of neighborhood characteristics is considered, including workplace accessibility, homeownership rate, median monthly rent, and percent of black residents, as well as selected attributes of the chosen suburban town. The methodological approach in this study is also more sophisticated.[7] The results suggest that both workplace accessibility and racial composition are critical to neighborhood choice. These renter households were more likely to choose areas closer to their workplaces and more likely to choose neighborhoods with greater representation of their racial group. Interestingly, there appear to be no differences in the racial composition of the *towns* selected by black and white households.

Lerman's analysis of household choice (1979) considers a sample of renters and homeowners living in Washington, D.C. in 1968. Several neighborhood attributes are considered: per-pupil school expenditure, the difference between a household's income and the average income in a tract, residential density, and the percentage of non-white residents in a tract. As expected, the study finds that income levels and residential density matter, with households preferring to live in less dense areas and to have neighbors with incomes higher than their own. School expenditures do not appear to matter, but given that many middle-class households in the District of Columbia send their children to private school, this is perhaps not all that surprising. Finally, consistent with the other findings, racial composition seems to be a critical factor in location decisions, even after income, density, and school expenditures are taken into account; blacks tend to choose to live in tracts with more blacks, and whites choose to live in tracts with more whites.

The final study that considers the choice of census tract uses somewhat more recent data (covering 1977–1979) from the Housing Allowance Experiment in South Bend, Indiana (Ottensmann, Good, and Gleeson 1990). The methodological approach of this study differs from those discussed earlier. Unlike the prior studies, which model the household choice of neighborhood, it models the probability that a given vacancy will be filled by a white or black household. But if the methodology is different, the conclusions are basically the same. Specifically, vacancies are much more likely to be filled by blacks as the percentage of blacks in the neighborhood increases. Interestingly, the authors consider the choice of blocks as well, and they arrive at an almost identical result.

In short, neighborhood factors in general, and racial composition in particular, consistently emerge as critical in housing choice. Every study that has explored racial composition has found it to be a significant predictor of locational choice for both black and white households. These results should be qualified somewhat, however. First, one study discussed discovers that racial composition is a good deal less important once the quality of local schools is taken into account (Jud and Bennett 1986). Second, the studies that actually consider the choice of census tracts are all fairly dated. Finally, it is important to stress that these choice models assume that all individuals have unfettered access to the full set of communities. Given the evidence on housing market discrimination, information gaps, and perceptions of racial hostility, such an assumption is clearly suspect. Thus, it is probably not appropriate to interpret these results as measures of revealed preference. But they still may be appropriate as predictors of actual household behavior.

Evidence from Studies Exploring Unit-Level Choice

Three other studies have explored the impact of racial considerations on household location decisions, but they consider the choice at the level of the housing unit. They examine, that is, the probability that a household of one race will replace a household of another race in a particular housing unit. Actual neighborhood characteristics are not taken into account. To some extent, the race of the previous occupant may be viewed as a clear proxy for the racial composition of the neighborhood. If a white household has been living in a housing unit, the chances are pretty good that the unit is located in a predominantly white neighborhood. But it is possible that the race of the departing occupant signifies something in itself, a possibility that will be discussed at greater length below.

Two of the studies use versions of the same data set that is used in this study to explore housing and neighborhood choices—the American Housing Survey (AHS). Since the AHS is a panel of housing units located around the country, it is a natural data set to use to trace the successive occupants of a given home. The first, Spain's analysis (1980), uses successive years of the AHS to calculate the probability of an urban housing unit turning over between 1973 and 1977 from white occupancy to black and from black to white. Consistent with surveys of racial preferences, the results suggest that whites are particularly unlikely to move into units vacated by blacks, with black-to-white turnover occurring less than one-quarter as often as would be expected in a color-blind world.[8] While this figure is strikingly small, it is considerably larger than the ratio a few years earlier—between 1967 and 1971, black-to-white turnover reportedly occurred only one-tenth as often as expected.

In a similar analysis of the AHS during the mid-1970s, Marullo (1985) finds that turnover is somewhat more frequent. In this study, whites replace blacks about one-third as often as would be expected given the number of black and white in-movers in the sample. In contrast to the first study, this analysis is not limited to central cities, which might explain the disparity in results.

As to where and under what conditions turnover is most likely to occur, white-to-black turnover is most common in the South and least common in the West, while black-to-white shifts are most common in the West. Significantly, these tendencies may be more a reflection of the relative numbers of blacks and whites living in these areas, rather than a statement about the relative openness of the housing markets in the regions. Similarly, white-to-black turnovers are more likely to occur within central cities, probably because of their larger minority populations. As for neighborhood conditions, blacks appear more likely to move into units previously occupied by whites when the original white occupant rates the neighborhood less favorably. But it is hard to know how to interpret this finding, since it is not clear if this lower rating results from the fact that the neighborhood is already racially changing or if areas that are less desirable to whites in the first place are more susceptible to racial change. A final result, and one that is consistent with race-based neighborhood stereotyping, is that whites are even less likely to move into homes previously occupied by blacks when they are purchasing, as opposed to simply renting, the units.

In a third analysis, Rosenbaum (1992) considers racial turnover in New York City during the 1980s, using that city's Housing and Vacancy Survey (HVS), which is a panel survey of housing units very similar to the AHS. Once again, turnover is rare, with white households moving into black-vacated units only about 14 percent as often as predicted. While this figure is even lower than those implied by the national studies above, it does not necessarily mean that racial divisions are more pronounced in the New York City housing market or that housing markets have become even more divided over time. For since the New York City analysis considers Puerto Ricans and other Hispanics as separate racial groups, its results are not truly comparable to these earlier studies. And in fact, when the percentages are recalculated, placing Puerto Ricans in the same category as blacks and other Hispanics in the same group as whites, the ratio of actual to expected turnovers is virtually identical to that generated by the second study summarized earlier.[9]

Interestingly, in contrast to the national results reported by Marullo (1985), tenure status is generally not found to be important in black-to-white turnover. This difference might be explained by the unique nature of the rental housing market in New York, where many affluent residents rent units for extended periods of time and never become homeowners.[10]

Who Moves into Racially Mixed Areas?

As discussed earlier, the hypothesis of race-based neighborhood stereotyping predicts that the white households moving into mixed areas will tend to be young, childless, and renters. Black households opting for mixed areas are likely to be more affluent than those moving to largely black areas, and they may be more likely to have children and own their homes.

Table 7.3 presents a comparison of the characteristics of white and black in-movers to integrated and segregated communities. Once again, the sample of thirty-four metropolitan areas from the national AHS (the neighborhood-coded version) is used. The racial mix of a neighborhood is defined by its proportion of blacks in 1990, and the entering households move in between 1989 and 1993.

The comparisons indicate that white households moving into integrated areas tend to be somewhat younger and less affluent than their counterparts opting for predominantly white environments. And consistent with race-based neighborhood stereotyping, they are both less likely to have children and less likely to be homeowners. As for black households, there is no clear difference in the tenure status and the number of children of those living in mixed and segregated areas. The main difference seems to be status—black families living in mixed areas have higher incomes on average than the black families living in largely black communities. Given the typically higher incomes of white households, this result is not surprising.[11] It is possible too, that

Table 7.3 Comparison of characteristics of households moving into integrated and segregated neighborhoods

Characteristic	Non-Hispanic white in-movers		Black in-movers	
	Integrated	White segregated	Integrated	Black segregated
Mean age	37.2*	38.8	35.8*	39.0
% Married	41.9	46.4	31.7*	19.1
Mean income	$35,412*	$46,184	$26,746*	$20,311
% of households with children	29.9*	36.9	54.3	58.9
% Homeowners	25.3*	42.7	15.6	15.2
Number of households	391	1,540	199	309

Source: Ellen (2000b).

*Difference between integrated and segregated neighborhoods statistically significant at the 5 percent level.

lower-status blacks are particularly susceptible to racial discrimination when trying to enter white communities.

While I found that no other study considers the characteristics of households moving into integrated areas, a few compare the characteristics of white households presently living in integrated and segregated environments. Because some households in integrated areas may have actually chosen to move into segregated areas and simply remained as the neighborhood unexpectedly changed, the characteristics of current residents may be quite distinct from those of in-movers. Still, the results of these comparisons are fairly consistent with those reported here. In Taylor's study of integrated communities in Omaha (1981), for instance, whites living in integrated neighborhoods are found to be more likely to be single, under age thirty-one, and college educated.

An analysis of a national sample of households living in racially mixed areas, meanwhile, finds that white households in integrated areas are more likely than their counterparts in segregated communities to be single, to live in smaller households, and to be renters. In seeming contradiction to the findings here, however, the authors report that white households in mixed areas tend to be older (Bradburn, Sudman, and Gockel 1971). Actually, this observation is not at all inconsistent with my findings. For given urban history, the current residents of a mixed area are likely to be made up of two groups of people: those who chose to move into the mixed area, and those who chose originally to move into a white area, but have simply stayed as the area has become mixed. According to case-study accounts, it is elderly whites who because of strong emotional ties opt to remain in integrated areas; their younger white counterparts, especially those with school-age children, typically move to predominantly white areas (see Aldrich 1975, p. 337; Levine and Harmon 1992, p. 311; Cummings 1998).

Analysis of Neighborhood Choice

While the previous section relates the characteristics of the black and white residents who are likely to choose to live in racially mixed areas, it tells us little about the willingness of households in general to move into mixed areas and offers little insight into the kinds of mixed neighborhoods that might be more attractive to whites and blacks. To answer these questions, we need to consider the choice of housing unit and neighborhood.

Incidence of Housing Unit Turnover

This section considers racial turnover in housing units and examines whether such turnover has become more common since the 1960s, 1970s, and mid-1980s when the three studies summarized earlier were undertaken. Racial turnover is defined as a household of one race moving into a unit previously occupied by a household of another race. Table 7.4 shows the actual probabilities of racial turnover between 1989 and 1993 as well as the expected probabilities given the overall racial distribution of the in-mover population.[12] The expected probability, in other words, is the proportion of blacks that we would expect to see moving in, assuming a color-blind world. The table also computes the ratio of actual to expected probabilities.

In the case of owner-occupied units, only 3.7 percent of units vacated by non-Hispanic white households during this time period were re-occupied by black homeowners.[13] Black households of course made up only a small fraction of homeowners moving into new homes. But the expected proportion—7.1 percent—was nearly twice the proportion of the white-vacated homes that were in fact re-occupied by blacks. (White-vacated here refers to units originally occupied

Table 7.4 Expected and actual percentages of housing units undergoing racial turnover, 1989–1993

	Race of incoming Household		
	White	Black	Other
	Owner-occupied units		
Actual percentage of entrants			
White-vacated unit	88.5	3.7	7.8
Black-vacated unit	16.9	75.7	7.4
Other-vacated unit	37.8	5.2	57.0
Expected percentage of entrants	82.0	7.1	10.9
Ratio of actual/expected percentage			
White-vacated unit	1.08	0.52	0.72
Black-vacated unit	0.21	10.70	0.68
Other-vacated unit	0.46	0.73	5.20
	Rental units		
Actual percentage of entrants			
White-vacated unit	81.5	7.6	10.9
Black-vacated unit	25.5	63.5	11.1
Other-vacated unit	33.1	10.2	56.7
Expected percentage of entrants	67.1	15.8	17.1
Ratio of actual/expected percentage			
White-vacated unit	1.20	0.48	0.64
Black-vacated unit	0.38	4.00	0.65
Other-vacated unit	0.49	0.65	3.30

Note: In this table, white refers to non-Hispanic white household.

by non-Hispanic white households.) Similarly, the frequency of blacks moving into white-vacated rental units was also about half that expected.

The discrepancies are even larger for homes vacated by black households. A unit vacated by a black renter, for instance, was four times more likely than expected to be re-occupied by another black, and about one-third as likely as predicted to be re-occupied by a non-Hispanic white household. In the case of homeowners, meanwhile, the differences are starker still—black households were more than *ten times* more likely than expected to re-occupy owner-occupied units vacated by black households, while non-Hispanic white households entered such units only one-fifth as often as expected. Once again, it appears that white homeowners are uniquely resistant to racial mixing.

How do these figures compare to earlier times? Does racial turnover appear more common today than it was ten or twenty years ago? Because of methodological and sample differences between this study and earlier analyses, it is difficult to directly compare these results.[14] When making adjustments for consistency, however, turnover appears more common in our sample than the study discussed earlier suggested it was in New York City between 1978 and 1987. But it is not clear whether this is a reflection of a genuine shift or an indication of a difference between New York City and the rest of the country.

As for comparisons with the earlier national results, it appears that turnover occurred more frequently during the early 1990s than it did during the 1960s. But the evidence concerning the 1970s is ambiguous, since the two national studies of the 1970s arrive at quite different conclusions. If we consider the Spain results (1980) to be the appropriate comparison, then the results here suggest that turnover from black to white occupancy during the early 1990s was more prevalent than it was during the 1970s. But if we use the Marullo results (1985) instead as a comparison, then turnover appears to have occurred at about the same rate in 1989–1993 as it did during the 1970s. In short, there is little evidence here to suggest any shift in the rate of racial turnover since the 1970s.

Modeling Neighborhood Choice

The crucial question, of course, is how to interpret these numbers. Why is the race of the departing occupant so significant in predicting the race of the subsequent resident? Is it merely a proxy measure for the racial composition of the neighborhood, or are other factors at play here? Do these stark differences in the probabilities of black households moving in persist when the price and quality of the unit are considered? How about when neighborhood racial composition and other community characteristics are taken into account? The answers to these questions require a multivariate analysis of housing unit choice that permits us to consider the characteristics of the neighborhoods surrounding the housing units.

To tackle the difficult problem of modeling such choice, this study estimates a logistic regression of the probability of a black household's moving into a housing unit vacated between 1989 and 1993 as a function of unit and neighborhood characteristics (as measured in 1990).[15] Although this approach might not be ideal from a theoretical standpoint, it is sensible when considering a sample of house-holds from thirty-four different metropolitan areas, since defining the neighborhood choices faced by such varied households would be vir-tually impossible.

Since small changes in racial composition may have very differ-ent effects on the probability of black entry when the proportion of blacks differs, the regression allows the relationship between a com-munity's racial composition and the probability of black entry to dif-fer in predominantly white tracts (less than 10 percent black), inte-grated tracts (10–50 percent black), and majority black tracts.[16]

Table 7.5 shows selected coefficients from the logistic regression of black entry.[17] For ease of interpretation, only blacks and whites are considered here—white Hispanics are classified as white, and Asians

Table 7.5 Regression of probability of black entry into vacant unit, 1989–1993, selected coefficients

	Owner-occupied units		Rental units	
	Coeff.	Std. error	Coeff.	Std. error
% Black, 1990	.272***	(.064)	.176***	(.03)
Spline 1:(% Black-10)[a]	−.25***	(.073)	−.144***	(.034)
Spline 2: (% Black-50)[b]	.112*	(.059)	.036**	(.017)
1980–1990 change in % black	.0465*	(.026)	.011	(.009)
Departing black household	2.87***	(.603)	1.33***	(.198)
% Other, 1990	.027	(.018)	.008	(.006)
Public housing unit	NA	NA	.848**	(.332)
Central city	.32	(.4)	.45***	(.173)
Poor quality neighborhood	.928*	(.52)	.565***	(.186)
Poverty rate	−.066*	(.039)	−.04***	(.01)
1980–1990 change in poverty rate	.01	(.05)	.002	(.015)
N	896		1,760	

Source: Ellen (2000b).

[a]This spline variable is zero for tracts in which the percentage black is less than 10 percent. For tracts in which the percentage black is greater, the variable is defined as the percentage of blacks minus 10.

[b]This spline variable is zero for tracts in which the percentage black is less than 50 percent. For tracts in which the proportion of black residents is greater, the variable is defined as the percentage of blacks minus 50.

Note: Regression also controls for the estimated value of the owner-occupied units, the gross rent of the rental unit, whether the unit is a single-family home, and whether the household judges it to be of poor quality.

*, **, *** Statistically significant at the 10, 5, and 1 percent levels.

are omitted. But the general conclusions are no different when Hispanics and Asians are considered to be a third distinct ethnic group. The results for the non-racial variables are largely as expected: black entry is more probable in central cities, public housing, and poor-quality neighborhoods. The one surprising result is that units in tracts with higher poverty rates are *less* likely to be re-occupied by blacks (after controlling for all of these other unit and neighborhood characteristics).

As for the measures of racial mix, present racial composition emerges as relevant in the case of entry decisions, in contrast to the case of exit decisions. This suggests that when racial transition occurs, it is driven largely by entry and not exit decisions. (Indeed, a simulation constructed from these results shows that this is the case [Ellen 2000b]). Yet inspection of the coefficients on the spline variables shows that entry decisions are not sensitive to racial composition within neighborhoods that are racially integrated. For the estimated effect of small differences in the proportion of blacks for tracts that are between 10 and 50 percent black is the sum of the coefficient on percent black and the first spline variable. As shown then, the predicted effect of additional black residents falls to approximately zero among these racially integrated tracts.[18]

Since the coefficients for logistic regressions are difficult to interpret (especially with spline regressions), Figure 7.1 shows the effect of racial composition on the predicted probability of a black household purchasing a typical owner-occupied housing unit.[19] The two lines on the graph show how the probability of black entry into a typical unit vacated by a black household and the probability of black entry into a typical unit vacated by a white household vary with the proportion of black residents in the census tract. Two points are worth noting. First, the slope of both graphs is relatively flat for racially integrated census tracts. That is, the predicted probability of black entry into units is not much different in neighborhoods that are 10 percent black than in those that are 50 percent black. When the neighborhood is more than 50 percent black, however, the effect of racial composition is quite dramatic. Consider that the predicted probability of black entry into a unit previously occupied by a white household that is located in a 70 percent black tract is 73 percent, compared to just 15 percent in a tract that is half black.[20]

The second point worth noting is the stark difference between the

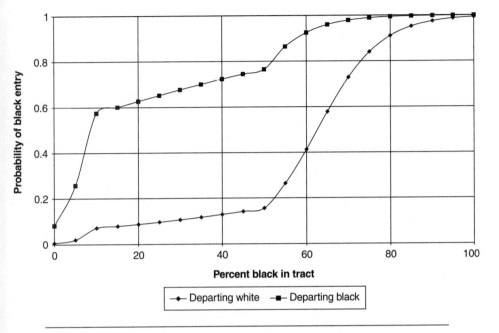

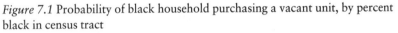

Figure 7.1 Probability of black household purchasing a vacant unit, by percent black in census tract

two curves. The fact that the race of the prior occupant remains so critical, even after controlling for the racial mix of the tract, is somewhat surprising. Consider the average owner unit in a neighborhood that is 20 percent black. If the out-going occupant is white, the chance of a black household moving in is just 9 percent; if the out-going family is instead black, the chance of another black family moving in increases to 63 percent. It is possible that the race of the departing occupant serves as a proxy for the racial mix of the block or the subneighborhood within a census tract, or that the in-movers aware of the race of the prior occupant may at least use it as a signal of that mix.[21] It is also possible that the very fact that a prior occupant is black indicates that the agent handling the unit deals with minority customers, or in the case of rental units, that the particular building or development is welcoming to minorities. Finally, the relevance of the race of the out-going occupant may also speak to the power of word-of-mouth in the housing market. For to the extent that word-of-mouth plays a significant role in housing transactions, and to the extent that people tend to associate with those of their same race, we would expect whites to replace whites and blacks to replace blacks. Whatever their ultimate cause, however, these differences certainly make evident the importance of considering the race of a home's previous occupant when modeling racial change.

It is possible too that the effect of racial composition and other neighborhood characteristics is different depending on the race of the out-going occupant. Perhaps, for instance, white households are very sensitive to neighborhood conditions in general but steadfastly refuse to move into a home previously occupied by a black family, regardless of the neighborhood environment. To explore this possibility, the regression is estimated separately for units initially occupied by white households and those initially occupied by black households. The results (not shown) turn out to be fairly different.[22] Specifically, in the case of black departures, whether the unit is in the central city, whether it is owner occupied, and whether it is publicly owned are all irrelevant. Similarly, the poverty rate, the share of non-black minorities present, and the growth in the black population over the previous decade are all inconsequential. Yet all of these variables emerge as relevant in the case of units that initially have white occupants. The key implication is that whites appear unwilling to enter black-vacated units, and few circumstances seem to change their minds. The likelihood of racial turnover in white-vacated units, in contrast, seems very influenced by the neighborhood environment. Most significantly, black households are far less likely to move into units vacated by whites when they are located in neighborhoods considered to be of high quality.

I also tested for differences between rental and owner units. In general, the conclusions are fairly similar for both kinds of housing. Small differences in racial composition appear to have little effect in racially integrated neighborhoods. Yet a tract's racial composition has a substantial impact on the probability of black entry for units located in predominantly white areas as well as those situated in majority black areas. There is one important difference between rental and owner units, however. Consistent with race-based neighborhood stereotyping, it appears that home buyers are more sensitive than prospective renters to *changes* in racial composition. Indeed, in the case of rental units, the coefficient on the growth in black population between 1980 and 1990 is not significantly different from zero. There is no evidence, in other words, that recent changes in racial composition make a difference to white or black renters. But such changes appear quite important to prospective home buyers. Consider that the probability of black entry into the typical owner unit is 9.5 percent in a neighborhood that has been 25 percent black for ten years, but is just 14.5 percent in a neighborhood that is presently 25 percent black but that was 15 percent black ten years ago.[23]

That homeowners and not renters should be sensitive to racial change makes sense. For we would expect homeowners, who are making a financial investment in a community and who are likely to remain in place for a longer period of time, to be more concerned with *future* neighborhood characteristics. Thus when searching for a home, prospective home buyers are likely to pay more attention to recent trends in neighborhood conditions.

The analysis of neighborhood entry supports many of the predictions of the race-based neighborhood stereotyping hypothesis. First, and perhaps most significantly, the analysis demonstrates that racial composition is far more central to neighborhood entry decisions than to exit choices. Yet racial mix does not appear quite as critical as generally assumed—at least *within* integrated neighborhoods. There is little difference, that is, between the probability that blacks will move into neighborhoods that are 10 percent black and the probability that they will move into neighborhoods that are 50 percent black. Second, while changes in racial composition appear to matter to homeowners, they seem largely irrelevant to the probability of racial turnover in rental units. Third, the results show that certain white households—in particular, those that are younger, those that rent their homes, and those that do not include children—are far more likely to opt for mixed areas.

CHAPTER EIGHT

Conclusions and Policy Implications

The previous chapters suggest that racial mixing is fragile, largely because white households tend to resist moving into integrated areas. Yet racially integrated neighborhoods are not, as once thought, inevitably doomed to rapid resegregation. This book has hopefully shed some light on the underlying dynamics of change in racially mixed areas and suggested several circumstances under which such areas are likely to be more stable. This chapter explores some of the policy implications of these findings. What do they imply about the likely efficacy of traditional government or community actions aimed at bolstering racial stability? And what do they suggest about the likely impact on racial stability of public actions designed to achieve other goals? Finally, just because government can intervene in a productive way to promote integration does not necessarily mean that it should. Thus, after summarizing the factors correlated with racial stability, the chapter begins its analysis of public action by exploring the moral and economic justifications for policies designed to promote the stability of racial integration.

Characteristics of Comparatively Stable Integrated Neighborhoods

The previous four chapters identify five key factors—consistent with race-based neighborhood stereotyping—that are linked to neighborhood racial stability, and in particular to maintaining white demand in racially mixed communities. The first, and perhaps most critical, is a community's past racial stability. The longer a community is integrated, the more likely it is to remain integrated in the future. Analysis of individual decision making confirms this claim. Controlling for present racial composition, white households are both less likely to leave a mixed community and more likely to enter one if its black population has been fairly constant. Indeed, with respect to the rate of white departures from a community, the actual size of the black population appears largely irrelevant. Whites, that is, appear perfectly content to live in a neighborhood that is 40 or 50 percent black, as long as that proportion has been steady in the past and thus seems likely to remain steady in the future.

A second and related factor is a neighborhood's distance from an area's central minority concentration, with integrated neighborhoods located farther from black inner-city communities more likely to remain stable. This location may also be linked to expectations. Neighborhoods closer to black inner-city communities are naturally perceived as more apt to gain black population and more vulnerable to experiencing the social dislocation that whites associate with such gain. These expectations are not entirely unfounded. In the past, neighborhoods bordering on existing black areas were the first communities opened to blacks and thus often experienced rapid minority growth. Furthermore, even without such discriminatory exclusion, it seems likely that black households might choose to move into mixed areas that are nearer to largely minority areas, since these areas are likely to be nearer to friends, relatives, and past community ties. It may also be that these inner communities are located in fiscally weaker jurisdictions and are thus less able to maintain the services necessary to attract (typically wealthier) white households.[1]

A third factor is the predominance of rental housing. This is not to say that communities with high rates of homeownership are destined to resegregate. But it does appear that white homeowners are particularly averse to racial mixing, and thus that neighborhoods with relatively larger proportions of rental housing are more likely to remain integrated.

A fourth factor is a thriving housing market and, more generally, a secure set of neighborhood amenities. Large stabilizing institutions, such as universities or military bases, may provide just such security because they promise to provide a continual flow of people—both white and black—into the community. It is possible that other neighborhood characteristics, such as a prized stock of historic housing or the presence of highly regarded magnet schools, may also help to bolster confidence in an area's structural strength and thus stabilize racial mixing.

The fifth factor concerns the nature of racial relations in the larger metropolitan area in which the community is located. In particular, racially mixed communities appear to be more stable if they are located in metropolitan areas that have smaller black populations, are less segregated, and lack a history of intense racial competition for housing and widespread neighborhood racial change. This latter factor may explain the greater stability of racially integrated neighborhoods located in the western region of the country.

As discussed in Chapter 7, it is also true that the whites who appear most resistant to racial mixing tend to have children—an observation that suggests that concern about local school quality may be a key factor underlying resistance to racial mixing. But, as discussed already, it does not necessarily follow that mixed communities with larger shares of these sorts of households are bound to be less stable. For the very fact that large numbers of married white households with children have chosen a particular integrated community is a good indication that it has other features that promise to bolster its institutions and property values.

To some extent, the same argument could be made about homeowners—that racially integrated neighborhoods with more homeowners are not necessarily going to be less stable over time. But the difference here is that the homeownership rate is not simply a characteristic of the underlying population; it is also a function of the housing stock. A neighborhood filled with high-rise apartments is likely to have only a small share of homeowners.

Justification for Public Action

Before addressing what policymakers can do with this information, it is important to take a step back and probe what in fact they should do. What kinds of government intervention, if any, are warranted to promote integration?

As with any government action, there are two sorts of arguments for government intervention to promote integration: moral (or justice-based) arguments, and economic arguments. The moral argument relates primarily to the causes of racial transition. As stressed throughout these pages, the key force undermining the stability of racially integrated neighborhoods is the private choice of white households to avoid racially integrated areas. Many researchers and policymakers who agree have thus tended to assume that the unraveling of integration is beyond the scope of government action.

Certainly, if the transition occurring in racially integrated communities is simply the result of benign private household preferences (or differences in income), then the market is operating just like it does in every other arena—merely sorting people according to their desires and means. In this case, it is hard to justify government intervention, or even official concern. As a matter of political morality, moreover, there seems to be nothing wrong with wanting to be near others who share your customs and ways of life. Do we care (enough to motivate government action), for instance, that Russian immigrants choose to cluster in Brooklyn's Brighton Beach neighborhood?

But as argued throughout, whites' motivation to resist sharing neighborhoods with blacks does not seem to stem from some benign desire to live exclusively among other whites or to live among those with similar incomes and tastes. White resistance to integrated living appears to be more the result of negative racial attitudes, and in particular, race-based neighborhood stereotyping. As such, white decisions to avoid integrated neighborhoods seem clearly objectionable in a way that decisions, say, to cluster voluntarily with other members of one's own ethnic group are not.

As explained in Chapter 1, how objectionable these decisions are depends in part on the extent to which the neighborhood stereotypes that whites adopt are true. On the one hand, if it were really the case that black neighborhoods, after controlling for income levels and other socioeconomic factors, do have inferior schools, lower property value appreciation, and higher crime than white neighborhoods, one might conclude that whites are simply choosing to live, in a colorblind fashion, in higher-quality neighborhoods. In such a situation perhaps significant government intervention would not be justified. The point should not be pressed too far, however, since any disparities that exist between black and white neighborhoods are to a significant degree rooted in negative racial attitudes and discrimination and therefore may themselves merit public action. For example, one obvious reason that black neighborhoods might provide inferior services is that they have been denied the same political power as white neighborhoods to attract the necessary resources to sustain and improve neighborhood services and quality of life. Moreover, even if there is some truth to the stereotypes about largely black communities, there is something troubling about households making blanket assumptions about the quality of black neighborhoods without examining the specifics of the neighborhood in question. Given our nation's sorry racial past and the continued role that such blanket assumptions play in perpetuating racial inequality, it is not unreasonable to demand a little more diligence.

On the other hand, if the stereotypes are in fact false, then the case is clear-cut. Certainly we should care if whites are everywhere inaccurately branding black neighborhoods as "bad," based on the same kind of insidious assumptions about black inferiority that underlie racial prejudice against individuals.

Unfortunately, the data here cannot reveal with certainty the quality of schools and the level of crime in largely black or racially integrated areas. But the evidence reported in Chapter 5 seems to suggest that after controlling for the level of poverty, racial composition is not in fact related to satisfaction with neighborhood conditions and amenities. And while white households report lower neighborhood quality in neighborhoods with growing black populations, black households do not, suggesting that whites may unfairly exaggerate the degree to which community decline accompanies racial change.

So far in this discussion, as well as throughout much of this book, the decisions of white households to avoid racially integrated neighborhoods have been treated as purely individual matters. But as is also noted throughout, discriminatory actions on the part of landlords, realtors, lenders, and even employers have shaped these individual preferences by perpetuating racial disparities and undermining minority communities. To the extent that discrimination plays a role in racial transition and to the extent that such discrimination has been sanctioned by the state (consider the underwriting guidelines issued by the Federal Housing Administration in the postwar period that urged lenders to avoid racially diverse communities), the case for government intervention is naturally strengthened.

Finally, at the most general level, there is something morally troubling about the two races living in such different worlds, especially in light of this country's appalling racial legacy. Segregation among Latinos may be growing too, but the history of African Americans makes the meaning and responsibilities different. As Nathan Glazer has written, the social status of African Americans is the "most enduring reproach to the egalitarian ideals of American society" (Glazer 1998, p. 24). And similarly, the persistence of such high levels of segregation seems an affront to the fairness of American institutions.

In short, there is a sound case to be made for at least concern about residential integration, and there may be a moral case for modest government intervention to promote racial stability. It should be noted, however, that one of the implications of the race-based neighborhood stereotyping hypothesis, which emphasizes worries about neighborhood quality, is that our concern about white household decision making should perhaps not be as great as if transition were driven by simple racism.

There may also be an economic rationale for public action. There may be, that is, social benefits to increasing integration. Recent research provides strong evidence that neighborhood segregation contributes to racial differences in education and labor market outcomes (Galster and Keeney 1988; Galster 1991; O'Regan and Quigley 1996b; Cutler and Glaeser 1997). The mechanism, however, is unclear. As John Kain first argued in his 1968 article, it may be that low-skilled blacks who remain constrained to inner-city neighborhoods are seriously disadvantaged as blue-collar and other low-skilled jobs continue to move to the suburbs. They may not hear about jobs available in suburban areas, and it is likely to entail considerable time and expense to commute to suburban jobs, especially given that our transportation systems are designed to move workers from suburbs to central city downtowns and not the reverse (Kain 1968; Wilson 1987; Hughes 1989; Kasarda 1989; Ihlanfeldt and Sjoquist 1990).

Others contend that racial segregation confines blacks to live in more economically deprived communities (Massey and Eggers 1990; Massey 1990; Massey and Denton 1993). According to these researchers, "concentrated poverty among African-Americans follows ultimately from the racial segmentation of urban housing markets, which interacts with high and rising rates of black poverty to concentrate poverty geographically" (Massey, Gross, and Shibuya 1994). Put simply, when a highly segregated group has a high rate of poverty, the inevitable result is geographically concentrated poverty. And since concentrated poverty tends to bring with it a range of social problems—joblessness, welfare dependency, crime, drugs, and single parenthood—African Americans are exposed to a social and economic environment that is far more distressed than that enjoyed by whites. Even affluent minorities have been found to live in communities that are significantly less prosperous than those of whites, with lower median home values, more widespread single parenthood, and a far higher proportion of low-performing high school students (Massey and Denton 1993, pp. 152–153).

Does growing up or living in such communities make a difference? Because it is methodologically difficult to dissect the effects of a neighborhood from the effects of personal and family characteristics that lead people to live in certain kinds of neighborhoods, this question is difficult to answer. But in general, a growing number of studies are finding that children growing up in socially and economically deprived communities suffer disadvantages, even after controlling for family background.[2] The evidence suggests that teenagers growing up in poor communities are more likely to drop out of school and more likely to get pregnant as teenagers (Datcher 1982; Case and Katz 1991; Crane 1991; Clark 1992; Brooks-Gunn et al. 1993; Duncan 1994; Aaronson 1997; Duncan, Connell, and Klebanov 1997; Ellen and Turner 1997). And some studies have also found a relationship between the characteristics of the neighborhood in which one grows up and subsequent employment outcomes (Datcher 1982; Corcoran et al. 1989).

There is evidence that simply living in (as opposed to growing up in) poor neighborhoods may also reduce the employment opportunities of minorities (Case and Katz 1991; Massey, Gross, and Eggers 1991; O'Regan and Quigley 1996a). Since word-of-mouth is a critical mechanism through which adults as well as adolescents learn about employment opportunities, the very fact of living in a neighborhood in which few people work in decent-paying jobs is a disadvantage. Moreover, the absence of working neighbors also means the absence of people who can vouch for one's reliability and character. Such recommendations, especially from in-house workers, have been shown to be critical for finding jobs (Sullivan 1989; Wial 1991; Kasinitz and Rosenberg 1996).

Significantly, a few of these studies have also suggested that the costs of poverty concentration do not lie solely with those in poor neighborhoods. For there is some evidence that there are significant threshold effects—that neighborhood poverty harms people only after it exceeds a certain level. If so, then the deconcentration of poverty that results from a reduction of racial segregation may lead to decreased levels of poverty and its consequent problems not only in the streets of Anacostia (in Washington, D.C.) and East St. Louis but in society overall (Hogan and Kitagawa 1985; Crane 1991; Galster 1997).

But even if racial segregation does not ultimately leave blacks isolated from jobs or concentrated in poorer communities, the simple fact of racial isolation may be detrimental in that it fosters racial prejudice. Although the evidence here is somewhat mixed, several studies have found that people, or at least white people, typically become less prejudiced as a result of living among and being exposed to others of different racial groups (Deutsch and Collins 1951; Ford 1973; Hamilton and Bishop 1976; Robinson and Preston 1976; Sigelman and Welch 1993; Smith 1994; Wilson 1996). The direction of causality in many of these studies is admittedly murky (do those with more liberal racial attitudes simply seek out more inter-racial interaction?), but the clearest studies seem to suggest that diminished racial prejudice follows from inter-racial contact and not the reverse.[3] Thus, even if reducing segregation may cause some discomfort in the short run, it may still remain optimal from a longer-run perspective.[4]

Finally, to the extent that fears of racial isolation and neighborhood structural decline drive racial segregation, the collective consequences of individual residential choices may result in fewer integrated neighborhoods than is optimal. The key point, as emphasized throughout this book, is that many white and black households might in fact prefer to live in racially mixed environments, but because of a widespread lack of faith in the harmony and stability of these areas, these environments are more rare (despite real progress) than they should be.

In short, there are many reasons to believe that racial segregation may be harmful to blacks and ultimately to society overall. Yet it is important to point out that there are reasonable economic arguments on the other side as well. Economic theory certainly does not predict that the segregation of particular racial groups is necessarily bad. It is possible, for instance, that racial segregation in fact produces more economic integration, by keeping rich and poor blacks together when they would otherwise live apart. William Julius Wilson, for instance, argued in his 1987 book that the flight of middle-class blacks from inner-city communities to integrated suburbs has increased the class segregation of blacks and thereby worsened the plight of poor blacks. Others have posited that segregation may help minorities by insulating their budding businesses from white competition (Glazer and Moynihan 1963). Racial segregation may also afford minority groups a greater voice in the political process by giving them the concentration they need to elect a representative sensitive to their interests. Finally, segregated communities may provide minorities with stronger social networks and support.

But while these are certainly sound arguments, the best evidence to date suggests that racial segregation is in fact linked to greater social and economic isolation and adverse outcomes for blacks, and has little effect on whites (Galster and Keeney 1988; Galster 1991; LaVeist 1992; Cutler and Glaeser 1997). It seems that W. E. B. Du Bois was right in arguing that in the long run, "the greatest human development is going to take place under experiences of widest individual contact" (Lewis 1995, p. 558).

Policies directed at promoting integration are also sometimes criticized as unjustified exercises in social engineering. William Bradford Reynolds, assistant attorney general for civil rights in the Reagan Justice Department, for instance, has asserted that as long as people are not denied free choice of housing, "government [should not] be about the business to reorder society or neighborhoods to achieve some degree of racial proportionality" (Polikoff 1986, p. 49). Certainly, whites' decisions to move away from, or not to move into, mixed neighborhoods because of racial prejudice, or decisions not to be welcoming to blacks who move into their neighborhoods, are hardly the kind of decisions that can be made legally actionable; to do so would severely curtail freedom of movement and thought. Nonetheless, there is a range of non-coercive government actions, such as incentive-based programs and information dissemination efforts, that can help to support integration and that are perfectly consistent with the protection of individual liberty.

Policies to promote neighborhood racial mixing have also been attacked for being demeaning to minorities, that is, for presuming that there is something inherently wrong with all-black communities.

As Justice Clarence Thomas charged in a 1995 Supreme Court opinion concerning court-ordered school desegregation efforts, "It never ceases to amaze me that the courts are so willing to assume that anything that is predominantly black must be inferior" (*Missouri v. Jenkins* 1995). Such charges have been leveled from the other side of the political spectrum as well. The Chicago chapter of the Southern Christian Leadership Council, for instance, has charged that the very concept of integration maintenance suggests that black communities are somehow undesirable and thereby "reinforces the myth of white supremacy and black inferiority" (Polikoff 1986, p. 45).

Any policy undertaken to promote integration must be sensitive to such concerns. But the idea that all efforts to stem racial transition are premised on the notion of black neighborhood inferiority is not sustainable. Indeed, the core theme of this book is that racial transition is fundamentally caused by precisely such stereotypes (held by white households) about the inferiority of black neighborhoods, and that any justified government intervention must be designed to challenge and overcome these stereotypes, not propagate them. Moreover, promoting integration also requires efforts to help open all-white segregated neighborhoods.

The debate about efforts to support racial integration continues to rage in academic journals, actual communities, and courts of law. This book by no means aims to resolve it, but merely to suggest that there is an arguable case for modest government intervention.

Past Efforts to Maintain Integration

The range of integration maintenance programs that have been implemented over the years is fairly wide, and thus blanket support or rejection is not appropriate. This section reviews the various policy tools that have been adopted in different communities to try to stem the pace of racial change. (The next section then evaluates which of these tools, based on the evidence and arguments presented above, are likely to be most effective.) The strategies may be divided into two camps: the race neutral and the race conscious.

Race-Neutral Policies

The aim of race-neutral integration maintenance policies is not race neutral at all. It is explicitly to maintain the racial mix of a community and to forestall resegregation. The means, however, are neutral with respect to race, in that they do not treat any single racial group differently from any other. There are six main examples of these race-neutral efforts:

- restrictions on realtor solicitation
- bans on the display of "For Sale" signs
- equity insurance programs
- aggressive public relations campaigns
- community betterment projects
- general community building

The first policy listed is restrictions on unsolicited efforts by realtors to encourage homeowners to sell, efforts that, in the past, drove block-busting and panic selling. Several communities have passed ordinances to this end. Maywood, Illinois, for instance, requires brokers to first request permission from both the town and specific households before soliciting a homeowner to list her home for sale. In Teaneck, New Jersey, residents may file an affidavit with the town clerk stating that they do not wish to be solicited, and realtors are responsible for making sure that they do not bother these homeowners (Lake and Winslow 1981). Park Forest, Illinois, tried to ban realtor solicitation altogether, but this broad ban on realtor contact with homeowners was found by a federal district court in 1989 to be an unconstitutional violation of free speech. While the federal appeals court ultimately upheld these bans, it made clear that such bans are subject to some degree of court scrutiny.

The second policy, banning the display of "For Sale" signs on front lawns, similarly aims to stem panic selling. Such policies may also in fact work to decrease black demand, since minority households tend to rely more than whites on such signs in their housing searches (Lake 1981). Naturally, the communities that have instituted such bans—Southfield, Michigan; Willingboro, New Jersey; Gary, Indiana; Shaker Heights, Ohio; and Oak Park, Illinois; to name a few—have stressed the more laudable aim of preventing panic. Like prohibitions on realtor solicitations, however, these restrictions also risk violating constitutionally protected free speech, and the courts have declared some bans to be unconstitutional. For example, in 1977, the Supreme

Court struck down the sign ban instituted in Willingboro, New Jersey. But the Court did not determine that such prohibitions were always invalid and in fact it referred to neighborhood integration as both a "vital goal" and "an important government objective" (Polikoff 1986, p. 56). It found instead that the town failed to establish that the ban was necessary to maintain integration.

The remaining race-neutral policies listed earlier aim largely to counter white fears about structural decline in racially changing communities. The third option, for instance, is to insure homeowners against possible losses of equity in their homes. The idea was advanced by Adam Yarmolinsky in a 1971 article as a way to moderate racial change. Yarmolinsky argued that such a program would take away the chief legitimate (even if unfounded) fear about racial change and help to prevent block-busting. "Even where economic concerns are pure rationalizations by white racists, there is something to be said for calling their bluff," Yarmolinsky wrote. "There is also something to be said for removing the commercial incentives that lead block-busting real estate operators to seek rapid turnover in an atmosphere of panic and hate" (Yarmolinsky 1971, p. 106).

While Yarmolinsky's call for a national program never came to life (or at least has yet to), Oak Park, Illinois—an affluent suburb of Chicago—instituted an equity insurance program in 1978. As stated in the ordinance establishing the program, the aim was "to insure the single-family residences in the Village of Oak Park against the possibility of economic loss, and thereby help to eliminate irrational fears of racial change" (Lake and Winslow 1981, p. 314). Under the original terms of the program, a participating homeowner would pay the village approximately $100 for an appraisal. If after at least five years the owner were to sell the home for less than the appraised value, the village would use bond funds to reimburse her for 80 percent of the difference between the appraised value and the sale price. In fact, very few homeowners have actually participated in the program, perhaps because property values (at least until the late 1980s) have risen in the community by about 10 percent each year. By 1986, only 135 out of an eligible 10,500 homeowners in the village had signed up for the program, and no one had yet filed a claim (Lieber 1990). But it is still possible that the program's very existence has worked to reassure whites and thus has helped to stabilize Oak Park, which remained 18 percent black in 1990 (Keating 1994).

The next policy on the list is aggressive public relations campaigns to counter the public perception—especially by whites—that mixed neighborhoods inevitably decline or are otherwise unappealing. These efforts range from offering widely publicized home tours, to lobbying for historic landmark designation, to hiring professional marketing firms to sell a mixed community's image through advertisements and glossy brochures (Saltman 1990). The promotional literature designed by Oak Park is an interesting example because it explicitly mentions and celebrates its racial diversity, in an apparent attempt to attract those white households who desire stable racial mixing. The village has also aggressively marketed itself as a diverse community to employers, hospitals, and universities throughout the Chicago metropolitan area, and has even placed advertisements in national publications such as the *New Republic* and the *Saturday Review* to try to attract educated liberal (and presumably white) residents (Goodwin 1979).

A more recent example is that of Matteson, Illinois, a town located forty miles south of Chicago. In 1980, Matteson was 12 percent black; by 1997, it was estimated to be 48 percent black and its residents—both white and black—were growing concerned about the long-term implications. So in the spring of 1996, the town launched a $37,000 advertising campaign largely aimed at whites. As in the case of Oak Park, the ads explicitly trumpeted Matteson's racial diversity and celebrated the town's schools, parks, safety, and low taxes. But the placement of the ads was clearly aimed at whites. (In this respect, public relations campaigns are not entirely race-neutral.) Ads were placed for instance, in the *Chicago Tribune* and the *Chicago Reader.* They were not to be found in the *Chicago Sun Times,* which is especially popular in minority neighborhoods, or the *Chicago Defender,* a historically black newspaper (Terry 1996).

The fifth strategy is to undertake community betterment projects that aim directly to bolster residents' confidence in their community's strength and security. For if, as argued above, people's fears about racial mixing stem largely from their fear of the structural decline that they associate with minority neighborhoods, then improving the appearance of the neighborhood should be vital to stability. As a resident of one racially mixed neighborhood in Chicago put it, "The issues come down to quality of life. . . . Is there a good quality of life here? Is it safe for kids? . . . Are gangs a problem? That's what human beings are looking for, no matter what color they are" (Maly and Nyden 1996, pp. 26–27). And simple signs of disorder—a vacant lot, public drinking, a burned-out street lamp, uncollected litter—can lead residents to quickly lose faith in their community. A single unrepaired "broken window," as George Kelling and James Q. Wilson have persuasively argued (1982, p. 31), is a strong sign to both residents and vandals that no one in the community really cares.[5]

West Mount Airy, a nationally renowned, stably diverse community in Philadelphia, has taken the community betterment approach. The neighborhood did not, that is, try to attract whites into the community or in any way to discourage blacks; it simply tried to heighten overall demand for its housing. Similarly, Teaneck, New Jersey, has invested heavily in enhancing neighborhood amenities, such as street lighting, playgrounds, and traffic patterns. The most common campaigns, however, are targeted at public safety. Prospect–Lefferts Gardens in Brooklyn, for instance, has developed an active community crime-prevention program, with frequent foot patrols and marked cars (Saltman 1990). And suburban jurisdictions, such as Oak Park, have raised expenditures for police and increased their patrols in racially changing neighborhoods (Goodwin 1979).

The final strategy is related to these community betterment efforts, but its focus is less on the physical aspects of the community or the crime rate than on the level of social cohesion or social capital in the community. The notion is that social cohesion and interaction in and of themselves enable residents to bolster each other's confidence in their neighborhood and can provide a powerful counter to prevailing negative stereotypes about racial mixing. Almost every case study of diverse communities has identified an active community group. Consider, for example, the community association in the Park Hill neighborhood in Denver, which in the late 1980s had an organized network of block workers on over three hundred of the neighborhood's five hundred blocks, held monthly town meetings, distributed a monthly newsletter, and sponsored welcoming parties for in-movers three times each year (Saltman 1990).

Race-Conscious Remedies

Not surprisingly, the more controversial efforts to maintain integration are those that take race explicitly into account and treat racial groups differently. Three main types of race-conscious policies have been instituted to promote racial mixing:

- ceiling quotas
- affirmative marketing
- pro-integrative mortgage incentives

The first and most direct technique of race-conscious integration maintenance is the "benign housing quota," which limits the proportion of blacks that may live in a specified community or housing complex. These quotas are generally applied to individual housing projects, rather than entire neighborhoods. The village of Oak Park seriously considered imposing a 30 percent ceiling on black occupancy in a portion of the village bordering on Chicago. In the face of harsh criticism in the Chicago-area press, however, the village's community relations commission ultimately defeated the proposal (Goodwin 1979; Lake and Winslow 1981).

Still, several housing developments—both public and private—have instituted ceilings on racial occupancy. The most renowned case is that of Starrett City, a large middle-income apartment complex in Brooklyn. The private owners of Starrett City (which was built with large federal and state subsidies) established quotas from the outset in order to alleviate white fears of a predominantly minority project. Specifically, they set a distribution of 70 percent white, 22 percent black, and 8 percent Hispanic (Husock 1990a). But the demand for the project was far greater from minorities—especially blacks—than from whites, even after the development added extensive amenities and advertised heavily in nearby white neighborhoods. As a result, the typical wait for an apartment in the early 1980s was 20 months for a black family and just two months for a white (Yinger 1995). In 1979, five black applicants, with the support of the NAACP, filed a suit charging the development, and New York State as well, for racial discrimination. After five years of litigation, the parties arrived at a settlement that allowed Starrett City to continue using a quota, but required eighty-six other predominantly white, state-sponsored projects to institute affirmative action programs. The Reagan Justice Department quickly moved to challenge the agreement, however, charging that it continued to rely on an illegal quota system. A federal district court agreed, explaining that the Starrett City developers, "as private landlords, were not empowered to establish quotas limiting the number of apartments to be made available to eligible minority applicants, in disregard of the Fair Housing Act" (Husock 1990b, p. 1). The decision was subsequently upheld by a federal appeals court, by a 2 to 1 margin, and the Supreme Court declined to review the ruling.

The second race-conscious approach, affirmative marketing, has been more favorably received by the courts. Unlike quotas that bar black entry, affirmative marketing involves merely encouraging home seekers to consider areas in which their racial group is under-repre-sented. Several racially mixed, suburban communities support hous-ing centers that engage in this sort of "benign steering." In some cases, the housing centers are part of the municipal government. More typi-cally, they are non-profit organizations, supported by corporate con-tributions, foundation grants, and Community Development Block Grant funds.

Some of these organizations have aimed to persuade minorities to look for housing outside of their community altogether, in surround-ing, predominantly white suburban areas. The community relations committee of Calumet Park, Illinois, for instance, stated in a 1980 newsletter that the main purpose of the suburb's housing center was "to attract white prospective buyers and renters . . . and to assist mi-norities to locate housing in racially 'closed' villages to reverse steer-ing practices on the part of the real estate industry" (Lake and Wins-low 1981, p. 315). To take another example, the village of Park Forest South, Illinois, amended its fair housing ordinance to require realtors to develop plans to encourage the entry of racial groups that were un-der-represented in the community (in comparison to the Chicago met-ropolitan area as a whole). Given the racial composition of the village at the time, this policy effectively required local realtors to recruit whites. The policy did not last long, however, for the village ulti-mately repealed the ordinance in response to the protests of these realtors (*Harvard Law Review* 1980).

More often, communities have taken more subtle approaches. The housing office in Shaker Heights, Ohio, for instance, regards it as part of its mission to offer assistance to interested minority buyers in locat-ing new homes in their community. Given the office's aim to "foster stable and orderly integration," however, it will not show housing to minorities in specified "target neighborhoods" that have a disproportionate minority population (Lake and Winslow 1981, p. 316). The housing center in Oak Park has similar objectives, as reflected in the text of the card it gives clients: "The policy of the Oak Park Housing Center is to assist in stabilizing integration in the village. To this end, there will be encouragement of white clients to move into buildings or areas that are already integrated, and the encouragement of black clients to move into buildings or areas which are not substantially integrated. Listings will be provided in keeping with this policy, with the understanding that under both local and federal laws, all clients are free to pursue the housing of their choice" (Goodwin 1979, p. 174).

The legality of such benign steering has been approved by a federal appeals court. Reviewing a 1989 district court decision upholding the affirmative marketing activities of the South Suburban Housing Center in the Chicago area, the Court maintained that the affirmative marketing plan did not violate the Fair Housing Act, since it "does not exclude minorities from housing opportunities." "We see nothing wrong," the Court wrote, "[in] attempting to attract white persons to housing opportunities they might not ordinarily know about and thus choose to pursue" (*South Suburban Housing Center* 1991).

The final race-conscious policy tool on the list takes such encouragement a step further, and actually provides financial incentives to home buyers willing to make pro-integrative moves. In the 1960s and 1970s, a few non-profits began small-scale efforts to provide such subsidies. In 1960, for instance, neighborhood groups in Shaker Heights began making loans to white home buyers on a small scale. The Fund for an Open Society in Philadelphia, meanwhile, began in 1978 to subsidize the movement of black households into predominantly white areas. The first fund to be directly supported by a local government was established by the city of Shaker Heights in 1986. This program offers low-interest loans of $3,000 to $6,000 to home buyers making pro-integrative moves within their community, and unlike its predecessors, is open to both blacks and whites. Still, the vast majority of the over one hundred loans awarded have gone to white buyers (Chandler 1992). There is some evidence that the program has been effective. According to one econometric analysis, it has increased the probability that white home purchasers will buy in integrated areas of Shaker Heights (Cromwell 1990).

The Shaker Heights program was, of course, limited in what it could achieve, since its influence could not really extend beyond its own borders. Thus, the regional program sponsored by the Ohio Housing Finance Agency promised to be more effective. The program was initiated in response to charges that the agency's loans had been contributing to racial segregation. According to the terms of the program, the agency would set aside 10 percent of the Cuyahoga County share of state low-interest-mortgage revenue bond funds for pro-integrative moves throughout the county (later extended to the full Cleveland metropolitan area and a few other metropolitan areas in Ohio).[6] To be eligible, white home buyers would be required to purchase homes in school districts that were more than 50 percent black, and black home buyers would be required to purchase homes in school districts that were less than 25 percent black (Husock 1989).[7] The impact of this program has not been definitively studied. But one preliminary analysis suggested that it did not alter the residential patterns of the overall region, since participants were overwhelmingly moving to Shaker Heights and two other nearby suburbs that had been engaged in affirmative marketing efforts for years (Chandler 1992).

Wisconsin has launched the only other state-supported program to provide mortgage incentives. As part of a 1987 settlement to a school segregation suit, the state agreed to set aside a $5 million pool to provide low-interest mortgages to home buyers making pro-integrative moves in the Milwaukee metropolitan area.

Policies for the Future

As discussed, there is certainly a case for concern about racial transition, and at least a modest case to be made for carefully tailored government interventions. This section explores the policies described above in more detail, analyzing which policies are more or less carefully tailored in light of the book's findings.

Before discussing particular policy options, however, it is worth noting a few general criteria suggested by this and the previous chapters. First, for obvious reasons, policies that restrict people's freedom to live where they want should be avoided. There are ample promising strategies that are not coercive in this way; they rely instead on information and incentives to promote integration. Similarly, race-neutral policies are preferable to race-conscious ones, for, among other reasons, race-neutral policies generally aim to benefit both whites and blacks (while promoting integration). It is also worth noting that, as a legal matter, race-neutral policies are probably more sustainable than those that explicitly take race into account. Courts apply strict scrutiny to policies using race as a classification, and approve such policies only in special circumstances and when it can be demonstrated that more race-neutral efforts cannot work.

Third, integration maintenance efforts are likely to be more promising if they target the entry decision, a decision shown earlier to be considerably more sensitive to racial composition and more critical to long-run stability than the choice whether to remain in or leave a particular community. In crude terms, the focus should be on strengthening white demand for integrated communities, rather than on forestalling white flight from such communities.

Finally, the results from the previous chapters suggest that a critical element in promoting integration is addressing whites' fears about community decline. In this regard, decisions about expenditures on public services may be communities' most powerful tool for promoting integration.

One set of policies that meets all of the above criteria is community betterment projects. These are non-coercive, race-neutral efforts that aim at strengthening white demand by improving the community. To be sure, major community betterment projects—especially capital projects such as the construction of a new school building—are obviously quite costly and need to be justified on their own merits. Still, in close cases, when it is not clear whether such projects are worthwhile, a community might want to take into account the positive effects that the investment is likely to have on neighborhood racial stability. And of course, more modest and inexpensive betterment projects like playground maintenance can be justified more easily.

Along similar lines, the recent apparent successes of New York City and other cities in reducing crime rates are noteworthy. New York City's "broken windows" strategy of targeting low-level crime may be particularly helpful, and not simply in reducing actual crime. For it may be precisely these small signs of disorder that signal that a community is not merely changing its racial mix but also slipping out of control. Similarly, establishing neighborhood watch programs or community policing initiatives may be effective. Such visible signs of safety will help to bolster residents' sense of control over their communities, as well as make neighborhoods more attractive to outsiders.

It is critical, however, that these efforts are undertaken carefully and in cooperation with the selected communities. Aggressively targeting small problems in the way that the New York Police Department has done runs the risk of increasing police-community tensions.[8] In addition, both blacks and whites must be actively engaged in any law enforcement efforts, so that they are not perceived as racially motivated or biased. Given the long history of harassment, blacks tend to view law enforcement officials with ambivalence. Even middle-class blacks—particularly men—commonly believe that they have more to fear from the police than to gain, because they know that race is often used as mark of suspicion.[9] To black Americans (and particularly, black American males), the police are "the most prominent reminder of his second class citizenship," as one former police officer has put it (Kennedy 1997, p. 152). Thus, community safety efforts must be especially careful to involve and gain support from African Americans. If not, as one racially mixed community in northern Florida learned, these efforts run the risk of alienating black residents. That community established a citizens' patrol program in the late 1980s to counter fears about growing crime. But all of the volunteers were white and so, not surprisingly, the patrols were scorned by black residents in the community, who came to view them as a vehicle for harassing local blacks. If anything, the patrols served to fuel racial tensions (Boyum 1990).

Although bolstering the quality of local schools is perhaps harder (and more expensive), it is possibly even more important for racial integration, given that families with children, and particularly those with children in public school, are most averse to racial mixing. In this regard, one effective strategy for a mixed neighborhood might be to try to persuade state and county officials to place a magnet school in the community. The experience of Prince Georges County, however, suggests that the presence of such schools may not prove to be sufficient; whites in this suburban county have all but withdrawn from even magnet schools located in substantially integrated areas.

Another possibility is to introduce school choice, at least within the public school system. For if it is true, as this research suggests, that much of white resistance to neighborhood integration is rooted in fear about the quality of integrated schools, then breaking the link between residence and school should make white households much more open to living in racially diverse environments. Of course, this strategy is only relevant for larger areas, with multiple schools, and is best implemented at a broader scale (see later in this chapter). Even in large municipalities, white households have all but disappeared from the public school system. Consider the case of Detroit. In the 1996–1997 school year, over 90 percent of the city's public school population was minority (Orfield and Yun 1999). In this context, allowing for school choice will clearly do little to help integrate neighborhoods.

Investments aimed at safety and education are not the only community betterment projects that are likely to help stabilize racial mixing. Improvements to the physical appearance of a community—from restoring local playgrounds, to cleaning up commercial strips, to fixing Wilson and Kelling's "broken windows"—are likely to be effective as well, for visible signs of decline can significantly undermine people's faith in a neighborhood's strength. Less tangible but potentially important are general community-building efforts. Although the data used in this book cannot speak to the impact of local community groups, the findings suggest that community confidence and expectations are key to racial stability. And such groups, by building social capital, can help to foster commitment to a neighborhood and faith in its future. Moreover, if both whites and minorities are actively involved, these community groups can help to support just the sort of social interaction that builds mutual trust and may even, as discussed above, help dissolve racial prejudice.

Such projects are naturally less useful if nobody, especially prospective residents, knows about them. Thus, publicizing major investments and more generally advertising a community's strengths—its housing stock, parks, community solidarity—can be important too. Such public relations campaigns are directly aimed at countering people's perceptions that racially integrated communities are inherently unstable, deteriorating, and unsafe. Furthermore, these public relations efforts are primarily addressed at those outside of the community, and thus target the entry decision.

One of the more ambitious policies that might be effective is the establishment of a national equity insurance program for homeowners across the country. Some economists have attempted to develop such a program (Harney 1994). The idea is to allow homeowners to insulate themselves against all declines in the market value of their homes and thus make the housing market more efficient.[10] To the extent that white homeowners resist racial integration because of fears about declining equity, such a program would also support racial mixing. Under one variant, the federal government would not actually provide this insurance, but rather would play a key facilitating role in setting up the rules for such a market—deciding premiums, for instance, and the procedure for evaluating claims.

But although such an insurance program represents a potentially promising approach when implemented at a broad level, the example of Chicago shows that such a proposal, when offered at the local level, may prove offensive to minority groups. In the late 1980s, a proposal to institute an equity insurance program in several Chicago neighborhoods was quickly labeled "black insurance" and generated heated opposition from African-American politicians who viewed it as an official statement that blacks lower property values (Lieber 1990). After a racially divisive debate, the proposal was narrowly passed by the city council and then vetoed by acting mayor Eugene Sawyer. At the national level, because it is not specifically targeted at racial change, the program would probably not encounter the same resistance.

Finally, affirmative marketing and incentive programs—though race conscious—are potentially effective. One key point to emphasize is that despite being race conscious, these proposals do not directly limit minority choice. And so long as they include incentives to encourage black households to move into all-white areas, they should not prove objectionable to minorities.[11] Significantly, such efforts are likely to be far more promising when undertaken not at the level of the individual neighborhood or suburban town, but rather at the level of the metropolitan area. For when covering a broader geographic area, a program can obviously offer more alternatives to households and have a more significant impact on residential patterns. By this reasoning, such affirmative marketing programs would be most effective if operated at the national level so that white households in almost exclusively white Salt Lake City, for example, can be informed about housing options in the black District of Columbia (and vice versa). Encouraging people to make such long distance moves, however, is simply not realistic and arguably not desirable.

As suggested earlier, there may be a certain wisdom in pairing affirmative marketing proposals designed to encourage white households to consider racially integrated communities with efforts to encourage black households to move into all-white areas.[12] In the long run, such a two-pronged approach is likely to be more effective, since a reduction in the number of totally white areas may itself help to promote the stability of racial mixing elsewhere, as white households will have fewer all-white suburban enclaves to move to. Moreover, a single integrated community that is "advertising" for whites runs the risk of sending a message that there is something wrong with predominantly black communities. Consider the protest of one black resident in Matteson, Illinois, when her town launched a marketing campaign aimed at recruiting whites: "They're saying that white is stability and black is liability. It's degrading" (Terry 1996).

Such policies are also likely to be more effective if they recognize the nature and source of both black and white fears. Efforts to attract blacks should be careful to make families feel welcome and safe in their new communities. And attempts to attract whites are likely to be more productive when accompanied by the kinds of community betterment and public relations campaigns described earlier and by careful efforts to calm the fears of potential white home buyers—even if these fears are irrational and based on prejudice.

I should also add here that some of the other factors discussed in earlier chapters are still highly relevant—for example, the fact that racial mixing is more tenable in areas farther away from central cities than in areas closer. Any efforts to promote racial mixing should also be initiated early. As suggested, expectations are key, and once a neighborhood is perceived by whites to be racially changing, bolstering white demand will be that much more difficult.

The subject of designing policies that promote integration cannot be concluded without a discussion of anti-discrimination efforts. While specific acts of housing discrimination may not be the chief cause of racial change in particular integrated communities, they do undeniably contribute to it. Such discrimination powerfully limits the ability of minorities to move into predominantly white areas and maintains all-white areas as an option to which whites can escape. And while the nature of discrimination may have changed somewhat over the last few decades, the best evidence suggests that it remains widespread. In particular, a national audit study sponsored by the U.S. Department of Housing and Urban Development in 1989 (and conducted by the Urban Institute and Syracuse University) suggests that discrimination by real estate agents did not diminish between 1977 and 1989 (Turner and Wienk 1993; Yinger 1995). Thus, continued government efforts to eradicate racial discrimination in housing sales, rentals, and lending are likely to promote integration.

Finally, policies promoting integration are not the province of local governments alone. Anti-discrimination efforts, for example, are most effectively focused at the state and federal levels. As for community betterment and affirmative marketing, while these strategies are probably more effective when implemented at the local or regional level, the federal government could obviously help by providing funding. Particular program features could be left up to individual recipients, subject only to a few limited restrictions such as on the use of legally questionable quota systems. And governments at all levels can certainly do their part in educating children to be racially tolerant; publicizing the existence of thriving and stable racially integrated communities; correcting negative stereotypes about people and neighborhoods; and providing visible support for the principle of racial integration. For as argued throughout this book, it is ultimately these negative, and often uninformed, attitudes that prove to be the greatest blocks to stable racially integrated communities.

It is important to note what is left out of this list of policies. It does not include bans on "For Sale" signs or restrictions on realtor solicitation. Because these policies are aimed largely at stemming white flight, they are not likely to be as effective as other, entry-focused strategies. They do little to change the image of the community in the eyes of outsiders, and indeed may even contribute to general negative perceptions. Moreover, as discussed above, these regulations are particularly vulnerable to legal challenges under the First Amendment.

Quotas are also omitted. Why? First, because such restrictions do indeed limit minority housing options, even ardent pro-integrationists should feel uneasy from a racial justice perspective. Second, the Starrett City decision and the recent Supreme Court decisions regarding racial distinctions in government contracting and the designation of voting districts suggest that the courts would not look favorably upon a program that specifically set a ceiling on the number of minorities allowed in a community. Lastly, the empirical evidence detailed earlier suggests that such specific quotas are probably not very useful. Specifically, the results here suggest that there is no set level, or quota, of black representation beyond which whites will be unwilling to live in an area. Instead, the maximum percentage of minorities that whites will feel comfortable living with varies depending on the particular situation of the community and the circumstance of the households.

Finally it is critical for policymakers to recognize how various governmental policies entirely unrelated to race can sometimes influence the racial makeup of urban and suburban communities. For example, since the evidence presented here suggests that homeowners are more averse to racial mixing than renters, government programs that promote homeownership may actually exacerbate segregation. The largest such program is the federal subsidy for homeownership provided through the mortgage interest income-tax deduction, which amounts to some $60 billion every year (U.S. Congress 1999).

At the close of Chapter 1, the point was made that the true portrait of America's neighborhoods, while far from depicting a color-blind society, tells a more optimistic and dynamic story than has been told of late. In short, there is a substantial and increasing minority of neighborhoods that are currently integrated and likely to stay that way for many years. Further, the racial transition that does take place seems to have more to do with negative neighborhood stereotyping than with other, more disturbing causes such as racial hatred. Policymakers who take account of these points will be better equipped to devise sound policies that foster racial integration, or at least better able to avoid unwittingly undermining it.

Notes

References

Index

Notes

2. The Extent and Stability of Racial Integration

1. In 1990, 12 percent of the total U.S. population was black. But 13 percent of the population living in metropolitan areas was black (U.S. Bureau of the Census 1990).

2. This method fails to distinguish between blacks replacing whites and Hispanics replacing whites. Yet it seems more compatible with theories of racial change, which typically focus on white household behavior in the face of racial mixing.

3. Perhaps the most critical limitation is the fact that the 1970 Census did not ask all households whether or not they were of Spanish origin. Thus, while it is possible to get good estimates of the black and white populations in 1970, it is not possible to separate Hispanics from these two categories. Another issue is that it is easier to shift 1990 tracts back to 1980 boundaries than it is to shift 1970 tracts up to 1980 boundaries (see discussion of Underclass Data Base in text).

4. The figures in Table 2.3 reflect the share of total whites, including Hispanics, since the 1970 data do not have reliable information on Hispanic origin. Using the total white population does not seem to distort the results much, however. In 1980 and 1990, the proportions of total whites and blacks living in neighborhoods of differing racial mix are almost identical to the proportions of non-Hispanic whites and blacks living there.

5. While the percentage of blacks living in metropolitan areas increased slightly over this period, the increase was far too small to account for this rise in the number of integrated neighborhoods. Between 1980 and 1990, the proportion of blacks rose by 0.3 percentage points, or 2.4 percent (U.S. Bureau of the Census 1980; U.S. Bureau of the Census 1990).

6. Because, as noted already, Hispanics cannot be reliably identified in the 1970 Census, the figures cited here refer to changes in the total white population. (As a result, they differ somewhat from the figures cited earlier for non-Hispanic whites.)

7. Calculations from Tables 25 and 26 of their book suggest that 18.8 percent of census tracts that initially have at least 250 non-whites (but in which less than 90 percent of the population is non-white) failed to gain a significant number of black residents between 1940 and 1950, compared with only 9.0 percent between 1950 and 1960.

8. In an all white tract, the proportion of residents classified as "black" or "other" is less than 10 percent. In a predominantly black or other tract, the minority group in question represents a majority of the population, while the remaining minority group represents less than 10 percent. In the mixed white and minority tracts, the minority group represents between 10 and 50 percent of the population, while the remaining minority group represents less than 10 percent. In the mixed black and other tracts, the black and other minority group populations each represent at least 10 percent of the total population, while non-Hispanic whites represent less than 40 percent. Finally, in the mixed multiethnic communities, the black and other minority group populations each represent at least 10 percent of the population, while non-Hispanic whites represent at least 40 percent.

9. This is consistent with some prior empirical work (e.g., Denton and Massey 1991), but it runs sharply counter to the hypothesis that non-black minorities provide a buffer in inter-racial environments, making whites more willing and comfortable to live among blacks (Farley and Frey 1994).

10. When weighting by population, the mean dissimilarity index is somewhat higher: 72.7.

11. Their sample includes 211 metropolitan areas in 1970, 284 in 1980, and 313 in 1990.

12. It is also true that the dissimilarity index tends to underestimate shifts over time, because it does not change in response to population shifts across neighborhoods that are above or below the average racial composition (see Schnare 1980). Thus, we would not expect increases in the stability of integrated neighborhoods—even significant shifts—to necessarily be reflected in the dissimilarity index.

3. Toward a Theory of Racial Change

1. The four Northern cities include Detroit, Cleveland, Philadelphia, and St. Louis. The definitions used by Taeuber and Taeuber differ from those in this study. They define a mixed tract as one in which there are at least 250 non-whites, but in which the percentage of non-whites is less than 90 percent. The percentages reported here also exclude mixed tracts that were stable or gained white population. But these tracts amounted to a very small share of the communities they examine.

2. Consistent with popular belief, Levine and Harmon maintain that the BBURG line covered basically the entirety of Boston's Jewish community. (Some argue that this Jewish area was no longer profitable to the banks, because so many of the residents had paid off their mortgages. Others maintain that the Jews were considered more willing to accept blacks than either of Boston's two other major ethnic groups—the Italians and Irish.) But in his careful historical analysis, Gamm (1999) demonstrates that in fact about half of those living within the BBURG line were white Catholics. He thus argues that BBURG clearly did not cause the rapid Jewish exodus from Mattapan. Nonetheless, if most *believed* that the line covered the Jewish area, BBURG still may have been an important force contributing to the loss of the Jewish population.

3. Yinger's "Prejudice and Discrimination in Urban Housing Markets" (1979) provides a good summary of the different types of economic models that describe racial preferences.

4. Earlier works also offer economic models of racial transition based on the notion that whites dislike living near or among blacks (Bailey 1959; Muth 1969).

5. Such discrimination takes many forms, and Yinger (1995) usefully divides them into three broad categories. First, realtors may show or recommend fewer housing units to minority households than they have provided to equivalent white households. At the most blatant, realtors may feign that units are unavailable or even refuse to serve minority customers altogether. Second, minority households may be offered different terms and conditions—higher rents, larger security deposits, and so on. (More subtly, realtors may simply make less of an effort to complete transactions by, for instance, making fewer follow-up calls.) Similarly, lenders may offer minorities less favorable mortgage terms. The third form of discrimination is racial steering, or when a realtor directs or "steers" a customer toward neighborhoods in which his or her racial group is over-represented. A minority customer, that is, may only be shown homes in minority communities, even though plenty of homes in her price range are available in white areas and she has not voiced any preference for particular neighborhoods.

6. The comments made by realtors may also dissuade whites from moving into largely black areas. The Housing Discrimination Study found that when a neighborhood is largely black, white customers hear significantly more negative comments about the neighborhood than do blacks.

7. One might argue that this theory ultimately comes down to racial preferences. It is simply that some whites—those who belong to a particular ethnic group or those living in a tight-knit community, for instance, have a particularly strong preference for living among their own kind.

8. Gamm (1999) shows that at least in Boston, white Jewish neighborhoods lost white population much more rapidly than did white Catholic areas. As discussed in the next chapter, he attributes this greater solidarity of the Catholic population to fundamental differences in Catholic and Jewish institutions.

As discussed later, his argument—and emphasis on institutions—is ultimately very consistent with race-based neighborhood stereotyping.

9. Throughout this chapter, racial stereotypes that people hold and how people and households react to minority populations are discussed. For the most part, the emphasis is on white households and individuals. But because it is possible that some black households are also averse to neighborhoods with growing minority populations, "households" and "individuals" are often used to include both blacks and whites.

10. More recent studies suggest there may be a negative relationship between growing black populations and housing prices (Schnare 1976; Chambers 1992; Sander 1994). Kiel and Zabel (1995) find widely varying results in three different metropolitan areas. In an interesting study, Chambers (1992) finds no relationship between racial composition and housing prices. He does find, however, that house values decline in response to racial change and to location near to the central area of black residents. Rents are less sensitive. As will be shown in subsequent chapters, these results are consistent with the findings of this book.

11. Significantly, Kennedy also stresses that this discrimination may be rational, since young black men commit a disproportionate share of street crimes. As discussed in Chapter 1 and Chapter 8, the evidence concerning neighborhood stereotypes is less certain. On average, black neighborhoods are certainly of lower quality than white areas. But the differences if any, after controlling for income, are significantly diminished.

12. This study is certainly not the first to note the importance of white entry, at least to the long-run stability of neighborhoods. The Kerner Commission wrote in 1968 that "efforts to stop massive transition by persuading present white residents to remain will ultimately fail unless whites outside the neighborhood can be persuaded to move in" (National Advisory Commission on Civil Disorders 1968, p. 119).

13. Gamm (1999) and Sugrue (1996) both highlight the role of religious institutions, and in particular Catholic churches, in bolstering a neighborhood.

14. Paul Courant's search model shows how discrimination by just a few sellers in white neighborhoods can increase the search costs of black buyers and discourage them from even looking in these communities.

4. Correlates of Racial Stability

1. Rapkin and Grigsby (1960) find that the price and quality of the local housing stock are the critical factors (slow transition is linked on the one hand to expensive homes, which blacks cannot afford, and on the other to low-quality homes, for which financing is difficult to obtain). Grier and Grier (1960), meanwhile, find that the economic status of the minority population is most critical.

2. Rapkin and Grigsby (1960) also stress the importance of expectations, stat-

ing that the predictions of white families concerning the eventual racial mix of a neighborhood and their fear of possibly being outnumbered by minorities in a community might be "more significant than any other factor in determining the level of white demand (p. 118)." They do not, however, explore the further implications of this claim.

3. Gamm (1999) also argues persuasively that the actual structure of a Catholic church is a more sacred and permanent structure than a synagogue. In Jewish law, the Torah is holier than any synagogue structure, and Torah rolls are totally portable. Therefore, synagogues, unlike Catholic churches, were not viewed as very powerful anchors in their communities.

4. An index of segregationist sentiment is developed through a two-step process. First, Galster estimates a regression equation that models individual responses to questions about racial integration in a National Opinion Research Center survey as a function of a variety of demographic and socioeconomic dummy variables. He then uses these coefficients as weights that multiply the share of individuals in a tract with the relevant characteristic (for instance, percent with less than a high-school diploma or percent foreign born). The resulting index may be interpreted as the expected attitudes of the average individual in the tract.

5. Steinnes interprets this as a reflection of the greater mobility of the more affluent whites. Significantly, Steinnes distinguishes between factors that correlate with initial black entry into predominantly white communities and those that seem to accelerate the pace of change once minorities are present. He finds that higher median income and other neighborhood characteristics make it more likely that blacks will enter a particular tract in the first place, but that once blacks reach about 10 percent of the population, the variation in the rate of racial turnover is determined largely by the distance to the ghetto. The tipping model, that is, seems to be an accurate depiction of the course of racial change in racially mixed communities, which is precisely the change that this study aims to explain.

6. The difference may be explained by the fact that Denton and Massey (1991) include suburban neighborhoods in the analysis—and in these neighborhoods, underlying growth patterns may be more critical.

7. Denton and Massey (1991) study racial change in sixty metropolitan areas. Galster (1990b) examines racial change in neighborhoods in suburban and central city Cleveland.

8. See Chapter 2 for a list of the thirty-four metropolitan areas included.

9. As explained in Chapter 2, this measure treats a tract that moves from 90 to 89 percent non-Hispanic white as experiencing the same loss as one that moves from 10 to 9 percent. This latter change is arguably a more significant one, however, because the decline represents a larger share of the white population in that case, and moreover, because as the white population shrinks to a certain size, further declines might be considerably less likely. (Certain white residents, for instance, face inordinately high financial or psychological

moving costs.) Note that another potential problem with using the loss in percentage of white residents as a dependent variable is censoring. Because the ending proportion of non-Hispanic whites must fall between 0 and 100, the dependent variable is limited on both the top and bottom. The censoring problem is negligible in this sample, however, because only three census tracts in the sample actually fall at these extremes. Despite these limitations, as explained in Chapter 2, this alternative was viewed as preferable to other alternatives.

10. Denton and Massey (1991) use a third alternative to represent neighborhood racial change—the log of the ratio of the 1980 to the 1970 black population. But this metric does not control for the simultaneous growth in the white population. A doubling of the black population represents a very different kind of change in a tract in which the white population also doubles than in one in which the white population is constant. A fourth alternative is that used by White (1984): the logit of the black proportion in 1990. With this specification, additional increments in the independent variables are required to generate the same change in the percentage of black residents as this percentage approaches 0 or 100. This specification was estimated, and again the conclusions were much the same.

11. The dissimilarity index is used here to measure racial segregation. As mentioned in Chapter 2, it ranges from 0 to 100 and may be understood as the proportion of blacks who would have to move in order to achieve perfect integration (i.e., a world in which every neighborhood contains the same proportion of blacks).

12. A fixed effects model with dummy variables for each metropolitan area was also estimated to capture the many differences across metropolitan areas that might influence the pace of white loss. The results were nearly identical (Ellen 1996).

13. The spline regression constrains white loss to be equal at the endpoints of adjacent segments. See Greene (1993) for an explanation.

14. Neither the coefficients on the percent black variable nor any of those on the seven splines were statistically significant. The remaining coefficient estimates were virtually identical to those estimated in the regressions discussed earlier (Ellen 1996).

15. A different definition of Hispanics was used in the 1970 Census than in 1980 and 1990, and therefore it is not possible to assess changes in this population during the 1970s.

16. The model was also estimated with the white-black differential in these two measures, and the conclusions were the same—tracts are less likely to lose non-Hispanic white population when blacks are less educated and less affluent relative to whites. (The differential was defined as the percent of blacks attaining the status level—say, earning at least $25,000—subtracted from the share of whites attaining the same status level.)

17. It is possible that the growth in the black population is less important as a

driver of racial change simply because we are not seeing the kind of rapid growth that we did in many Northern cities in the 1950s and 1960s.

18. All of the other coefficients are largely the same when estimating this regression for the full set of metropolitan areas in the country.

19. One important difference, for instance, is that several of these other studies consider the universe of census tracts or communities in a given metropolitan area, rather than simply those that are racially mixed. This sample selection is likely to matter, with whites sensitive perhaps to changes in racial composition when the proportion of blacks is quite small. Yet even the prior studies that focus exclusively on racially mixed areas find that the initial black proportion matters. Another relevant difference is the inclusion here of a variable measuring recent change in racial composition.

20. Because of missing data, the sample is somewhat smaller here as well, covering just thirty-one metropolitan areas. (Census tracts in Chicago, Charlotte, and Milwaukee are omitted.)

21. In addition, the comparison model does not include the proportion of other minorities, the proportion of recent movers, and the proportion of blacks with some college education. Finally, rather than including particular characteristics of a metropolitan area, a fixed effects model is estimated for each decade that includes a dummy variable for each of the metropolitan areas in the sample.

22. The same result holds when considering the percent change in the proportion of white residents. In a regression of the percent loss in the proportion of whites on the same set of independent variables, the coefficient on the initial proportion of black residents was significantly different from zero in the 1970–1980 model but not in the 1980–1990 model.

23. This map and the others following were all constructed by the author by linking census tract data on racial composition taken from the Urban Institute's Underclass Data Base (UDB) to 1990 census tract boundary maps produced by MapInfo. Since the UDB data correspond to 1980 boundaries, conversions were made when necessary.

24. In Washington, D.C., this occurred in a section of the Catholic University campus, where the population of students and faculty appears to be largely white and the surrounding community is largely black.

25. Block-group data obtained from *1990 U.S. Census of Population and Housing*, CD-ROM. U.S. Bureau of the Census, 1990.

26. Most of the staff at Walter Reade actually live in a complex located just across the border in Maryland, but they are counted as living in D.C. for the purposes of the census.

27. The internal point is basically the centroid of the tract. When a tract's centroid falls outside of its boundaries, however, the Census Bureau defines the internal point as the point on the boundary closest to the centroid.

28. A weighted mean was also calculated that used the product of the poverty rate and the share of black residents in the tract as weights in order to ac-

count for the fact that people might have particularly negative associations with poor black neighborhoods. The resulting mean was located in almost the identical spot as the mean calculated using the black population in the tract as a weight.

29. At least part of the reason that blacks gravitated toward Prince Georges County was its relatively affordable housing. In 1984, the median sales price for all housing in Prince Georges County was $82,000, the lowest of all counties in the metropolitan area. The median price was $118,000 in Montgomery County and $124,000 in Fairfax County (Gale 1987, p. 127). Another reason may have been that realtors systematically steered blacks into the county.

5. Racial Composition and Neighborhood Satisfaction

1. Hedonic analysis of housing prices has also been used to measure household preferences for different neighborhood characteristics. In such hedonic models, the sale price or contract rent of a housing unit is regressed on variables describing the unit's characteristics—its number of bedrooms, its size, its age—as well as its neighborhood environment. In many cases, the coefficients of the neighborhood variables—including those for racial composition, crime, and school quality—have been insignificant or have displayed unexpected signs, suggesting that these neighborhood attributes may not be important to consumers. The problem with the hedonic approach, however, is that it measures the views of the marginal buyer, which may not be the same as those of the average household. If traffic is uncorrelated with housing prices, for instance, this indicates that the marginal consumer does not mind noise from traffic. It is still possible, however, that most people are in fact bothered by such noise.

2. The other study suggests that racial composition does matter to neighborhood rating (Boehm and Ihlanfeldt 1991). Their study is similar to this one in that it examines data from a version of the 1985 American Housing Study. Unlike the analysis here, however, this earlier study did not have access to data about households' actual neighborhoods. Thus they relied on reports from both the occupants and enumerators regarding services and particular problems in the neighborhood, such as crime, schools, noise, and litter. For a sub-sample of households, they also had information about a cluster of approximately ten of the household's neighbors. Their results suggest that many neighborhood attributes (crime, rundown housing, street noise, and litter) consistently influence household utility and that the race of one's neighbors matters to white and not black households. In particular, whites whose sample of neighbors is more than 75 percent white rank the quality of their neighborhoods higher than do other white households. As interesting as this study is, however, it does not have a measure of the racial composition of the overall neighborhood and it is not able to control for the objective indica-

tors of neighborhood quality that are included in the Harris study or in the analysis presented later in this chapter.

3. The inclusion of these non-racial determinants does reduce the magnitude of the effect of racial composition.

4. In addition to the national sample, the AHS selects a sample of households in forty-four major metropolitan areas and returns to each area about once every four years. This study, however, relies exclusively on the national survey.

5. The only geographic information available on the public use files of the national AHS is the metropolitan area.

6. Because the households are quite thinly spread across neighborhoods in my sample, there is little reason to worry about clustering and consequently little reason to employ hierarchical methods of estimation.

7. This interpretation follows from Boehm and Ihlanfeldt (1991), who also use a version of the American Housing Survey to study the determinants of neighborhood satisfaction. In an earlier paper, they show a link between changes in the AHS neighborhood quality rating and mobility decisions (Boehm and Ihlanfeldt 1986). Given the substantial costs of moving, they interpret these results as evidence that changes in the AHS neighborhood rating are linked to changes in individual household utility.

8. A continuous measure of income is not used because the effects are not necessarily linear. Low-income households, for instance, may also rate their neighborhoods more critically because they depend on them more for their services and social support.

9. This anomalous coefficient may be the result of insufficient variation in the data, and in particular the relatively high correlation between the change in the poverty rate, the poverty rate itself, and the growth in the black population.

10. Chambers (1992) finds a similar result concerning housing prices. His analysis of housing prices suggests that households respond less to gradations in racial composition than to the pace at which the neighborhood is undergoing racial change.

6. Race, Neighborhood, and the Decision to Move

1. The most influential sociological study of mobility patterns is probably Peter Rossi's Why Families Move (1955).

2. Wurdock (1981) uses the data from the first Detroit Area Survey to investigate whether the survey's conclusions hold up when certain key characteristics of the respondents, such as tenure, age, and income, are taken into account. He finds that even after controlling for these factors, racial composition remains a key factor behind mobility intentions, lending support to the conventional view that white flight plays an important role in accelerating neighborhood racial transition.

3. In surveys of households in Kansas City in 1982 and Cincinnati in 1978, the

share of whites expressing an intention to move out if their neighborhood became 40 percent black was 40 and 25 percent, respectively (Clark 1986). Although they represent significant proportions of the white population, all of these figures are under the threshold beyond which the neighborhood would inevitably unravel.

4. The two other cities where households surveys were undertaken—Kansas City and Cincinnati—are also highly segregated, Midwestern cities (though not as segregated as Detroit). The views of households in these cities may therefore be similarly non-representative.

5. The findings of the Wilson study (1983) are actually mixed. He finds elevated mobility rates only for those tracts that would have been predicted to have low turnover.

6. Again, the households in the sample are spread quite thinly across census tracts. Accordingly, there is little reason to worry about clustering in the data here (and little need for hierarchical modeling).

7. Although *changes* in the family situation should in fact drive mobility, most authors include level variables instead (again, this is probably because of data issues). For many variables, the levels might be considered as proxies for changes. A household with young children, for instance, has recently experienced a growth in household size. The mobility models in this chapter were estimated using both levels and changes. The changes were surprisingly insignificant and since including them requires using a smaller and potentially biased sample—households remaining in their homes between 1985 and 1989—the chapter focuses on the level variable results instead.

8. Additionally, I estimated a regression that included dummy variables for each of the metropolitan areas in the sample. The results were essentially the same.

9. As mentioned, for instance, a fixed effects regression was estimated with dummy variables included for each metropolitan area in the sample. Several additional specifications are also discussed in the chapter, although the full results are not shown.

10. This is particularly significant given that both inter-metropolitan and intra-neighborhood moves are probably included in the data set, moves for which community context is unlikely to play a decisive role. As a result, the data is to some degree biased against finding any neighborhood effects.

11. The coefficient on the proportion of professional workers is negative and significant in two cases for black households, perhaps reflecting a preference for higher-status neighborhoods. By contrast, the coefficient on the proportion of professional workers in the tract is *positive* and significant in both years for white homeowners. But rather than indicating any aversion to communities with large shares of professionals, this probably reflects the fact that professional workers tend to live among other professionals and that professionals tend to be more mobile. Since more whites than blacks work in professional occupations, this effect is more apparent in the white household regressions.

12. There is some possibility that the growth in the black population is endogenous in the 1985–1989 model, since if a greater number of white households moved out during these years, it would have enabled the black population to increase more rapidly. But the positive coefficient on the change in the percentage of blacks cannot merely reflect the fact that the departure of whites opened up homes for black households, for then the coefficient would be just as significant in the white renter model. Additionally, the coefficient is positive and statistically significant at the 10 percent level in the 1989–1993 model, where the change in the percentage of blacks reflects the growth that occurred in the black population between 1980 and 1990—basically, the *previous* decade.

13. None of the coefficients on these specifically black socioeconomic status (SES) variables were statistically significant, and the estimated effect of the growth in the black population on white household mobility was essentially unchanged when these variables were included.

14. This argument of course underscores the importance of including *changes* in racial composition in any model of mobility, a variable that earlier studies have omitted.

15. Several studies have found that owners often overvalue their homes (e.g., Kain and Quigley 1972, Follain and Malpezzi 1980, DiPasquale and Somerville 1995, Kiel and Zabel 1995). But since there does not seem to be any correlation between the magnitude of overvaluation and particular occupant, housing, or neighborhood characteristics (with the exception of length of tenure), the use of owners' valuations may still be a reasonable proxy.

16. Moreover, the effect of black growth on reported housing values may not be linear and therefore not apparent.

17. To keep valuation consistent, the sample is limited to households that remained in place between 1985 and 1989.

7. Racial Composition and Neighborhood Choice

1. When reporting the racial composition of these hypothetical neighborhoods, it is not clear whether to report the racial percentages that exist as the respondent considers the neighborhoods—the share of blacks, that is, among the fourteen existing households, or the proportion that would be present *after* the respondent moves in. Because these studies report the latter percentages, the same is done in Table 7.1. Arguably, however, the former approach is more accurate, and the black proportions listed in table should be somewhat higher—7 percent, 21 percent, 36 percent, and 57 percent.

2. This analysis assumes that "mostly white" means 90 percent white.

3. In this survey, 35 percent of whites report that 50–50 neighborhoods are optimal, and 49 percent chose the county pattern of 75 percent white.

4. Although the degree of violence is less than it was a few decades ago, blacks moving into largely white neighborhoods still encounter hateful words and

acts of hostility (DeParle 1993; Fletcher 1996; Belkin 1999, pp. 208, 251; Ferguson 1999; Goldberg 1999).

5. In the Detroit Area Survey results from the 1990s, the top choice among blacks is not half black, as it was in the 1976 survey, but closer to two-thirds black.

6. Theoretically a household could choose any neighborhood in any metropolitan area, but it seems fair to presume that households first select the metropolitan area to live in (due to family and job concerns), and then choose their neighborhood.

7. In particular, a nested logit model is used, where household choice is divided into three stages—the choice of town, the choice of neighborhood given town, and the choice of dwelling given neighborhood and town.

8. This figure is not actually reported in the study. It is generated, however, using data included in the paper. Specifically, it is the ratio of the actual proportion of black-vacated units turning over to white households, and the expected number, based on the total numbers of black and white in-movers over the period.

9. Evidence from Rosenbaum's study and others suggests that Puerto Ricans are unique among Hispanic groups in their separation from whites. In addition, many Puerto Ricans classify themselves as black.

10. As for where turnovers occur, the New York City analysis is able to offer somewhat more insight than the earlier studies, since the HVS identifies the "sub-borough" in which each housing unit is located. These "sub-boroughs" are groups of neighborhoods that typically house about 100,000 people. (In other words, they are approximately twenty-five times as large as the census tracts used for this study.) The results suggest that white-to-black turnovers are most likely to occur in the sub-boroughs with more minorities, and black-to-white turnovers in predominantly white areas. Interestingly, the racial composition of the sub-borough is not a very good predictor of whether a minority occupied unit will turn over to an occupant of the same minority group or another. Finally, Rosenbaum also reports that turnover probabilities are unaffected by housing and neighborhood quality, but these results are not shown.

11. DiPasquale and Kahn (1995) find that the average black household lives in a community with a significantly lower quality of life than does the average white. As their income increases, black households are more likely to live in higher-quality environments, though they never attain the same community quality that whites enjoy.

12. Units that were occupied in 1989 but vacant in 1993 are omitted from the analysis.

13. The tenure of the in-moving household defines the tenure of the unit. If a household vacates the home that they own but a renter moves in, for instance, the unit is considered a rental. Few units in fact undergo such "tenure switches," and the results are virtually identical when these units are omitted.

14. These earlier studies do not consider separately owners and renters, thus the

results here must be aggregated. And to make the present figures comparable to the national studies undertaken in the 1970s, we must classify non-black minorities as black or white, since these earlier studies did not separately consider Asians and Hispanics. To accomplish this, I chose to omit Asians and other racial groups and classify white Hispanics as white.

15. This approach is also taken by Ottensmann, Good, and Gleeson 1990.

16. A spline function is again used here. For tracts that are less than 10 percent black, the effect of an increase in percentage black is estimated by the coefficient on the percent black variable. For those between 10 and 50 percent black, the effect is estimated by the sum of the coefficient on percent black and the coefficient on spline 1. Finally, for majority black tracts, the effect of added black representation is estimated by the sum of the coefficients on percent black, spline 1, and spline 2.

17. Significantly, a specification was again run that included dummy variables for every metropolitan area in the sample. The idea was to account for unobserved differences in metropolitan areas that might make racial turnover more likely in certain areas. The results are not shown here because they were virtually identical.

18. For majority black tracts, the effect again becomes positive—since the effect of added black representation for these tracts is estimated by the sum of the coefficients on percent black, spline 1, and spline 2.

19. All other variables are assumed to take on mean values. The one exception is recent growth in the black population, which is assumed to be zero.

20. To some extent, of course, the sudden kinks at 10 and 50 percent black are driven by the methodology here, which allows the curve to bend only at these points. These points are used to be consistent with our definition of racial integration. Additional spline points were tested, however, and not found to be statistically significant.

21. This possibility is to some degree undermined by the analysis of block-group data in Chapter 4, which suggests that most block-groups within integrated tracts are themselves racially integrated.

22. Using a chi-squared test, the null hypothesis that the coefficients are the same across the two samples is rejected.

23. For average unit and neighborhood characteristics, the partial derivative of the probability of black entry in 1993 with respect to black population growth between 1970 and 1980 is .0047 in the case of owner-occupied units and .0016 in the case of rental units.

8. Conclusions and Policy Implications

1. Orfield (1997) makes a persuasive case that these suburbs are in fact even more vulnerable than central cities, which receive substantial tax revenues from central business districts and have greater experience in addressing social problems.

2. See Ellen and Turner 1997 for a review of these studies.

3. Many of these studies have unfortunately been cross-sectional and therefore cannot determine if contact actually affects prejudice. But a few recent studies that attempt to sort out the causality have found evidence that intergroup contact does tend to reduce prejudice (Sigelman and Welch 1993; Ellison and Powers 1994; Wilson 1996).

4. Patterson (1997) questions the importance of residential integration, arguing that workplace integration may in fact be far more critical to producing relationships and such inter-racial contact. But two recent studies suggest that residence in integrated neighborhoods does shape the nature of people's contacts and leads to greater inter-racial contact and friendships (Rosenbaum et al. 1991; Sigelman et al. 1996).

5. Wilson and Kelling cite a study by Philip Zimbardo. Zimbardo left one abandoned car on the street in the Bronx and another on a street in Palo Alto. The car in the Bronx was attacked within ten minutes, while the car left in Palo Alto was left untouched. When he smashed part of the Palo Alto car with a sledgehammer, however, it was completely destroyed within hours.

6. Because of opposition from black real estate interests and one fair housing group, the state agreed to simultaneously sponsor an independent set-aside program that offered low-interest loans to minority home buyers without any restrictions on the location of their moves (Chandler 1992).

7. Initially, white home buyers could receive loans if they moved into census tracts that were more than 40 percent black, and blacks were eligible if they moved into tracts that were less than 10 percent black. But in response to opposition from black leaders who charged that "bribing" whites to move into a 40 percent black community was demeaning to minorities, the state increased the black percentages defining the eligible communities. At the same time, however, the program switched to using school district rather than census tract boundaries. This means that the eligible areas may have been left largely intact, since the share of blacks attending local schools tends to be greater than the share living in a community overall (both because black households generally have more children and because their children more commonly attend public school).

8. Mayor Giuliani's relations with minority groups has clearly been strained by his aggressive policing strategy (Siegel 1999). But certainly such efforts to target low-level crime are not inherently destined to mistreat and anger minority groups. Surely the administration could make a better effort to work with local communities without jeopardizing the key facets of its strategy.

9. Consider that in April 1999, New Jersey officials admitted that state police had unfairly singled out minority drivers (Peterson 1999).

10. Like the school choice option, which decouples public school enrollment from residential location, this would help to insulate a homeowner's equity investment from the residential environment. In both cases, the argument is that white households will become more open to racial mixing when these other factors are de-linked from residential location. (At the extreme, these

policies would make white homeowners with children in public school behave a little bit more like renters with children in private school.)

11. Of course, as suggested above by the case of Ohio, there is an issue about how to define largely white and largely black areas. At what level of black representation should whites be given incentives to move into the community? At what racial mix should blacks be offered incentives to move in? The Ohio Housing Finance Agency encountered considerable resistance in making these determinations (Husock 1989).

12. Surveys of racial preference suggest that many African Americans are understandably not comfortable being the very first of their group to join an all-white community. But the degree of minority presence required for most blacks to be willing to move into such communities appears to be quite low, and the results in Chapter 2 show that few neighborhoods remain totally white. In any case, the barriers to getting blacks to consider largely white areas are likely to be much smaller than those to getting whites to consider substantially integrated areas. Indeed, the more formidable barriers to getting blacks into all-white areas are likely to be white, not black, attitudes.

References

Aaronson, Daniel. 1997. "Sibling Estimates of Neighborhood Effects." In Jeanne Brooks-Gunn, Greg Duncan, and Lawrence Aber, eds., *Neighborhood Poverty: Policy Implications in Studying Neighborhoods,* pp. 80–93. New York: Russell Sage Foundation Press.

Abrams, Charles. 1947. *Race Bias in Housing.* New York: American Civil Liberties Union.

——— 1955. *Forbidden Neighbors: A Study of Prejudice in Housing.* New York: Harper & Row.

Alba, Richard D. 1990. *Ethnic Identity.* New Haven: Yale University Press.

Alba, Richard D., and John R. Logan. 1993. "Minority Proximity to Whites in Suburbs: An Individual-Level Analysis of Segregation." *American Journal of Sociology* 98:1388–1427.

Albrecht, Don E., and Sean-Shong Hwang. 1991. "Neighborhood Selection and Residential Segregation." *Sociological Inquiry* 61:199–218.

Aldrich, Howard. 1975. "Ecological Succession in Racially Changing Neighborhoods: A Review of the Literature." *Urban Affairs Quarterly* 10:327–348.

Allport, Gordon. 1954. *The Nature of Prejudice.* New York: Doubleday Anchor.

Altshuler, Alan. 1970. *Community Control: The Black Demand for Participation in Large American Cities.* New York: Pegasus.

Anas, Alex. 1980. "A Model of Residential Change and Neighborhood Tipping." *Journal of Urban Economics* 7:358–370.

Anderson, Elijah. 1985. "Race and Neighborhood Transition." In Paul E. Peterson, ed., *The New Urban Reality,* pp. 99–127. Washington, D.C.: The Urban Institute Press.

——— 1990. *Streetwise: Race, Class, and Change in an Urban Community.* Chicago: University of Chicago Press.

Apgar, William C., and Henry O. Pollakowski. 1986. "Housing Mobility and Choice." Working Paper W86–6. Cambridge, Mass.: Joint Center for Housing Studies of MIT and Harvard University.

Bailey, Martin. 1959. "Note on the Economics of Residential Zoning and Urban Renewal." *Land Economics* 35:288–292.

Bartik, Timothy, J. S. Butler, and Jin-Tan Liu. 1992. "Maximum Score Estimates of the Determinants of Residential Mobility: Implications for the Value of Residential Attachment and Neighborhood Amenities." *Journal of Urban Economics* 32:233–256.

Bartik, Timothy, and V. Kerry Smith. 1987. "Urban Amenities and Public Policy." In Edwin S. Mills, ed., *Handbook of Regional and Urban Economics*, vol. 2, pp. 1207–1254. Amsterdam: North-Holland.

Becker, Gary. 1971. *The Economics of Discrimination.* Chicago: University of Chicago Press.

Belkin, Lisa. 1999. *Show Me a Hero: A Tale of Murder, Suicide, Race, and Redemption.* Boston: Little, Brown & Co.

Bell, David. 1982. "Regret in Decision Making under Uncertainty." *Operations Research* 30:961–981.

Berry, Brian J. 1976. "Ghetto Expansion and Single-Family Home Prices: Chicago, 1968–1972." *Journal of Urban Economics* 3:397–423.

Berry, Brian J., Carole Goodwin, Robert W. Lake, and Katherine B. Smith. 1976. "Attitudes toward Integration: The Role of Status in Community Response to Racial Change." In Barry Schwartz, ed., *The Changing Face of the Suburbs,* pp. 221–264. Chicago: University of Chicago Press.

Berry, Brian J., and John D. Kasarda. 1977. *Contemporary Urban Ecology.* New York: Macmillan Co.

Berry, Jeffrey, Kent Portney, and Ken Thomson. 1993. *The Rebirth of Urban Democracy.* Washington, D.C.: The Brookings Institution.

Birch, David L., Eric S. Brown, Richard P. Coleman, Dolores W. Da Lomba, William L. Parsons, Linda C. Sharpe, and Sheryll A. Weber. 1977. "The Behavioral Foundations of Neighborhood Change." Cambridge, Mass.: Joint Center for Urban Studies of MIT and Harvard University.

Bobo, Lawrence, Howard Schuman, and Charlotte Steeh. 1986. "Changing Racial Attitudes toward Residential Integration." In John M. Goering, ed., *Housing Desegregation and Federal Policy,* pp. 152–169. Chapel Hill: University of North Carolina Press.

Bobo, Lawrence, and Camille Zubrinsky. 1996. "Attitudes on Residential Integration: Perceived Status Differences, Mere In-Group Preference, or Racial Prejudice?" *Social Forces* 74:883–909.

Boehm, Thomas P. 1984. "Inflation and Intra-Urban Residential Mobility." *Housing Finance Review* 3:19–37.

Boehm, Thomas, and Keith Ihlanfeldt. 1986. "Residential Mobility and Neighborhood Quality." *Journal of Regional Science* 26:411–424.

——— 1991. "The Revelation of Neighborhood Preferences: An N-Chotomous Multivariate Probit Approach." *Journal of Housing Economics* 1:33–59.

Boehm, Thomas, and Jonathan Mark. 1980. "A Principal Component Logistic Analysis of the Mobility Decision in Transitional Neighborhoods." *AREUEA Journal* 8:299–319.

Bond, Eric W., and N. Edward Coulson. 1989. "Externalities, Filtering, and Neighborhood Change." *Journal of Urban Economics* 26:566–589.

Borjas, George. 1994. "Ethnicity, Neighborhoods, and Human Capital Externalities." Cambridge, Mass.: National Bureau of Economic Research.

Boyum, Ingrid. 1990. "Springfield Revitalization Strategy." Kennedy School case C96-90-1012. Kennedy School Case Program, Harvard University, 1990.

Bradburn, Norman, Seymour Sudman, and Galen Gockel. 1971. *Side by Side: Integrated Neighborhoods in America.* Chicago: Quadrangle Books.

Bradford, David, and Harry Kelejian. 1973. "An Econometric Model of Flight to the Suburbs." *Journal of Political Economy* 81:566–589.

Brooks, Roy L. 1996. *Integration or Separation? A Strategy for Racial Equality.* Cambridge, Mass.: Harvard University Press.

Brooks-Gunn, Jeanne, et al. 1993. "Do Neighborhoods Influence Child and Adolescent Development?" *American Journal of Sociology* 99(2): 353–395.

Brueckner, Jan. 1977. "The Determinants of Residential Succession." *Journal of Urban Economics* 4:45–59.

Butler, Edgar W., et al. 1969. *Moving Behavior and Residential Choice: A National Survey.* Washington, D.C.: Highway Research Board, National Research Council.

Caplan, Eleanor, and Eleanor Wolf. 1960. "Factors Affecting Racial Change in Two Middle-Income Housing Areas." *Phylon* 11:225–233.

Case, Anne, and Lawrence Katz. 1991. "The Company You Keep: The Effects of Family and Neighborhood Effects on Disadvantaged Youths." Working Paper 3705. Cambridge, Mass.: National Bureau of Economic Research.

Case, Karl E., and Robert Shiller. 1988. "The Behavior of Home Buyers in Boom and Post-Boom Markets." Working Paper 2748. Cambridge, Mass.: National Bureau of Economic Research.

Chambers, Daniel. 1992. "The Racial Housing Price Differential in Racially Transitional Neighborhoods." *Journal of Urban Economics* 32:214–232.

Chandler, Mittie Olion. 1992. "Obstacles to Integration Program Efforts." In George C. Galster and Edward W. Hill, eds., *The Metropolis in Black and White: Place, Power, and Polarization,* pp. 286–305. New Brunswick, N.J.: Center for Urban Policy and Research, Rutgers University.

Clark, Kenneth B. 1965. *Dark Ghetto: Dilemmas of Social Power.* New York: Harper & Row.

Clark, Rebecca. 1992. "Neighborhood Effects on Dropping Out of School among Teenage Boys." Washington, D.C.: The Urban Institute.

Clark, William A. 1986. "Residential Segregation in American Cities: A Review and Interpretation." *Population Research and Policy Review* 5:95–127.

——— 1991. "Residential Preferences and Neighborhood Racial Segregation: A Test of the Schelling Segregation Model." *Demography* 28:1–19.

———— 1992. "Residential Preferences and Residential Choices in a Multiethnic Context." *Demography* 29:451–466.

———— 1993. "Neighborhood Transitions in Multiethnic/Racial Contexts." *Journal of Urban Affairs* 15:161–172.

Clark, W. A. V., and W. F. J. Van Lierop. 1986. "Residential Mobility and Household Location Modelling." In Peter Nijkamp, ed., *Handbook of Regional and Urban Economics*, vol. 1, pp. 97–132. Amsterdam: North-Holland.

Cloutier, Norman R. 1982. "Urban Residential Segregation and Black Income." *Review of Economics and Statistics* 64:282–288.

Coleman, Richard. 1978. "Attitudes toward Neighborhoods: How Americans Choose to Live." Working Paper 49, March. Cambridge, Mass.: Joint Center for Urban Studies of MIT and Harvard University.

Conley, Dalton. 1999. *Being Black, Living in the Red: Race, Wealth, and Social Policy in America*. Berkeley: University of California Press.

Corcoran, Mary, Roger Gordon, Deborah Laren, and Gary Solon. 1989. "Effects of Family and Community Background on Men's Economic Status." Working Paper 2896. Cambridge, Mass.: National Bureau of Economic Research.

Courant, Paul. 1978. "Racial Prejudice in a Search Model of the Urban Housing Market." *Journal of Urban Economics* 5:329–345.

Courant, Paul N., and John Yinger. 1977. "On Models of Racial Prejudice and Urban Residential Structure." *Journal of Urban Economics* 4:272–291.

Cowgill, Donald O., and Mary S. Cowgill. 1951. "An Index of Segregation Based on Block Statistics." *American Sociological Review* 16:825–831.

Crane, Jonathan. 1991. "The Epidemic Theory of Ghettos and Neighborhood Effects on Dropping Out and Teenage Childbearing." *American Journal of Sociology* 96:1226–1259.

Cromwell, Brian A. 1990. "Prointegrative Subsidies and Their Effect on Housing Markets: Do Race-Based Loans Work?" Working Paper 9018. Cleveland: Federal Reserve Bank of Cleveland.

Cummings, Scott. 1998. *Left Behind in Rosedale: Race Relations and the Collapse of Community Institutions*. Boulder, Colo.: Westview Press.

Cutler, David M., Douglas Elmendorf, and Richard J. Zeckhauser. 1993. "Demographic Characteristics and the Public Bundle." Supplement to *Public Finance* 48:178–198.

Cutler, David M., and Edward L. Glaeser. 1997. "Are Ghettos Good or Bad?" *Quarterly Journal of Economics* 112(3):827–872.

Cutler, David M., Edward L. Glaeser, and Jacob L. Vigdor. 1999. "The Rise and Decline of the American Ghetto." *Journal of Political Economy* 107:455–506.

Daniels, Charles B. 1975. "The Influence of Racial Segregation on Housing Prices." *Journal of Urban Economics* 2:105–122.

Danielson, Michael N. 1976. *The Politics of Exclusion*. New York: Columbia University Press.

Darden, Joe T. 1987. "Choosing Neighbors and Neighborhoods: The Role of Race in Housing Preference." In Gary A. Tobin, ed., *Divided Neighborhoods: Changing Patterns of Racial Segregation,* pp. 15–42. Newbury Park, Calif.: Sage Publications.

Datcher, Linda. 1982. "Effects of Community and Family Background on Achievement." *Review of Economics and Statistics* 64:32–41.

Deane, Glenn D. 1990. "Mobility and Adjustments: Paths to Resolution of Residential Stress." *Demography* 27:65–79.

DeMarco, Donald L., and George C. Galster. 1993. "Prointegrative Policy: Theory and Practice." *Journal of Urban Affairs* 15:141–160.

Denowitz, Ronald M. 1980. "Racial Succession in New York City, 1960–70." *Social Forces* 59:440–455.

Dent, David J. 1992. "The New Black Suburbs." *New York Times Magazine,* June 14, pp. 18ff.

Denton, Nancy, and Douglas Massey. 1988. "Residential Segregation of Blacks, Hispanics, and Asians by Socioeconomic Status and Generation." *Social Science Quarterly* 69:797–818.

—— 1989. "Racial Identity among Caribbean Hispanics: The Effect of Double Minority Status on Residential Segregation." *American Sociological Review* 54:790–808.

—— 1991. "Patterns of Neighborhood Transition in a Multiethnic World: U.S. Metropolitan Areas, 1970–1980." *Demography* 28:41–63.

DeParle, Jason. 1993. "An Underground Railroad from Projects to Suburbs." *New York Times,* December 1, pp. A1, B8.

Desforges, Donna M., Charles G. Lord, Shawna L. Ramsey, Julie A. Mason, Marilyn D. Van Leeuwen, and Sylvia C. West. 1991. "Effects of Structured Cooperative Contact on Changing Negative Attitudes toward Stigmatized Social Groups." *Journal of Personality and Social Psychology* 60(4):531–544.

Deutsch, Morton, and Mary Collins. 1951. *Interracial Housing: A Psychological Evaluation of a Social Experiment.* Minneapolis: University of Minnesota Press.

DiPasquale, Denise, and Matthew E. Kahn. 1999. "Measuring Neighborhood Investments: An Examination of Community Choice." *Real Estate Economics* 27(3):389–424.

DiPasquale, Denise, and Tsur Somerville. 1995. "Do House Price Indices Based on Transacting Units Represent the Entire Stock? Evidence from the American Housing Survey." *Journal of Housing Economics* 4:195–229.

Downs, Anthony. 1960. "An Economic Analysis of Property Values and Race (Laurenti)." *Land Economics* 36:181–189.

—— 1973. *Opening Up the Suburbs: An Urban Strategy for America.* New Haven: Yale University Press.

—— 1981. *Neighborhoods and Urban Development.* Washington, D.C.: The Brookings Institution.

———— 1992. "Policy Directions Concerning Racial Discrimination in U.S. Housing Markets." *Housing Policy Debate* 3(2):685–745.

Duncan, Greg. 1994. "Families and Neighbors as Sources of Disadvantage in the Schooling Decisions of White and Black Adolescents." *American Journal of Education* 103:20–53.

Duncan, Greg, Jim Connell, and Pamela Klebanov. 1997. "Conceptual and Methodological Issues in Estimating Causal Effects of Neighborhoods and Family Conditions on Individual Development." In Jeanne Brooks-Gunn, Greg Duncan, and Lawrence Aber, eds., *Neighborhood Poverty: Context and Consequences for Children,* pp. 219–250. New York: Russell Sage Foundation Press.

Duncan, Greg J., and Sandra J. Newman. 1976. "Expected and Actual Mobility." *Journal of the American Institute of Planners* April: 174–186.

Duncan, Otis D., and Beverly Duncan. 1955. "A Methodological Analysis of Segregation Indices." *American Sociological Review* 20:210–217.

———— 1957. *The Negro Population of Chicago: A Study of Residential Succession.* Chicago: University of Chicago Press.

Duneier, Mitchell. 1992. *Slim's Table: Race, Respectability, and Masculinity.* Chicago: University of Chicago Press.

Edwards, Ozzie. 1972. "Family Composition as a Variable in Residential Succession." *American Journal of Sociology* 77:731–741.

Ellen, Ingrid Gould. 1996. "Sharing America's Neighborhoods: The Changing Prospects for Stable, Racial Integration." Ph.D. diss., Harvard University.

———— 1998. "Stable Racial Integration in the Contemporary United States: An Empirical Overview." *Journal of Urban Affairs* 20:27–42.

———— 2000a. "A New White Flight? The Dynamics of Neighborhood Change in the 1980s." In Nancy Foner and Ruben Rumbaut, eds., *Immigration Research for a New Century: Multidisciplinary Perspectives.* New York City: Russell Sage Foundation.

———— 2000b. "Race-Based Neighbourhood Projection: A Proposed Framework for Understanding New Data on Racial Integration." *Urban Studies* 36(9).

Ellen, Ingrid Gould, and Margery Austin Turner. 1997. "Does Neighborhood Matter? Assessing Recent Evidence." *Housing Policy Debate* 8:833–866.

Ellison, Christopher G. and Daniel A. Powers. 1994. "The Contact Hypothesis and Racial Attitudes among Black Americans." *Social Science Quarterly* 75:(2)385–400.

Farley, John E. 1995. "Race Still Matters: The Minimal Role of Income and Housing Cost as Causes of Housing Segregation in St. Louis, 1990." *Urban Affairs Review* 31:244–254.

Farley, Reynolds. 1986. "The Residential Segregation of Blacks from Whites: Trends, Causes, and Consequences." In *Issues in Housing Discrimination,* pp. 14–28. U.S. Commission on Civil Rights. Washington, D.C.: Government Printing Office.

Farley, Reynolds, and William Frey. 1994. "Changes in the Segregation of Whites from Blacks during the 1980s: Small Steps toward a More Integrated Society." *American Sociological Review* 59:23–45.

Farley, Reynolds, Tara Jackson, Keith Reeves, Charlotte Steeh, and Maria Krysan. 1994. "Stereotypes and Segregation: Neighborhoods in the Detroit Area." *American Journal of Sociology* 100:750–780.

Farley Reynolds, Howard Schuman, Suzanne Bianchi, Diane Colasanto, and Shirley Hatchett. 1978. "'Chocolate City, Vanilla Suburbs': Will the Trend toward Racially Separate Communities Continue?" *Social Science Research* 7:319–344.

Farley, Reynolds, Charlotte Steeh, Tara Jackson, Maria Krysan, and Keith Reeves. 1993. "Continued Racial Residential Segregation in Detroit: 'Chocolate City, Vanilla Suburbs' Revisited." *Journal of Housing Research* 4:1–38.

Feinberg, Lawrence. 1983. "Math Scores Show Increase in Virginia SATs." *Washington Post*, September 28, pp. C1, C6.

Ferguson, P. H. 1999. "Ethnic Tensions on the Rise in Antelope Valley Hub." *Los Angeles Times*, April 11, p. B4.

Fishman, Joshua. 1961. "Some Social and Psychological Determinants of Intergroup Relations in Changing Neighborhoods." *Social Forces* 40:107–139.

Fletcher, Michael A. 1996. "A Neighborhood Slams the Door: Racist Acts Drive Philadelphia Family Out of White Area." *Washington Post*, May 18, pp. A1, A12.

Follain, James R., and Stephen Malpezzi. 1980. *Dissecting Housing Value and Rent: Estimates of Hedonic Indexes for 39 Large SMSAs*. Washington, D.C.: The Urban Institute.

Ford, W. Scott. 1973. "Interracial Public Housing in a Border City." *American Journal of Sociology* 78:426–444.

——— 1986. "Favorable Intergroup Contact May Not Reduce Prejudice: Inconclusive Journal Evidence, 1960–1984." *Sociology and Social Research* 70:256–258.

Fredland, Daniel. 1974. *Residential Mobility and Home Purchase*. Lexington, Mass.: D.C. Heath and Company.

Freiberg, Fred. 1993. "Promoting Residential Integration: The Role of Private Fair Housing Groups." In G. Thomas Kingsley and Margery Austin Turner, eds., *Housing Markets and Residential Mobility*. Washington, D.C.: The Urban Institute Press.

Frey, William H. 1979. "Central City White Flight: Racial and Non-Racial Causes." *American Sociological Review* 44:425–448.

——— 1980. "Black In-Migration, White Flight, and the Changing Economic Base of the Central City." *American Journal of Sociology* 85:1396–1417.

——— 1992. "Minority Suburbanization and Continued "'White Flight' in U.S. Metropolitan Areas: Assessing Findings from the 1990 Census." Research Report 92-247. Ann Arbor: University of Michigan Population Studies Center.

Frey, William H., and Reynolds Farley. 1993. "Latino, Asian, and Black Segregation in Multi-Ethnic Metro Areas: Findings from the 1990 Census." Research Report 93-278. Ann Arbor: University of Michigan Population Studies Center.

Gabriel, Stuart, and Stuart Rosenthal. 1989. "Household Location and Race: Estimates of a Multinomial Logit Model." *Review of Economics and Statistics* 71(2):240–249.

Gale, Dennis. 1987. *Washington, D.C.: Inner-City Revitalization and Minority Suburbanization.* Philadelphia: Temple University Press.

Gallup Poll Social Audit. 1997. "Black/White Relations in the United States 1997." Princeton, N.J.: The Gallup Organization. June.

Galster, George C. 1977. "A Bid-Rent Analysis of Housing Market Discrimination." *American Economic Review* 67:144–155.

——— 1979. "Interracial Variations in Housing Preferences." *Regional Science Perspectives* 9:1–17.

——— 1982. "Black and White Preferences for Neighborhood Racial Composition." *AREUEA Journal* 10:39–66.

——— 1986a. "More than Skin Deep: The Effect of Discrimination on the Extent of Racial Residential Segregation in the United States." In John M. Goering, ed., *Housing Desegregation and Federal Policy*, pp. 119–138. Chapel Hill: University of North Carolina Press.

——— 1986b. "What Is a Neighborhood?" *International Journal of Urban and Regional Research* 10:243–263.

——— 1987a. *Homeowners and Neighborhood Investment.* Chapel Hill: Duke University Press.

——— 1987b. "The Ecology of Racial Discrimination in Housing: An Exploratory Model." *Urban Affairs Quarterly* 23:84–107.

——— 1988. "Residential Segregation in American Cities: A Contrary Review." *Population Research and Policy Review* 7:93–112.

——— 1990a. "Federal Fair Housing Policy: The Great Misapprehension." In Denise DiPasquale and Langley C. Keyes, eds., *Building Foundations: Housing and Federal Policy*, pp. 137–155. Philadelphia: University of Pennsylvania Press.

——— 1990b. "Neighborhood Racial Change, Segregationist Sentiments, and Affirmative Marketing Policies." *Journal of Urban Economics* 27:334–361.

——— 1990c. "White Flight from Racially Integrated Neighborhoods in the 1970s: The Cleveland Experience." *Urban Studies* 27:385–399.

——— 1991. "Housing Discrimination and Urban Poverty of African-Americans." *Journal of Housing Research* 2:87–122.

——— 1992. "The Case for Racial Integration." In George C. Galster and Edward W. Hill, eds., *The Metropolis in Black and White: Place, Power, and Polarization*, pp. 270–285. New Brunswick, N.J.: Center for Urban Policy and Research, Rutgers University.

——— 1997. "Assessing MTO's Impacts on Sending and Receiving Neighborhoods: A Response to Turner and Ellen." Paper presented at HUD's Conference on the Moving to Opportunity Program. November.

—— 1998. "A Stock/Flow Model of Defining Racially Integrated Neighborhoods." *Journal of Urban Affairs* 20:43–52.

Galster, George, and Heather Keeney. 1993. "Subsidized Housing and Racial Change in Yonkers, New York." *Journal of the American Planning Association* 59:172–181.

Galster, George, and W. Mark Keeney. 1988. "Race, Residence, Discrimination, and Economic Opportunity: Modeling the Nexus of Urban Residential Phenomena." *Urban Affairs Quarterly* 24:87–117.

Gamm, Gerald. 1999. *Urban Exodus: Why the Jews Left Boston and the Catholics Stayed.* Cambridge, Mass.: Harvard University Press.

Gans, Herbert. 1961. "The Balanced Community: Homogeneity or Heterogeneity in Residential Areas?" *Journal of the American Institute of Planners* 27:176–184.

—— 1962. *The Urban Villagers: Group and Class in the Life of Italian Americans.* New York: Free Press.

—— 1967. *The Levittowners: Ways of Life and Politics in a New Suburban Community.* New York: Pantheon Books.

Glazer, Nathan. 1974. "On 'Opening Up' the Suburbs." *Public Interest* 37:89–111.

—— 1998. "In Defense of Preference." *New Republic,* April 6.

Glazer, Nathan, and Daniel Patrick Moynihan. 1963. *Beyond the Melting Pot: The Negroes, Puerto Ricans, Jews, Italians, and Irish of New York City.* Cambridge, Mass.: MIT Press.

Goering, John M. 1978. "Neighborhood Tipping and Racial Transition: A Review of Social Science Evidence." *Journal of the American Institute of Planners* 44:68–78.

Goldberg, Carey. 1999. "Boston Settles Lawsuit by Harassed Minority Tenants." *New York Times,* July 27, p. A14.

Goodman, John L. 1976. "Housing Consumption Disequilibrium and Local Residential Mobility." *Environment and Planning A* 8:855–874.

Goodman, John L., and Mary L. Streitwieser. 1983. "Explaining Racial Differences: A Study of City-to-Suburb Mobility." *Urban Affairs Quarterly* 18:301–325.

Goodwin, Carole. 1979. *The Oak Park Strategy: Community Control of Racial Change.* Chicago: University of Chicago Press.

Gramlich, Edward, Deborah Laren, and Naomi Sealand. 1992. "Moving into and out of Poor Urban Areas." *Journal of Policy Analysis and Management* 11:273–287.

Greenberg, Michael R., and Thomas D. Boswell. 1972. "Neighborhood Deterioration as a Factor in Intraurban Migration: A Case-Study of New York City." *Professional Geographer* 24:11–16.

Greene, William H. 1993. *Econometric Analysis.* New York: Macmillan.

Greenfield, Robert. 1961. "Factors Associated with Attitudes toward Desegregation in a Florida Residential Suburb." *Social Forces* 49:31–42.

Grier, George, and Eunice Grier. 1960. *Privately Developed Interracial Housing: An Analysis of Experience.* Berkeley: University of California Press.

Grodzins, Morton. 1957. "Metropolitan Segregation." *Scientific American* 197:33–41.

Gronberg, Timothy J., and Robert Reed. 1992. "Estimation of Duration Models Using the American Housing Survey." *Journal of Urban Economics* 31:311–324.

Guest, Avery M. 1978. "The Changing Racial Composition of the Suburbs." *Urban Affairs Quarterly* 14:195–206.

Guest, Avery M., and James J. Zuiches. 1974. "Another Look at Residential Turnover in Urban Neighborhoods: A Note on 'Racial Change in a Stable Community' by Harvey Molotch." *American Journal of Sociology* 77:457–467.

Guterbock, Thomas M. 1976. "The Push Hypothesis: Minority Presence, Crime, and Urban Deconcentration." In Barry Schwartz, ed., *The Changing Face of the Suburbs,* pp. 137–155. Chicago: University of Chicago Press.

Hacker, Andrew. 1992. *Two Nations: Black and White, Separate, Hostile, Unequal.* New York: Ballantine Books.

Hamilton, David L., and George D. Bishop. 1976. "Attitudinal and Behavioral Effects of Initial Integration of White Suburban Neighborhoods." *Journal of Social Issues* 32:47–67.

Hanushek, Eric, and John Quigley. 1978. "An Explicit Model of Intra-Metropolitan Mobility." *Land Economics* 54:411–429.

Harney, Kenneth R. 1994. "Equity Insurance Offers Hedge against Falling Property Values." *Washington Post,* January 8, p. E1.

Harris, David R. 1997a. "The Flight of Whites: A Multilevel Analysis of Why Whites Move." Research Report 97-386. Population Studies Center, University of Michigan.

——— 1997b. "'Property Values Drop When Blacks Move In Because . . .': Racial and Socioeconomic Determinants of Neighborhood Desirability." Research Report 97-387. Population Studies Center, University of Michigan.

——— 1997c. "Racial and Nonracial Determinants of Neighborhood Satisfaction among Whites, 1975–1993." Research Report 97-388. Population Studies Center, University of Michigan.

Harvard Law Review. 1980. Comment. "Benign Steering and Benign Quotas: The Validity of Race-Conscious Government Policies to Promote Residential Integration." 93:938–965.

Helper, Rose. 1969. "The Problem in National Perspective." In *Racial Policies and Practices of Real Estate Brokers,* vol. 1, pp. 3–14. Minneapolis: University of Minnesota.

——— 1979. "Social Interaction in Racially Mixed Neighborhoods." *Housing and Society* 6:20–38.

—— 1986. "Success and Resistance Factors in the Maintenance of Racially Mixed Neighborhoods." In John M. Goering, ed., *Housing Desegregation and Federal Policy,* pp. 170–194. Chapel Hill: University of North Carolina Press.

Hirsch, Arnold R. 1983. *Making the Second Ghetto: Race and Housing in Chicago, 1940–1960.* Cambridge: Cambridge University Press.

Hochschild, Jennifer L. 1995. *Facing Up to the American Dream: Race, Class, and the Soul of the Nation.* Princeton, N.J.: Princeton University Press.

Hogan, Dennis, and Evelyn Kitagawa. 1985. "The Impact of Social Status, Family Structure, and Neighborhood on the Fertility of Black Adolescents." *American Journal of Sociology* 90(4):825–855.

Holmes, Steven A. 1997. "Leaving the Suburbs for Rural Areas." *New York Times,* October 19, p. 34.

Hughes, Mark Alan. 1989. "Misspeaking Truth to Power: A Geographical Perspective on the 'Underclass' Fallacy." *Economic Geography* 65(3):187–207.

Hunt, Chester L. 1959. "Negro-White Perceptions of Interracial Housing." *Journal of Social Issues* 15:24–29.

Hunter, Albert. 1974. *Symbolic Communities: The Persistence and Change of Chicago's Local Communities.* Chicago: University of Chicago Press.

Husock, Howard. 1989. *Integration Incentives in Suburban Cleveland.* Cambridge, Mass.: Kennedy School Case Program, Harvard University.

—— 1990a. *Occupancy Controls and Starrett City.* Cambridge, Mass.: Kennedy School Case Program, Harvard University.

—— 1990b. *Occupancy Controls and Starrett City: Epilogue.* Cambridge, Mass.: Kennedy School Case Program, Harvard University.

Huttman, Elizabeth D., and Terry Jones. 1991. "American Suburbs: Desegregation and Resegregation." In Elizabeth D. Huttman, Wim Blauw, and Juliet Saltman, eds., *Urban Housing Segregation of Minorities,* pp. 335–366. Durham: Duke University Press.

Ihlanfeldt, Keith R., and David L. Sjoquist. 1990. "Job Accessibility and Racial Differences in Youth Employment Rates." *American Economic Review* 80(1):267–276.

"Illinois Town, Fearing Racial Imbalance, to Advertise for Whites." 1997. *New York Times,* April 30, late ed., sec. 1: 36.

Jackman, Mary R., and Marie Crane. 1986. "'Some of My Best Friends are Black . . .': Interracial Friendship and Whites' Racial Attitudes." *Public Opinion Quarterly* 50:459–486.

Jackson, Kenneth T. 1985. *Crabgrass Frontier: The Suburbanization of the United States.* New York: Oxford University Press.

Jacoby, Tamar. 1998. *Someone Else's House: America's Unfinished Struggle for Integration.* New York: The Free Press/Simon & Schuster.

Jahn, Julius. 1950. "The Measurement of Ecological Segregation: Derivation of an Index Based on the Criterion of Reproducibility." *American Sociological Review* 15:100–104.

James, David R., and Karl E. Taeuber. 1985. "Measures of Segregation." In Nancy Tuma, ed., *Sociological Methodology.* San Francisco: Jossey Bass, pp. 1–32.

Jargowsky, Paul. 1994. "Ghetto Poverty among Blacks in the 1980s." *Journal of Policy Analysis and Management* 13:288–310.

Jaynes, Gerald David, and Robin M. Williams, eds. 1989. *A Common Destiny: Blacks and American Society.* Washington, D.C.: National Academy Press.

Jencks, Christopher, and Susan E. Mayer. 1990. "The Social Consequences of Growing Up in a Poor Neighborhood." In Laurence E. Lynn and Michael G. H. McGeary, eds., *Inner-City Poverty in the United States,* pp. 111–186. Washington, D.C.: National Academy Press.

Jud, G. Donald., and D. Gordon Bennett. 1986. "Public Schools and the Pattern of Intraurban Residential Mobility." *Land Economics* 62:362–370.

Kahneman, Daniel, and Amos Tversky. 1979. "Prospect Theory: An Analysis of Decision under Risk." *Econometrica* 47:263–291.

Kain, John F. 1968. "Housing Segregation, Negro Unemployment, and Metropolitan Decentralization." *Quarterly Journal of Economics* 82:175–197.

――― 1976. "Race, Ethnicity, and Residential Location." In Ronald Grieson, ed., *Public and Urban Economics,* pp. 267–292. Lexington, Mass.: Lexington Books.

――― 1985. "Black Suburbanization in the Eighties: A New Beginning or a False Hope?" In John Quigley and Daniel Rubinfeld, eds., *American Domestic Priorities,* pp. 253–284. Berkeley: University of California Press.

――― 1986. "The Influence of Race and Income on Racial Segregation and Housing Policy." In John M. Goering, ed., *Housing Desegregation and Federal Policy,* pp. 99–118. Chapel Hill: University of North Carolina Press.

――― 1987. "Housing Market Discrimination and Black Suburbanization in the 1980s." In Gary A. Tobin, ed., *Divided Neighborhoods: Changing Patterns of Racial Segregation,* pp. 68–94. Newbury Park, Calif.: Sage Publications.

Kain, John F., and Joseph J. Persky. 1969. "Alternatives to the Gilded Ghetto." *Public Interest* 14:74–87.

Kain, John, F., and John M. Quigley. 1972. "Note on Owners' Estimates of Housing Value." *Journal of the American Statistical Association* 67:803–806.

――― 1975. *Housing Markets and Racial Discrimination: A Microeconomic Analysis.* New York: Columbia University Press.

Kantrowitz, Nathan. 1979. "Racial and Ethnic Segregation in Boston: 1830–1970." *Annals of the American Academy of Political and Social Science* 441:41–54.

Karlen, David H. 1968. "Racial Integration and Property Values in Chicago." Urban Economics Report 7. Chicago: University of Chicago.

Kasarda, John D. 1989. "Urban Industrial Transition and the Underclass." *Annals of the American Academy of Political and Social Science* 501:26–47.

Kasinitz, Philip and Jan Rosenberg. 1996. "Missing the Connection: Social Isolation and Employment on the Brooklyn Waterfront." *Social Problems* 43(2):180–196.

Katzman, Martin T. 1980. "The Contribution of Crime to Urban Decline." *Urban Studies* 17:277–286.

Keating, W. Dennis. 1994. *The Suburban Racial Dilemma: Housing and Neighborhoods.* Philadelphia: Temple University Press.

Keller, Suzanne. 1968. *The Urban Neighborhood: A Sociological Perspective.* New York: Random House.

Kennedy, Randall. 1997. *Race, Crime, and the Law.* New York: Pantheon Books.

Kern, Clifford. 1981. "Racial Prejudice and Residential Segregation: The Yinger Model Revisited." *Journal of Urban Economics* 10:164–172.

Kern, Clifford, and George D. Moulton. 1977. "Racial Discrimination and the Price of Ghetto Housing in City and Suburb: Some Recent Evidence." Discussion Paper D77–2. Cambridge, Mass.: Department of City and Regional Planning, Harvard University.

Kiel, Katherine A. 1994. "The Impact of Housing Price Appreciation on Household Mobility." *Journal of Housing Economics* 3:92–108.

Kiel, Katherine A., and Richard T. Carson. 1990. "Examination of Systematic Differences in the Appreciation of Individual Housing Units." *Journal of Real Estate Research* 5:301–318.

Kiel, Katherine A., and Jeffrey E. Zabel. 1996. "House Price Differentials in U.S. Cities: Household and Neighborhood Racial Effects." *Journal of Housing Economics* 5(2):143–165.

—— 1997. "Evaluating the Usefulness of the American Housing Survey for Creating House Price Indices." *Journal of Real Estate Finance and Economics* 14:189–202.

King, Gary. 1997. *A Solution to the Ecological Inference Problem: Reconstructing Individual Behavior from Aggregate Data.* Princeton, N.J.: Princeton University Press.

King, Thomas, and Peter Mieszkowski. 1973. "Racial Discrimination, Segregation, and the Price of Housing." *Journal of Political Economy* 81:590–606.

Ladd, William. 1962. "The Effect of Integration on Property Values." *American Economic Review* 52:801–808.

Lake, Robert W. 1981. *The New Suburbanites: Race and Housing in the Suburbs.* New Brunswick, N.J.: Center for Urban Policy and Research, Rutgers University.

Lake, Robert W., and Jessica Winslow. 1981. "Integration Management: Municipal Constraints on Residential Mobility." *Urban Geography* 12:311–326.

Lapham, Victoria. 1971. "Do Blacks Pay More for Housing?" *Journal of Political Economy* 79:1244–1257.

Lauber, Daniel. 1992. "Racially Diverse Communities: A National Necessity." In Philip Nyden and Wim Wiewel, eds., *Challenging Uneven Development: An Urban Agenda for the 1990s.* New Brunswick, N.J.: Rutgers University Press.

Laurenti, Luigi. 1960. *Property Values and Race.* Berkeley: University of California Press.

LaVeist, Thomas A. 1992. "The Political Empowerment and Health Status of African-Americans: Mapping a New Territory." *American Journal of Sociology* 97(4):1080–1095.

Leacock, Eleanor, Martin Deutsch, and Joshua A. Fishman. 1959. "The Bridgeview Study: A Preliminary Report." *Journal of Social Issues* 15:30–37.

Leadership Council for Metropolitan Open Communities. 1987. "The Costs of Housing Discrimination and Segregation: An Interdisciplinary Social Science Statement." In Gary A. Tobin, ed., *Divided Neighborhoods: Changing Patterns of Racial Segregation,* pp. 268–280. Newbury Park, Calif.: Sage Publications.

Lee, Barrett. 1985. "Racially Mixed Neighborhoods during the 1970s: Change or Stability?" *Social Science Quarterly* 66:346–364.

Lee, Barrett, R. S. Oropesa, and James Kanan. 1994. "Neighborhood Context and Residential Mobility." *Demography* 31:249–270.

Lee, Barrett, and Peter Wood. 1990. "The Fate of Residential Integration in American Cities: Evidence from Racially Mixed Neighborhoods, 1970–1980." *Journal of Urban Affairs* 12:425–436.

—— 1991. "Is Neighborhood Racial Succession Place-Specific?" *Demography* 28:21–39.

Leigh, Wilhelmina A., and James D. McGhee. 1986. "A Minority Perspective on Residential Racial Integration." In John M. Goering, ed., *Housing Desegregation and Federal Policy,* pp. 31–42. Chapel Hill: University of North Carolina Press.

Lemann, Nicholas. 1991. *The Promised Land: The Great Black Migration and How It Changed America.* New York: Alfred A. Knopf.

Lerman, Steven R. 1979. "Neighborhood Choice and Transportation Services." In David Segal, ed., *The Economics of Neighborhood,* pp. 83–118. New York: Academic Press.

Leven, Charles L., James T. Little, Hugh O. Nourse, and R. B. Read. 1976. *Neighborhood Change: Lessons in the Dynamics of Urban Decay.* New York: Praeger.

Levine, Hillel, and Lawrence Harmon. 1992. *The Death and Life of a Jewish Community: A Tragedy of Good Intentions.* New York: Free Press.

Lewis, David Levering, ed. 1995. *W. E. B. Du Bois: A Reader.* New York: Henry Holt.

Liao, Tim Futing. 1994. *Interpreting Probability Models: Logit, Probit, and Other Generalized Linear Models.* Thousand Oaks, Calif.: Russell Sage.

Lieber, James. 1990. *Mayor Harold Washington and the Guaranteed Home Equity Program.* Cambridge, Mass.: Kennedy School Case Program, Harvard University.

Lieberson, Stanley. 1980. *Piece of the Pie: Black and White Immigrants since 1880.* Berkeley: University of California Press.

Little, James T. 1976. "Residential Preferences, Neighborhood Filtering, and Neighborhood Change." *Journal of Urban Economics* 3:68–81.

Logan, John R., Richard D. Alba, and Shu-Yin Leung. 1996. "Minority Access to White Suburbs: A Multiregional Comparison." *Social Forces* 74:851–881.

Logan, John R., and Linda Brewster Stearns. 1981. "Suburban Racial Segregation as a Nonecological Process." *Social Forces* 60:61–73.

Logan, John R., and Mark Schneider. 1984. "Suburban Racial Segregation and Black Access to Public Resources." *Social Science Quarterly* 63:762–770.

Loomes, Graham, and Robert Sugden. 1982. "Regret Theory: An Alternative Theory of Rational Choice under Uncertainty." *Economic Journal* 92:805–824.

Maly, Michael T., and Philip Nyden. 1996. "Racial and Ethnic Diversity in Urban Communities: Challenging the Perceived Inevitability of Segregation." Unpublished manuscript on file with the author.

Mankiw, N. Gregory, and David Weil. 1989. "The Baby Boom, the Baby Bust, and the Housing Market." *Regional Science and Urban Economics* 19:235–258.

Mark, Jonathan, Thomas Boehm, and Charles Leven. 1979. "A Probability Model for Analyzing Interneighborhood Mobility." In David Segal, ed., *The Economics of Neighborhood,* pp. 43–56. New York: Academic Press.

Marshall, Harvey. 1979. "White Movement to the Suburbs: A Comparison of Explanations." *American Sociological Review* 44:975–994.

Marshall, Harvey, and Robert Jiobu. 1975. "Residential Segregation in U.S. Cities: A Causal Analysis." *Social Forces* 53:449–460.

Marullo, Sam. 1985. "Targets for Racial Invasion and Reinvasion: Housing Units where Racial Turnovers Occurred, 1974–77." *Social Forces* 63:748–774.

Massey, Douglas S. 1983. "A Research Note on Residential Succession: The Hispanic Case." *Social Forces* 66:825–833.

——— 1990. "American Apartheid: Segregation and the Making of the Underclass." *American Journal of Sociology* 96:329–358.

Massey, Douglas S., Gretchen A. Condran, and Nancy A. Denton. 1987. "The Effect of Residential Segregation on Black Social and Economic Well-Being." *Social Forces* 66:29–56.

Massey, Douglas S., and Nancy Denton. 1985. "Spatial Assimilation as a Socioeconomic Outcome." *American Sociological Review* 50:94–106.

——— 1987. "Trends in the Residential Segregation of Blacks, Hispanics, and Asians: 1970–1980." *American Sociological Review* 52:802–825.

——— 1988. "The Dimensions of Residential Segregation." *Social Forces* 67:281–315.

——— 1993. *American Apartheid: Segregation and the Making of the Underclass.* Cambridge, Mass.: Harvard University Press.

Massey, Douglas S., and Mitchell L. Eggers. 1990. "The Ecology of Inequality: Minorities and the Concentration of Poverty, 1970–1980." *American Journal of Sociology* 95:1153–1189.

Massey, Douglas S., and Andrew B. Gross. 1991. "Explaining Trends in Racial Segregation, 1970–1980." *Urban Affairs Quarterly* 27:13–35.

Massey, Douglas S., Andrew B. Gross, and Mitchell L. Eggers. 1991. "Segregation, the Concentration of Poverty, and the Life Chances of Individuals." *Social Science Research* 20:397–420.

Massey, Douglas S., Andrew B. Gross, and Kumiko Shibuya. 1994. "Migration, Segregation, and the Concentration of Poverty." *American Sociological Review* 59:425–455.

Massey, Douglas S., and Brendan P. Mullan. 1984. "Processes of Hispanic and Black Spatial Assimilation." *American Journal of Sociology* 89:836–873.

Mayer, Albert. 1960. "Russel Woods: Change without Conflict." In Nathan Glazer and Davis McEntire, eds., *Studies in Housing and Minority Groups,* pp. 198–220. Berkeley: University of California Press.

Mayer, Susan E. 1991. "How Much Does a High School's Racial and Socioeconomic Mix Affect Graduation and Teenage Fertility Rates?" In Christopher Jencks and Paul E. Peterson, eds., *The Urban Underclass,* pp. 321–341. Washington, D.C.: The Brookings Institution.

McEntire, Davis. 1960. *Residence and Race.* Berkeley: University of California Press.

McHugh, Kevin, Patricia Gober, and Neil Reid. 1990. "Determinants of Short- and Long-Term Mobility Expectations for Homeowners and Renters." *Demography* 27:81–95.

McKelvey, Richard D., and William Zavoina. 1975. "A Statistical Model for the Analysis of Ordinal Level Dependent Variables." *Journal of Mathematical Sociology* 4:103–120.

McKinney, Scott. 1989. "Changes in Metropolitan Area Residential Integration, 1970–1980." *Population Research and Policy Review* 8:143–164.

McKinney, Scott, and Ann B. Schnare. 1989. "Trends in Residential Segregation by Race, 1960–1980." *Journal of Urban Economics* 26:269–280.

Meer, Bernard, and Edward Freedman. 1966. "The Impact of Negro Neighbors on White Home Owners." *Social Forces* 45:11–19.

Metcalf, George R. 1988. *Fair Housing Comes of Age.* New York: Greenwood.

Meyer, Eugene L. 1983. "Poll Shows Majority Favors Modification of Revenue Freeze." *Washington Post,* August 16, pp. B1, B3.

Millen, James S. 1973. "Factors Affecting Racial Mixing in Residential Areas." In Amos H. Hawley and Vincent Rock, eds., *Segregation in Residential Areas: Papers on Socioeconomic and Racial Factors in the Choice of Housing,* pp. 148–171. Washington, D.C.: National Academy of Sciences.

Missouri v. Jenkins. 1995. 115 S. Ct. 2038.

Molotch, Harvey. 1969. "Racial Change in a Stable Community." *American Journal of Sociology* 75:226–238.

——— 1972. *Managed Integration: The Dilemmas of Doing Good in the City.* Berkeley: University of California Press.

Moore, Maurice, and James McKeown. 1968. *A Study of Integrated Living in Chicago.* Chicago: Community and Family Study Center, University of Chicago.

Morrill, Richard. 1965. "The Negro Ghetto: Problems and Alternatives." *Geographical Review* 55:339–361.

Munnell, Alicia, Lynn Browne, James McEneaney, and Geoffrey Tootell. 1996. "Mortgage Lending in Boston: Interpreting HMDA Data." *American Economic Review* 86:25–53.

Muth, Richard. 1969. *Cities and Housing.* Chicago: University of Chicago Press.

——— 1986. "The Causes of Housing Segregation." In *Issues in Housing Discrimination,* pp. 3–13. Washington, D.C.: U.S. Commission on Civil Rights.

National Advisory Commission on Civil Disorders. 1968. *Report of the National Advisory Commission on Civil Disorders.* New York: E. P. Dutton & Co.

National Commission on Neighborhoods. 1979. *People, Building Neighborhoods.* Final Report to the President and the Congress of the United States. Washington, D.C.: Government Printing Office.

Nyden, Philip, Michael Maly, and John Lukehart. 1997. "The Emergence of Stable, Racially and Ethnically Diverse Urban Communities: A Case-Study of Nine U.S. Cities." *Housing Policy Debate* 8:491–534.

O'Brien, David J., and Lynn Clough. 1982. "The Future of Urban Neighborhoods." In Gary Gappert and Richard V. Knight, eds., *Cities in the Twenty-first Century,* pp. 232–248. Beverly Hills, Calif.: Sage Publications.

O'Hare, William, and William H. Frey. 1992. "Booming, Suburban, and Black." *American Demographics* 14:30–38.

O'Regan, Katherine, and John Quigley. 1996a. "Spatial Effects upon Employment Outcomes: The Case of New Jersey Teenagers." *New England Economic Review* (May/June):41–58.

——— 1996b. "Teenage Employment and the Spatial Isolation of Minority and Poverty Households." *Journal of Human Resources* 31:692–702.

Oliver, Melvin L., and Thomas M. Shapiro. 1997. *Black Wealth/White Wealth: A New Perspective on Racial Inequality.* New York: Routledge.

Orfield, Gary. 1993. "The Growth of Segregation in American Schools: Changing Patterns of Separation and Poverty since 1968." *NSBA Council of Urban Boards of Education Publication.*

Orfield, Gary, and John T. Yun. 1999. "Resegregation in America's Schools." Cambridge, Mass.: The Civil Rights Project, Harvard University. www.law.harvard.edu/groups/civilrights/publications/resegregation99.html.

Orfield, Myron. 1997. *Metropolitics.* Washington, D.C.: Brookings Institution Press.

Orser, W. Edward. 1994. *Blockbusting in Baltimore: The Edmondson Village Story.* Lexington: University Press of Kentucky.

Ottensmann, John R., David H. Good, and Michael Gleeson. 1990. "The Impact of Net Migration on Neighbourhood Racial Composition." *Urban Studies* 27:705–717.

Park, Robert E. 1936. "Succession, An Ecological Concept." *American Sociological Review* 1:171–179.

Park, Robert E., Ernest W. Burgess, and Roderick D. McKenzie. 1925. *The City.* Chicago: University of Chicago Press.

Pascal, Anthony. 1967. *The Economics of Housing Segregation.* RM-5510-RC. Santa Monica, Calif.: The Rand Corporation.

Patterson, Orlando. 1997. *The Ordeal of Integration: Progress and Resentment in America's "Racial" Crisis.* Washington, D.C.: Civitas/Counterpoint.

Pedone, Carla I. 1977. "Neighborhood Dynamics: A Review of Previous Studies and Some Strategies for New Empirical Research." HUD Contract Report 243-2. Washington, D.C.: The Urban Institute.

Peterson, Iver. 1999. "Whitman Says Troopers Used Racial Profiling." *New York Times,* April 21, pp. A1, B8.

Pettigrew, Thomas F. 1971. *Racially Separate or Together?* New York: McGraw Hill.

——— 1973. "Attitudes on Race and Housing: A Social Psychological View." In Amos H. Hawley and Vincent Rock, eds., *Segregation in Residential Areas: Papers on Socioeconomic and Racial Factors in the Choice of Housing,* pp. 21–84. Washington, D.C.: National Academy of Sciences.

——— 1979. "Racial Change and Social Policy." *Annals of the American Academy of Political and Social Science* 441:114–131.

Phares, Donald. 1971. "Racial Change and Housing Values: Transition in an Inner Suburb." *Social Science Quarterly* 52:560–573.

Piven, Frances Fox, and Richard A. Cloward. 1966. "Desegregated Housing: Who Pays for the Reformers' Ideal?" *New Republic,* December 17, pp. 17–22.

Polikoff, Alexander. 1986. "Sustainable Integration or Inevitable Resegregation: The Troubling Questions." In John M. Goering, ed., *Housing Desegregation and Federal Policy,* pp. 44–71. Chapel Hill: University of North Carolina Press.

Poterba, James M. 1984. "Tax Subsidies to Owner-Occupied Housing: An Asset Market Approach." *Quarterly Journal of Economics* 99:729–752.

Pryor, Frederick L. 1971. "An Empirical Note on the Tipping Point." *Land Economics* 47:413–417.

Putnam, Robert. 1993. *Making Democracy Work: Civic Traditions in Modern Italy.* Princeton, N.J.: Princeton University Press.

Quigley, John. 1985. "Consumer Choice of Dwelling, Neighborhood, and Public Services." *Regional Science and Urban Economics* 15:41–63.

Quigley, John, and Daniel Weinberg. 1977. "Intra-Urban Residential Mobility: Review and Synthesis." *International Regional Science Review* 2:41–66.

Rapkin, Chester, and William Grigsby. 1960. *The Demand for Housing in Racially Mixed Neighborhoods.* Berkeley: University of California Press.

Rent, George S., and J. Dennis Lord. 1978. "Neighborhood Racial Transition and Property Value Trends in a Southern Community." *Social Science Quarterly* 59:51–59.

Research Report on Integrated Housing in Kalamazoo. 1959. Kalamazoo, Mich.: W. E. Upjohn Institute for Community Research. July.

Rieder, Jonathan. 1985. *Canarsie: The Jews and Italians of Brooklyn against Liberalism.* Cambridge, Mass.: Harvard University Press.

Robinson Jr., James Lee. 1980. "Physical Distance and Racial Attitudes: A Further Examination of the Contact Hypothesis." *Phylon* 4:325–332.

Robinson Jr., Jerry W., and James D. Preston. 1976. "Equal-Status Contact and Modification of Racial Prejudice: A Reexamination of the Contact Hypothesis." *Social Forces* 54(4):911–924.

Roof, Wade Clark. 1979. "Race and Residence: The Shifting Basis of American Race Relations." *Annals of the American Academy of Political and Social Science* 441:1–12.

Rose, Arnold. 1944. *The Negro in America.* Boston: Beacon Press.

Rose, Arnold M., Frank J. Atelsek, and Lawrence R. McDonald. 1953. "Neighborhood Reactions to Isolated Negro Residents: An Alternative to Invasion and Succession." *American Sociological Review* 18:497–507.

Rose-Ackerman, Susan. 1975. "Racism and Urban Structure." *Journal of Urban Economics* 2:85–103.

Rosenbaum, Emily. 1992. "Race and Ethnicity in Housing Turnover in New York City, 1978–1987." *Demography* 29:467–486.

Rosenbaum, James E. 1991. "Black Pioneers: Do Their Moves to the Suburbs Increase Economic Opportunity for Mothers and Children?" *Housing Policy Debate* 2:1179–1213.

Rosenbaum, James E., Susan J. Popkin, Julie E. Kaufman, and Jennifer Rusin. 1991. "Social Integration of Low-Income Black Adults in Middle-Class White Suburbs." *Social Problems* 38(4):448–461.

Rossi, Peter. 1955. *Why Families Move: A Study in the Social Psychology of Urban Residential Mobility.* Glencoe, Ill.: Free Press.

Saltman, Juliet. 1990. *A Fragile Movement: The Struggle for Neighborhood Stabilization.* New York: Greenwood.

Sampson, Robert J. 1991. "Linking the Micro- and Macrolevel Dimensions of Community Social Organization." *Social Forces* 70(1):43–64.

Sampson, William A. 1986. "Desegregation and Racial Tolerance in Academia." *Journal of Negro Education* 55(2):171–184.

Sander, Richard H. 1998. "Housing Segregation and Housing Integration: The Diverging Paths of Urban America." *University of Miami Law Review* 52:977–1010.

Sanders, Marion K. 1970. *The Professional Radical: Conversations with Saul Alinsky.* New York: Harper & Row.

Santiago, Anne M. 1989. "Patterns of Residential Segregation Among Mexicans, Puerto Ricans, and Cubans in U.S. metropolitan Areas." Working paper 1. East Lansing: Julian Somora Research Institute, Michigan State University.

Schelling, Thomas. 1971. "Dynamic Models of Segregation." *Journal of Mathematical Sociology* 1:143–186.

——— 1972. "The Process of Residential Segregation: Neighborhood Tipping."

In Anthony Pascal, ed., *Racial Discrimination in Economic Life,* pp. 157–184. Lexington, Mass.: D.C. Heath.

Schietinger, E. F. 1954. "Race and Residential Market Values in Chicago." *Land Economics* 30:301–308.

Schnare, Ann B. 1976. "Racial and Ethnic Price Differentials in an Urban Housing Market." *Urban Studies* 13:107–120.

—— 1978. *The Persistence of Segregation in Housing.* Washington D.C.: The Urban Institute.

—— 1980. "Trends in Residential Segregation by Race: 1960–1970." *Journal of Urban Economics* 7:293–301.

Schnare, Ann B., and C. Duncan McRae. 1978. "The Dynamics of Neighborhood Change." *Urban Studies* 15:327–331.

Schnare, Ann B., and Raymond J. Struyk. 1977. "An Analysis of Ghetto Housing Prices over Time." In Gregory K. Ingram, ed., *Residential Location and Urban Housing Markets,* pp. 95–133. New York: National Bureau of Economic Research.

Schuman, Howard, and Lawrence Bobo. 1988. "Survey-Based Experiments on White Racial Attitudes toward Residential Integration." *American Journal of Sociology* 94:273–299.

Schuman, Howard, Charlotte Steeh, Lawrence Bobo, and Maria Krysan. 1997. *Racial Attitudes in America: Trends and Interpretations.* Cambridge, Mass.: Harvard University Press.

Schwab, W. A., and E. Marsh. 1980. "The Tipping Point Model: Prediction of Change in the Racial Composition of Cleveland, Ohio, Neighborhoods, 1940–1970." *Environment and Planning A* 12:385–398.

Schwirian, Kent P. 1983. "Models of Neighborhood Change." *Annual Review of Sociology* 9:83–102.

Segal, David. 1979. "Introduction." In David Segal, ed., *The Economics of Neighborhood,* pp. 3–13. New York: Academic Press.

Shear, William B. 1983. "Urban Housing Rehabilitation and Move Decisions." *Southern Economic Journal* 49:1030–1052.

Shefrin, Hersh, and Meir Statman. 1985. "The Disposition to Sell Winners Early and Ride Losers Too Long: Theory and Evidence." *Journal of Finance* 40:777–790.

Shipler, David K. 1997. *A Country of Strangers: Blacks and Whites in America.* New York: Alfred A. Knopf.

Shlay, Anne B., and Denise A. DiGregorio. 1985. "Same City, Different Worlds: Examining Gender- and Work-Based Difference in Perceptions of Neighborhood Desirability." *Urban Affairs Quarterly* 21(1):66–86.

Siegel, Fred. 1999. "Rudy Awakening." *New Republic.* April 19, pp. 14–18.

Sigelman, Lee, Timothy Bledsoe, Susan Welch, and Michael W. Combs. 1996. "Making Contact? Black-White Social Interaction in an Urban Setting." *American Journal of Sociology* 101(5):1306–1332.

Sigelman, Lee, and Susan Welch. 1991. *Black Americans' Views of Racial Inequality: The Dream Deferred.* Cambridge: Cambridge University Press.

——— 1993. "The Contact Hypothesis Revisited: Black-White Interaction and Positive Racial Attitudes." *Social Forces* 71:781–795.

Skogan, Wesley G. 1990. *Disorder and Decline: Crime and the Spiral of Decay in American Neighborhoods*. Berkeley: University of California Press.

Smith, Barton A. 1978. "Measuring the Value of Urban Amenities." *Journal of Urban Economics* 5:370–387.

Smith, Christopher B. 1994. "Back and to the Future: The Intergroup Contact Hypothesis Revisited." *Sociological Inquiry* 64(4):438–455.

Smith, Richard A. 1991. "The Measurement of Segregation Change through Integration and Deconcentration." *Urban Affairs Quarterly* 26:477–496.

——— 1993. "Creating Stable Racially Integrated Communities: A Review." *Journal of Urban Affairs* 15:115–140.

——— 1998. "Discovering Stable Racial Integration." *Journal of Urban Affairs* 20:1–26.

Smolla, Rodney A. 1985. "In Pursuit of Racial Utopias: Fair Housing, Quotas, and Goals in the 1980s." *Southern California Law Review* 58:947–1016.

Sniderman, Paul M., and Thomas Piazza. 1993. *The Scar of Race*. Cambridge, Mass.: The Belknap Press of Harvard University Press.

Solomon, Arthur P., and Kerry D. Vandell. 1982. "Alternative Perspectives on Neighborhood Decline." *Journal of the American Planning Association* 48:81–98.

South, Scott, and Kyle D. Crowder. 1997. "Escaping Distressed Neighborhoods: Individual, Community, and Metropolitan Influences." *American Journal of Sociology* 102(4):1040–1084.

South, Scott, and Glenn B. Deane. 1993. "Race and Residential Mobility: Individual Determinants and Structural Constraints." *Social Forces* 72:147–167.

South Suburban Housing Center v. Greater South Suburban Board of Realtors. 1991. 935 F.2d 868.

Soutner, Susan Blanche. 1980. "The Boston Banks Urban Renewal Group Homeownership Program: A Study of Racial Discrimination in an Urban Housing Market." Cambridge, Mass.: Department of City and Regional Planning, Harvard University.

Spain, Daphne. 1980. "Black-to-White Successions in Central-City Housing: Limited Evidence of Urban Revitalization." *Urban Affairs Quarterly* 15:381–396.

Speare, Alden. 1974. "Residential Satisfaction as an Intervening Variable in Residential Mobility." *Demography* 11(2):173–188.

Speare, Alden, Sidney Goldstein, and William H. Frey. 1975. *Residential Mobility, Migration, and Metropolitan Change*. Cambridge, Mass.: Ballinger.

St. John, Craig, and Nancy A. Bates. 1990. "Racial Composition and Neighborhood Evaluation." *Social Science Research* 19:47–61.

St. John, Craig, and Frieda Clark. 1984. "Race and Social Class Differences in the Characteristics Desired in Residential Neighborhoods." *Social Science Quarterly* 65:803–813.

Stahura, John M. 1988. "Changing Patterns of Suburban Racial Composition, 1970–1980." *Urban Affairs Quarterly* 23(3):448–460.

Stegman, Michael. 1969. "Accessibility Models and Residential Location." *Journal of the American Institute of Planners* April:22–29.

Steinnes, Donald. 1977. "Alternative Models of Neighborhood Change." *Social Forces* 55:1043–1057.

Sternlieb, George, and James W. Hughes. 1973. "Analysis of Neighborhood Decline in Urban Areas." New Brunswick, N.J.: Center for Urban Policy Research, Rutgers University.

Stipak, Brian, and Carl Hensler. 1983. "Effect of Neighborhood Racial and Socio-Economic Composition on Urban Residents' Evaluations of Their Neighborhoods." *Social Indicators Research* 12:311–320.

Straszheim, Mahlon. 1987. "The Theory of Urban Residential Location." In Edwin S. Mills, ed., *Handbook of Urban and Regional Economics*, vol. 2, pp. 717–782. New York: North-Holland.

Struyk, Raymond J., and Margery A. Turner. 1986. "Exploring the Effects of Racial Preferences on Urban Housing Markets." *Journal of Urban Economics* 19:131–147.

Sugrue, Thomas. 1996. *The Origins of the Urban Crisis: Race and Inequality in Postwar Detroit.* Princeton, N.J.: Princeton University Press.

Sullivan, Mercer L. 1989. *Getting Paid: Youth Crime and Work in the Inner City.* Ithaca, N.Y.: Cornell University Press.

Taeuber, Karl. 1968. "The Effect of Income Redistribution on Racial Residential Segregation." *Urban Affairs Quarterly* 4:5–15.

Taeuber, Karl, and Alma Taeuber. 1965. *Negroes in Cities: Residential Segregation and Neighborhood Change.* Chicago: Aldine.

Tatum, Beverly Daniel. 1997. *"Why Are All the Black Kids Sitting Together in the Cafeteria?' and Other Conversations about Race.* New York: Basic Books.

Taub, Richard, D. Garth Taylor, and Jan Dunham. 1984. *Paths of Neighborhood Change.* Chicago: University of Chicago Press.

Taylor, D. Garth. 1979. "Housing, Neighborhoods, and Race Relations: Recent Survey Evidence." *Annals of the American Academy of Political and Social Science* 441:26–40.

——— 1981. "Racial Preference, Housing Segregation, and the Causes of School Segregation: Recent Evidence from a Social Survey Used in Litigation." *Review of Public Data Use* 9:267–282.

Terry, Don. 1996. "In White Flight's Wake, a Town Tries to Keep Its Balance." *New York Times,* March 11, p. A12.

Thernstrom, Stephan, and Abigail Thernstrom. 1997. *America in Black and White: One Nation, Indivisible.* New York: Simon & Schuster.

Thomas, Paulette. 1992. "Blacks Can Face a Host of Trying Conditions in Getting Mortgages." *Wall Street Journal,* November 30, pp. A1, A8–A9.

Tobin, Gary A. 1987. "Introduction: Housing Segregation in the 1980s." In Gary

A. Tobin, ed., *Divided Neighborhoods: Changing Patterns of Racial Segregation,* pp. 8–14. Newbury Park, Calif.: Sage Publications.

Tobin, Mitch. 1993. "Users' Guide for the Urban Institute's Underclass Data Base." Washington, D.C.: The Urban Institute.

Turner, Margery, Raymond Struyk, and John Yinger. 1991. "Housing Discrimination Study: Synthesis." Washington, D.C.: U.S. Department of Housing and Urban Development.

Turner, Margery, and Ronald Wienk. 1993. "The Persistence of Segregation in Urban Areas: Contributing Causes." In G. Thomas Kingsley and Margery Austin Turner, eds., *Housing Markets and Residential Mobility,* pp. 193–216. Washington, D.C.: The Urban Institute Press.

U.S. Bureau of the Census. 1980. *1980 Census of Population: General Population Characteristics for Metropolitan Areas.* Washington, D.C.: Government Printing Office.

—— 1990. *1990 Census of Population: General Population Characteristics for Metropolitan Areas.* Washington, D.C.: Government Printing Office.

—— 1993. *Current Population Reports P20–505: Educational Attainment in the United States.* Washington, D.C.: Government Printing Office.

—— 1994. "Geographical Mobility: March 1992 to March 1993." *Current Population Reports,* P20–481. Washington, D.C.: Government Printing Office.

—— 1997. *Current Population Reports P60–201: Poverty in the United States.* Washington, D.C.: Government Printing Office.

—— 1998. *Current Population Reports P20–513: Educational Attainment in the United States.* Washington, D.C.: Government Printing Office.

U.S. Commission on Civil Rights. 1992. "Racial and Ethnic Tensions in American Communities: Poverty, Inequality, and Discrimination: A National Perspective." Executive summary and transcript of hearing held in Washington, D.C., May 21–22, 1992.

U.S. Congress, Joint Committee on Taxation. 1999. *Estimates of Federal Tax Expenditures for Fiscal Years 2000–2004.* Washington, D.C.: Government Printing Office.

U.S. Federal Bureau of Investigation. 1980. *Crime in the United States.* Washington, D.C.: Government Printing Office.

—— 1990. *Crime in the United States.* Washington, D.C.: Government Printing Office.

Vandell, Kerry D., and Bennett Harrison. 1976. "Racial Transition in Neighborhoods: A Simulation Model Incorporating Institutional Constraints." Working Paper 39. Cambridge, Mass.: Joint Center for Urban Studies of M.I.T. and Harvard University.

Varady, David P. 1979. *Ethnic Minorities in Urban Areas: A Case-Study of Racially Changing Communities.* Boston: Martinus Nijhoff.

Walsh, Edward. 1995. "Town Renowned for Integration Segregates Its Real Estate Sales Pitch." *Washington Post,* March 18, p. A3.

Washington, James Melvin, ed. 1986. *A Testament of Hope: The Essential Writings and Speeches of Martin Luther King, Jr.* San Francisco: HarperCollins.

Wegman, Robert. 1977. "Desegregation and Resegregation: A Review of the Research on White Flight from Urban Areas." In Daniel Levine and Robert Havighurst, eds., *The Future of Big City Schools,* pp. 11–54. Berkeley: McCutchan Publishing.

Weiher, Gregory. 1991. *The Fractured Metropolis.* Albany: State University of New York Press.

Weinberg, Daniel. 1979. "The Determinants of Intra-Urban Household Mobility." *Regional Science and Urban Economics* 9:219–246.

Weinberg, Daniel H., Joseph Friedman, and Stephen K. Mayo. 1981. "Intraurban Residential Mobility: The Role of Transactions Costs, Market Imperfections, and Household Disequilibrium." *Journal of Urban Economics* 9:332–348.

White, Michael. 1984. "Racial and Ethnic Succession in Four Cities." *Urban Affairs Quarterly* 20:165–183.

———— 1987. *American Neighborhoods and Residential Differentiation.* New York: Russell Sage Foundation.

White, Michelle. 1977. "Urban Models of Race Discrimination." *Regional Science and Urban Economics* 7:217–232.

"Why Can't We Live Together?" 1997. *Dateline NBC,* June 27. National Broadcasting Company.

Wial, Howard. 1991. "Getting a Good Job: Mobility in a Segmented Labor Market." *Industrial Relations* 30(3):396–416.

Williams, Roberton C. 1979. "A Logit Demand for Neighborhood." In David Segal, ed., *The Economics of Neighborhood,* pp. 17–41. New York: Academic Press.

Wilson, James Q., and George Kelling. 1982. "Broken Windows." *Atlantic Monthly.* March 1982:29–38.

Wilson, Thomas C. 1983. "White Response to Neighborhood Change." *Sociological Focus* 16:305–318.

———— 1996. "Prejudice Reduction or Self-Selection? A Test of the Contact Hypothesis." *Sociological Spectrum* 16:43–60.

Wilson, William Julius. 1987. *The Truly Disadvantaged: The Inner City, the Underclass, and Public Policy.* Chicago: University of Chicago Press.

Winship, Christopher. 1977. "A Reevaluation of Indexes of Residential Segregation." *Social Forces* 55:1058–1066.

Wolf, Eleanor P. 1960. "Racial Transition in a Middle-Class Area." *Journal of Intergroup Relations* 1:75–81.

———— 1963. "The Tipping Point in Racially Changing Neighborhoods." *Journal of the American Institute of Planners* 29:217–222.

———— 1965. "The Baxter Area, 1960–1962: A New Trend in Neighborhood Change?" *Phylon* 26:344–353.

———— 1981. *Trial and Error: The Detroit School Segregation Case.* Detroit: Wayne State University Press.

Wolfe, Alan. 1998. *One Nation, After All: What Middle-Class Americans Really Think About.* New York: Viking Penguin Books.

Wood, Peter B., and Barrett A. Lee. 1991. "Is Neighborhood Racial Succession Inevitable? Forty Years of Evidence." *Urban Affairs Quarterly* 26:610–620.

Wurdock, Clarence J. 1981. "Neighborhood Racial Transition: A Study of the Role of White Flight." *Urban Affairs Quarterly* 17:75–89.

Wynter, Leon. 1983. "Blacks Are Happier than Whites with Life in Prince Georges County, *Post* Poll Finds." *Washington Post,* August 8, pp. B1, B2.

Yale Law Review. 1980. Comment. "Tipping the Scales of Justice: A Race-Conscious Remedy for Neighborhood Transition." *Yale Law Review* 90:377–399.

Yarmolinsky, Adam. 1971. "Reassuring the Small Homeowner." *The Public Interest* 22:106–110.

Yinger, John. 1976. "Racial Prejudice and Racial Residential Segregation in an Urban Model." *Journal of Urban Economics* 3:383–406.

——— 1978. "Racial Transition and Public Policy." Cambridge, Mass.: Department of City and Regional Planning, Harvard University.

——— 1979. "Prejudice and Discrimination in the Urban Housing Market." In Peter Mieszkowski and Mahlon Straszheim, eds., *Current Issues in Urban Economics,* pp. 430–468. Baltimore: The Johns Hopkins University Press.

——— 1986. "On the Possibility of Achieving Racial Integration through Subsidized Housing." In John M. Goering, ed., *Housing Desegregation and Federal Policy,* pp. 290–312. Chapel Hill: University of North Carolina Press.

——— 1995. *Closed Doors, Opportunities Lost: The Continuing Costs of Housing Discrimination.* New York: Russell Sage Foundation.

Yinger, John M., George C. Galster, Barton A. Smith, and Fred Eggers. 1980. "The Status of Research into Racial Discrimination and Segregation in American Housing Markets: A Research Agenda for the Department of Housing and Urban Development." HUD Occasional Papers 6, pp. 55–175. Washington, D.C.: Government Printing Office.

Zimmer, Basil. 1973. "Residential Mobility and Housing." *Land Economics* 49:344–350.

Zubrinsky, Camille L., and Lawrence Bobo. 1996. "Prismatic Metropolis: Race and Residential Segregation in the City of Angels." *Social Science Research* 25(3):335–374.

Index

Abrams, Charles, 36–37
Affirmative marketing, 166, 167–168, 173–174, 175–176
African Americans. *See* Blacks
Alinsky, Saul, 1, 34
American Housing Survey (AHS), 94–95, 97–98, 101–102, 115–116, 140–141, 142
Asians, 29–31, 41, 57, 69–70, 147–148, 150; vs. blacks, 10, 17, 117, 133, 157

Banking practices, 38, 56, 61, 156, 174
Blacks: household decisions among, 2–3, 7–8, 10–11, 22, 46, 51, 55, 56–58, 86, 108, 111, 112, 114, 123, 126, 130, 131–132, 135–137, 142–143, 146–151, 159, 160, 164–165; attitudes toward racial integration, 3, 7, 10–11, 22–23, 56–58, 90, 92–93, 107, 108, 112, 126, 131, 135–137, 138–139, 142, 159, 164; socioeconomic status of, 3–4, 17, 42–43, 53–54, 56, 60, 61, 65–66, 67, 70, 71, 109, 123, 124, 132, 137, 142–143, 157–159; income of, 3–4, 17, 42–43, 53–54, 56, 60, 61, 67, 70, 71, 109, 123, 124, 132, 142–143, 157–159; as renters, 7, 97, 101, 118, 121, 123, 126, 138–139, 144–146, 149; as homeowners, 7, 97, 101, 118, 121, 123, 127–128, 130, 131, 142, 144–151, 150–151; as homeowners with children, 7, 127–128, 130, 131,

142; vs. Hispanics, 10, 17, 56–57, 117, 133; vs. Asians, 10, 17, 117, 133, 157; neighborhood satisfaction among, 48, 90, 91–93, 95–96, 101–102, 106, 111, 118, 156; average racial composition in neighborhoods of, 118, 121; expectations concerning racial transition, 126, 127, 128, 129–130, 131–132, 164; as homeowners without children, 127–128
Block-busting, 37–38, 39, 44, 162, 163
Block data, 80–81; vs. census tracts, 14, 33, 77–78, 139
Bolling Air Force Base, 80
Boston, Mass.: Mattapan neighborhood, 36, 37–38, 62; Dorchester neighborhood, 38, 62; Roxbury neighborhood, 38, 62; Catholics in, 62; Jews in, 62
Boston Banks Urban Renewal Group (BBURG), 38
Brooklyn, N.Y., 165, 166–167
Brown v. Board of Education, 29

Calumet Park, Ill., 167
Catholic University, 80
Ceiling quotas, 166–167, 175
Census data, 19, 62, 96, 138–140; census tracts vs. block data, 14, 33, 77–78, 139; census tracts as neighborhoods, 14, 66, 70; on Hispanics, 66, 75